GERMAN
IN WORLD WAR II

GERMAN PARATROOPS
IN WORLD WAR II

VOLKMAR KUHN

LONDON
IAN ALLAN LTD

First published 1974
English Edition 1978

ISBN 0 7110 0759 4

Translated by H. A. and A. J. Barker

© German Edition, Motorbuch Verlag, Stuttgart,
   West Germany, 1974

© English Edition, Ian Allan Ltd, 1978

Published by Ian Allan Ltd, Shepperton, Surrey,
and printed in the United Kingdom by
Ian Allan Printing Ltd, Shepperton, Surrey.

Contents

CHAPTER 1
The Background

In April 1889 the American balloonist Charles Leroux travelled to Berlin, taking with him a parachute which embodied a new type of harness he had designed and put together with his colleague, Joe Loyal. His intention was to demonstrate the novel technique of parachute jumping before an audience of senior German officers. The demonstration duly took place on 16 April at a field in front of the Berlin Headquarters of the German General Staff in Schöneberg. From the special enclosure a distinguished gathering waited while Leroux ascended in a balloon. The Chief of the General Staff, Graf von Waldensee, and the man who was to succeed him, General Graf von Schlieffen, were among those who watched Leroux make his jump from a height of 1,000 metres to land safely in front of them. The demonstration clearly impressed von Schlieffen and he commented in a report 'if one could only "steer" these things, parachutes could provide a new means of exploiting surprise in war, as it would be feasible for a few men to wipe out an enemy headquarters...'

Von Schlieffen's steering problem was resolved soon afterwards, when the development of the aeroplane made it possible for parachutists to be flown to the areas where they were to be dropped. From their gas-filled balloons the first parachutist pioneers graduated to the shaky box-like heavier-than-air machines, and by 1914 the parachute was a recognised safety device for those who took to the air in balloons and aeroplanes. Finally, during the course of World War I, the German aircraft designer Otto Heinicke perfected a parachute specifically for use by aviators jumping from aircraft, and Käthe Paulus — Germany's first female aeronaut and parachutist — organised the production of some 5,000 (!) parachutes to this design, during World War I.

The next chapter in the parachute saga was written in October 1918 by an American, Major-General William Mitchell, who at that time was commanding the American Army Air Forces in France. Mitchell saw an airborne assault as a means of breaking the deadlock on the western front. His plan was to equip all the infantry of the US 1st Division with parachutes, and drop them behind the German lines in the Menin-Roselare region. Machine guns, ammunition and other supplies would be dropped with them, and the operation would be supported by every available Allied fighter and bomber aircraft — of which, it was reckoned, there were about 2,000. Planning was well advanced, and Mitchell's grandiose operation was scheduled for February 1919, when the war ended. Had it been put into effect, Mitchell opined later, operation 'Panic Party' would have created havoc in the German rear areas and effected a break through in the Roselare area. As it was the operation was all but forgotten when the armistice came into effect, and it was not until Mitchell published his memoirs in 1930 that his views on the future of airborne operations were publicly revealed. Most people promptly dubbed him mad, and it was only in Russia that Mitchell's ideas found favour. Parachute jumping had developed into a national sport in the Soviet Union, and it was there that the 'free fall' technique was pioneered by Evdokimov who showed that it was possible to steer a course through the air by body movements. (Evdokimov was killed in an accident in 1934 when his parachute failed to open during a jump from 11,000m [36,000ft].)

By this time the Red Army had already formed a small parachute unit. Marshal Tuchatschewski, the commander-in-chief, had been attracted to the idea of a third dimensional combat force, and under his direction parachuting was encouraged under the auspices of the Ossaviachim — a pre-military training organisation which was active in all the major towns of the Soviet Union. Groups of young Russians, male and female alike, were trained to make parachute drops and taught to use radio. In 1930 paratroops took part in the Red Army's manoeuvres for the first time, when a lieutenant and a section of paratroops jumped on a target a few miles south of Moscow. Their role was almost exactly as von Schlieffen had forecast in 1889 — an assault on an enemy HQ — and the operation, the first in military history, was completely successful.

In manoeuvres during the following year, 1931, an officer and six men jumped from an Antonov 14, and within seven minutes of landing had brought a heavy machine gun into action— they had again demonstrated the ability of paratroops to play a decisive part in a battle. The result was intensified interest in this type of operation and in the equipment associated with it. Various types of parachutes were tested and those which fared best were adopted. Meantime, while development was going ahead, the Soviet Air Force commander, Marshal Michail Schtscherbakow, visited France, where Marshal Petain took him round the Maginot Line.

'These fortresses will prevent any incursion into our territory', he proudly declared to the Russian visitor.

General Schtscherbakow's smiling response was said to have shaken his host.

'Fortresses like these may well be superfluous in the future', Schtscherbakow said, 'if your potential adversary pursues General Mitchell's ideas and parachutes over them, to seize the hinterland they can be cut off, isolated and starved into submission'.

Petain's immediate reaction was to deploy additional anti-aircraft batteries to strengthen the air defence of the Maginot Line. Meanwhile, the Russians were training more parachutists, some of whom took part in the Red Army's manoeuvres in the Ukraine during the summer of 1935. And the following year considerable military interest was aroused by reports from military attachés attending the Red Army manoeuvres that no less than 1,000 paratroops had made a simultaneous and accurate drop on to an exercise objective. The parachute operation was unique in itself, but the subsequent airlift of 5,000 other troops on to the objective further enhanced its importance. In a letter to the British War Office, a certain Colonel Archibald Wavell who was destined to be the commander-in-chief of British forces in the Middle East, wrote: 'If I had not been an eye-witness of this event I would never have believed that such an operation was possible.'

German military observers attending the 1935 and 1936 Russian manoeuvres had reported in a similar vein to Berlin, where for some time the General Staff had been pondering on the potential of paratroops. A 'weapon' it seemed had been developed and was ready for use; all that was required was to select and train men to use it.

On 1 April 1935 a Prussian police formation was re-named the General Göring Air Regiment and formally constituted as a unit of the Wehrmacht. Six months later its commanding officer, Oberstleutnant Jacoby, was told by the Air Minister himself that the regiment was to be transferred to the Luftwaffe.

'You, Jacoby', Göring said, 'will call for volunteers from the regiment to train as paratroops. The Hermann Göring parachute battlion will be the nucleus of a German paratroop corps.'

The transfer was duly effected on 1 October, the regiment moved to the military training area at Altengrabow and Jacoby's verbal instructions were confirmed by a directive telling him to '.... develop an organisation and examine the potential of an infantry paratroop regiment'.

A few days later Jacoby's regiment paraded at Döberitz to watch a demonstration parachute jump, and many of the would-be volunteers had second thoughts when they saw the demonstrator injured in a hard landing. Nevertheless there were sufficient bold spirits among them to shrug the accident aside and 600 of the regiment — including nearly all the officers — stepped forward to declare their willingness to join the 1st Battalion of the General Göring Parachute Battalion. The principal appointments at that time were as follows:

Battalion Commander	Major Bruno Bräuer
Adjutant	Oberleutnant Vogel
Signals Officer	Leutnant Dunz
OC 1 Coy	Oberleutnant Walther
OC 2 Coy	Oberleutnant Kroh
OC 3 Coy	Oberleutnant Schulz
OC 4 Coy	Hauptmann Reinberger

When the regiment was reorganised in November (1935) the parachute battalion was re-named the 4th Battalion. (Subsequently, in April 1938 the battalion became the 1st Battalion FJR 1 (*Fallschirmjäger Regiment*) and ceased to be part of the General Göring Regiment. Nearly all the instructional personnel of the parachute training school at Stendal were provided by this unit.)

Although these General Göring paratroops started their training in 1935, the commemorative date for the raising of the German paratroop corps is recorded in the annals of German military history as 29 January 1936. On this day an Order of the Day, signed by Hermann Göring and reading as follows, authorised the foundation of the corps:

From The
Reichsminister, Commander-in-Chief of the Luftwaffe.

Berlin, 29 January 1936

LA Nr 262/36g III I.A.   *SECRET*

To: The Luftkreiskommando III
Air Sector Commander
Berlin.

The following preparations will be made for the training of the parachutist section of the General Göring Regiment:

a Fifteen officers, warrant officers and junior NCO volunteers are to be trained as paratroop instructors. Such volunteers must weigh less than 85kg fully clothed (187lb), and be physically fit; before final acceptance they must be medically certified as fit for flying duties.

b The first training course of eight weeks duration will probably commence on 1 April 1936. Of these eight weeks, the first four will be spent under the direction of the Luftwaffe Equipment Controller learning how to handle parachutes; the second four weeks will be devoted to practical training including jumping from an aircraft. The airfield at Neubrandenburg is allocated for this purpose, and a Ju52 will be provided under arrangements made by RLM(LC). Flying instructors will be furnished by the RLM(LA II).

c On 15 March 1936 LKKII will report:
 1 The names and ranks of the volunteers.
 2 The results of their medical examination.
 3 The suitability of the Neubrandenburg airfield for paratroop training. (Suggestions for an alternative airfield will be submitted to this office if Neubrandenburg is not considered suitable.)

d The expenses incurred in complying with these instructions will be defrayed by an allotment from Kap A2 Tit 34, Subdivision IVB.

e For the duration of the four weeks of practical training in parachute jumping pilots will be paid a flying allowance in accordance with Air Force Regulations. D.R.LLP.4010/35 11 Ag.v.3.5.35 Subsection IVb, is authorised.

(Signed) Milch.

The airfield at Stendal might well be designated the *Fallschirmjäger* birthplace, since the first volunteers were trained there. Following Milch's order, Hauptmanns Immans and Kuhno of the Luftwaffe established a training school on the lines indicated, while Major Bassenge developed a tactical doctrine for the employment of paratroops. As a result of his recommendations the duration of the course was extended to three months.

Meanwhile the 1st Parachute Battalion had moved into a camp near Stendal, and soon after their arrival the commanding officer, Major Bruno Bräuer, sent for the newly promoted Oberleutnant Lothar Schulz. Schulz, an engineer who commanded No 15 Company of the General Göring Regiment, had volunteered to become a parachutist but he did not know what Bräuer wanted him for until the latter said: 'Well, Schulz, we are going to incorporate a pioneer company in the battalion. And, as

Above: Paratroops leaving their planes. The Germans used a very different method of leaving the transports, diving headfirst as opposed to the Allied feet together and feet first.

Below: The paratroops hang in their 'chutes and float to earth.

11

you have volunteered yourself, I want you to go back to your company and ask for men to join you in forming the nucleus of a parachute engineer section.'

So Schulz returned to his unit, paraded his company and — after a short speech outlining Bräuer's proposals — appealed to those men who wished to join him in an exciting new venture to step forward. When everybody on parade promptly stepped forward Schulz merely said, 'Right! From today you are all parachutists!' In one fell swoop Bräuer had secured a complete pioneer company. Every man was fully trained; every man was a volunteer.

As the parachute training proceeded, various technical problems began to crop up, and experts were called in to resolve them. The first and most important decision to be taken concerned the type of parachute to be used. Apart from being safe and reliable, the paratrooper's parachute had to be suited to operational requirements. Up to then parachutes issued to aviators were operated manually, and there was a relatively long interval between pulling the ripcord and the time the canopy developed. This meant that below a height of 200m (660ft) such parachutes were not safe. Yet to cut down the time of descent it was obvious that paratroops would have to be dropped at comparatively low altitude. Suspended in mid-air they were helpless and ideal targets for an enemy on the ground. Fortunately the government department responsible for testing parachutes had been collaborating with the Luftwaffe since 1930 in the design and testing of improved safety measures for aviators. Thus, it was that a team comprising Professors Hoff and Madelung, the directors of this department, Dipl Engineer Friedrich Hoffman, an expert on parachute design, and two engineers, von Stryk and Herbert Klar, had already gone a long way towards identifying the problems involved in the design of a parachute suited to operational conditions. In a series of experiments conducted by two pilots, von Köppen and Bruntrock, dummies weighing 100kg (220lb) had been parachuted down to earth from heights of 80m (260ft) and 100m (330ft) from aircraft flying at speeds of 250kph to 400kph (155 to 250mph). By means of a recording instrument devised by Freize, an engineer working at the DVL in Adlershof, the forces to which the dummies were subjected were measured. Thus it was possible to gain a fairly comprehensive picture of what was happening during the drop and to construct a mathematical model illustrating the reactions of the human frame in such circumstances. By 1933 the performance of all German and every known type of foreign parachute had been tested and checked by Freize's recorder.

After 1933 responsibility for the development of military parachutes was centralised at the Technical Equipment Division of the German Air Ministry. Under the direction of this division specific research development and testing projects could be allocated to one or other of the following establishments:

a The German Institute for Air Experimentation in Berlin. (Oberst Robert Thelen and Dipl Eng Fritz Hellriegel were in charge of this establishment.)

b The Luftwaffe testing station in Rehlin, whose technical advisers for parachute projects were Dipl Eng Karl Achler, Eng Martin Ruck, Eng Biehl and the technician Willi Buss. (Biehl and Buss were test parachutists, as was Richard Kohnke, an old parachute pioneer, who specialised in jumping from great altitudes at varying speeds.)

Above: Folding a parachute. *Below:* Major Schulz after a jump.

c The Air-Technical Institute of the Technical University at Darmstadt, whose director was Professor Georgi.

d The newly established Zeppelin Research Institute at Stuttgart, whose director was Professor Madelung.

During 1933 the facilities of a new cine-theodolite measuring station were used to test parachutes. Film records were made as the parachute canopies unfolded, and relating these films to telemetered recordings of Freize's instruments every phase in the development of a canopy and the forces acting on it could be studied. And this work undoubtedly was a major contribution to the development of the round-cap parachute, the RZ1. With a diameter of 8.5m (28ft) and a canopy of 56 square metres (600sq ft) — the opening of which was triggered by a static line — this parachute was carried on the back. It was designed for use *without* a secondary reserve 'back-up' chute: the latter would have been superfluous, since the jumping height was fixed at 120m (400ft) and the paratroops were to use the relatively slow-flying Ju52 planes. Improved models — the RZ16 and RZ20 — quickly followed the RZ1 and in the course of the war the first triangular parachute was introduced as the RZ36. The latter, developed by Dipl Eng Wolf Schauenburg and patented in June 1943, had three attractive advantages in the way of reduced unfolding shock, less pendulum motion during descent, and softer landings.

In 1936 the General Staff was still considering the potential of paratroops, but when the decision to form a parachute battalion was taken, events moved quickly. The first operational parachute company under Oberleutnant Zahn — ably assisted by the well-known pentathlon winner Oberleutnant Pelz — made its debut in the Wehrmacht manoeuvres in Mecklenburg during the autumn of 1937. In the meantime the command of the General Göring Regiment had passed to Oberst Walther von Axthelm, and his attention was concentrated on the formation of his parachute battalion. From the military academy at Potsdam Major Richard Heidrich, a tactical instructor, was posted to command the first company formed. Heidrich was 41 years old but he sailed through the jumping course as easily as many younger men, and on 1 March 1938 he assumed command of the battalion. From then on the formations of parachute troops were to expand quickly. Initially the 1st Parachute Battalion was stationed at Stendal but it moved to Braunschweig-Riddagshausen as soon as the construction of new barracks was completed. The battalion — and the other battalions which were formed later — were Luftwaffe formations and parachute training continued throughout this period under the auspices of the Luftwaffe. The Wehrmacht who were following the development of the airborne arm with keen interest had no quarrel with the form that this training took. But when it came to questions of a tactical doctrine governing the future employment of parachutists, however, Luftwaffe and Wehrmacht opinions differed. The Luftwaffe visualised their employment in penny packets as saboteurs — destroying military installations and generally wreaking havoc behind the enemy's lines. The Wehrmacht, on the other hand, favoured their tactical deployment as conventional infantry. In manoeuvres during the autumn of 1937 Heidrich's company was able to demonstrate the possibilities of such tactics, and the flexibility of a parachute unit dropped on an objective behind enemy lines cooperating successfully with the main artillery force.

Above: Preparing for the next exercise drop.

Below: Parachutes need to be aired and dried. Every man had his own parachute which he looked after himself.

On 1 July 1938 Generalmajor Kurt Student [a Luftwaffe officer] was appointed to the overall command of German airborne forces. As a deceptive measure his new formation was officially designated the 7th Air Division (what we would now call an 'air landing' formation). As Student had recently completed an appointment as head of the Flying School Inspectorate he was already familiar with the Parachute School at Stendal and the arguments surrounding the development of the Wehrmacht's novel arm. The 7th Air Division was scheduled to be combat-ready by 15 September 1938, and by that date the divisional commander had to resolve the arguments concerning the employment of his troops. In effect his mind was already made up, and he summarised his views later:

'I could not accept the saboteur force concept. It was a daredevil idea but I did not see minor operations of this kind as worthwhile — they wasted individual soldiers and were not tasks for a properly constituted force. The chances of getting back after such missions appeared to be strictly limited; those taking part who survived would probably be captured and the prospect of then being treated as terrorists or spies would undermine the morale of even the best troops. Casualties are inevitable in war. But soldiers must be able to assume a real chance of survival, and an eventual return home. The employment of airborne troops on such limited missions did not seem to take account of their immense potential. From the very beginning my ideas went much, much further. In my view airborne troops could become a battle-winning factor of prime importance. Airborne forces made third-dimensional warfare possible in land operations. An adversary could never be sure of a stable front because paratroops could simply jump over it and attack from the rear where and when they decided. There was nothing new about attacking from behind of course — such tactics have been practised since the beginning of time and proved both demoralising and effective. But airborne troops provided a new means of exploitation and so their potential in such operations was of incalculable importance. The element of surprise was an added consideration; the more paratroops dropped, the greater the surprise. On the other hand there is always the danger that dropping a large number of men in close proximity to an alert and responsive enemy might produce an unpleasant surprise for the paratroops. I have considered all these important questions very carefully ...'

When General Student took command of the airborne forces the parachute battalion continued to be under the operational control of the Luftwaffe although the 7th Air Division was listed as a Wehrmacht formation. When the occupation of the Sudetenland was planned Hitler ordered Student to examine and submit proposals for an airborne operation to seize and knock out the Czech defences. D-day for this operation was set as 15 September 1938, and the division was made up to combat strength with an air landing battalion under the command of Oberstleutnant Sydow brigaded with the two parachute battalions which now existed. The 16th Infantry Regiment of the 22nd Infantry Division under Oberst Kreysing and — by Göring's special request — the *Standarte Feldherrnhalle* (Hall of Glory) SA Regiment were put through an emplaning and deplaning course to become the other two air landing brigades of Student's formation. Additionally the following Luftwaffe formations were allotted to him:

1 Reconnaissance Squadron
6 Transport Groups of Ju52s
1 Fighter-Bomber Wing of three Stuka Squadrons
1 Fighter Wing of three Squadrons.

During September, near Jüterbog, in the course of the preparations for the Sudetenland operation, General Student conducted the biggest airborne manoeuvres ever held. All units of his command participated, and Student was gratified to find that the men who flew the troop-carrying Ju52s — all experienced Lufthansa pilots — had little difficulty in mastering the technical problems which arose during the course of the exercise. Looking for ways of developing the airborne potential still further, Student — a glider enthusiast himself — hit on the idea of using gliders to carry both men and equipment. As it happened his Chief of Staff, Oberst Jeschonnek, was also a keen glider pilot, and when Student broached the subject, Jeschonnek is reported to have said: 'Nobody seems interested in gliders. It would be a good thing if you took charge of their development; otherwise nothing will be done ...'

In effect the prototype of a German glider, the DFS 230, which had been developed in 1933 by the German Research Institute for Gliding, already existed and seemed suited to operational use. Built by Hans Jacobs and test flown by Hanna Reitsch, this machine could carry a pilot and ten men. A number were produced and a well known gliding expert, Fritz Stamer of Darmstadt, initiated the first two pilots, Leutnant Kiess and Unteroffizier Flucke, into the mysteries of flying them. As soon as these two had learned how to handle the gliders, regular courses to train other glider pilots were begun, and a glider-training command under Leutnant Kiess was established as part of the 7th Air Division. Student himself visited the unit in its early stages at the Luftwaffe station at Prenzlau, and flew in a glider piloted by Kiess. That he was satisfied with all he had seen and heard may be deduced from the fact that he promptly decided to use gliders in the forthcoming Sudetenland operation. Kiess was told that his task would be to lead a flight of troop carrying gliders which would fly in and seize a prominent feature, Pt 698, south-east of Freudenthal.

In the event the agreement made at Munich in 1938 led to the cancellation of the proposed Sudetenland operation. The 7th Air Division occupied the Freudenthal area without firing a shot, and the only phase of the airborne assault carried out was conducted as an exercise. For security reasons Student forbade the paratroop drop and the glider-borne operation. But the air landing from 250 Ju52s of the remainder of the division took place as planned, and Göring, who watched as the planes landed and the troops deplaned, is said to have been fascinated by the smooth running organisation of the whole operation. 'This business has a great future', he said to Student.

The immediate repercussions of Göring's enthusiasm boded well for the 7th Air Division as a parachute force. On 1 January 1939 orders were issued establishing the 1st Parachute Regiment [Brigade] as a regular formation, and for the raising of a 2nd Parachute Regiment. Major Heidrich, the commanding officer of the 2nd Parachute

Battalion, was told that he had been earmarked for command of this 2nd Parachute Regiment, and he handed over to Hauptman Prager. (Prager's adjutant at this time was Leutnant Heckel and the signal officer was Leutnant Böhmler). In November the battalion had moved to Brunwick from Stendal.

At the same time as these changes were being made in the organisation of Student's 7th Air Division, the 22nd Infantry Division, commanded by Generalmajor Graf Sponeck, was reconstituted as an air landing division, and the 16th Infantry Regiment (loaned to Student for the Sudetenland operation) returned to its parent formation. Finally Student was nominated Inspector of Airborne Troops, and his 7th Air Division — which was not to consist solely of paratroops — was placed directly under operational control of the Luftwaffe. Subsequently, in compliance with Göring's orders, on 1 January the two existing parachute battalions were absorbed into the 1st Parachute Regiment under Oberst Bruno Bräuer, while Hauptman Karl Lothar Schulz in Gardelegen set about raising the third battalion of the 1st Regiment. Meantime in Tangermünde Hauptmanns Noster and Pietzonka were forming two more parachute battalions for the 2nd Parachute Regiment of the division.

All paratroopers were selected from those who volunteered to take a tough and intensive course at one of the parachute-training schools. Men who did not show the requisite physical qualities and mental outlook were weeded out on these courses. Further training for those who successfully completed the parachute course followed lines laid down by General Student:

'The first thing to do is to instil regimental spirit — to make a man proud of belonging to the Parachute Corps. This pride must stem from a comradeship which is wider and deeper than that of any other regiment or corps. Training must be based not on formal discipline based on fear and blind obedience but on the principle of mutual confidence.

'During the frequent visits I made to the parachute units', he said later, 'I tried to set an example by talking to individual paratroopers, discussing their personal problems and eliciting their opinions. I was pleased with the way this approach was received, and there is no doubt that the paratroop esprit de corps grew from strength to strength as the Paratroop Corps expanded. For a paratrooper to be expelled from the corps and transferred to another unit for some transgression of the rules came to be regarded as a disgrace. The subsequent success of the paratroops in action many be attributed to this attitude.'

Parallel with the expansion of the infantry element of the new corps, units of the supporting arms were formed to work specifically with paratroops. In the summer of 1938 the first airborne artillery battery under command of Leutnant Bruno Schram was raised. This battery, 'No 7', was equipped with 7.5cm Skoda guns drawn by horses and dog teams and was promptly dubbed 'Circus Schram'.

Paratroops made their official debut in a parade in Berlin on 20 April 1939 when — headed by Oberst Bräuer — they marched past Hitler.

The first airborne manoeuvres took place at Bergen three months later, in July 1939, and it was during these exercises that General von Kluge successfully staged a hoax which was to have considerable significance for the future. As a staff officer with the

7th Air Division Oberstleutant Heidrich had conceived the notion of dropping life-size dummies on parachutes as a deceptive measure and the idea was now tried out. During the course of the exercise dummies were dropped behind an 'enemy' regiment deployed for conventional defence. Believing his troops were menaced from the rear the regimental commander turned about to face the threat and while he was dealing with the dolls the 2nd Battalion of the FJR I was dropped to occupy the strategic heights which the 'enemy' was supposedly defending. General von Kluge was delighted with the success of the feint, and no doubt the news was passed back to the Führer. In the event Hitler did not comment, and his attitude towards the Parachute Corps at this time is not known since he had neither visited any of the units nor spoken to General Student about them.

When Germany mobilised on 26 August 1939 all units of the 7th Air Division were at their peacetime stations; they were trained but not yet up to full strength. In World War II the Parachute Corps was to prove itself in battle.

CHAPTER 2
Paratroops in Action

The Polish Campaign

At the start of the Polish campaign the German paratroop battalions were concentrated in camps on the motorway between Berlin and Breslau. They were standing by, ready to move to the airfields near Breslau from which they would emplane to take part in airborne assaults planned by General Student. One of these operations, codenamed Pulawy, had as its objective the capture of a strategically important bridge across the Vistula and the destruction of the Polish detachment guarding it. The paratroops assigned to this mission had already emplaned and their aircraft were waiting to take off when the operation was cancelled. No reason for the cancellation was given at the time but it transpired later that the invading German panzers, ahead of their schedule, had already seized the bridge. It was the same with the other operations in which the paratroops were to participate — the rapid advance of the ground troops obviated the need for their assaults.

As their operations were systematically called off there was considerable disappointment among the paratroopers waiting on the Silesian airfields. And this disappointment rapidly turned into angry frustration when what was termed a 'sale of the German Parachute Corps' followed. Paratroop units were broken up and sent off to perform what were considered to be relatively menial tasks: protecting the forward headquarters of Luftwaffe General von Richthofen being but one example. However, in mid-September some of the units of the 7th Air Division embussed in trucks which rolled eastwards on an operational mission. The objective was a ring of airfields between the Vistula and Bug rivers; these airfields were to be occupied and defended in the event of attacks by units of the now dispersed and straggling Polish army. In the course of this operation a paratroop patrol reconnoitring across the Vistula, clashed with a Polish artillery regiment and in the fighting which ensued the newly-blooded Paratroop Corps suffered its first casualties. Feldwebel Meusel is listed as the first paratrooper to be killed.

The 7th Division returned to Germany and dispersed to its peace-time stations during October. Anxious to see action before the war ended, some of the paratroopers now applied for transfers to infantry regiments. Little did they know that the Parachute

Corps' first big operation was being planned at that very time. On 27 October General Student had been called to the Reichschancellery to see Hitler, who told him why the paratroops had not been used as such in Poland. 'The paratroops are too valuable', the Führer declared, 'I shall only employ them when I think the time is opportune. The Wehrmacht managed very well on its own in Poland, and I did not want to disclose what amounts to a secret new weapon.'

Hitler then went on to tell Student what he had in mind for airborne troops during the forthcoming Western offensive. As the start of this offensive was scheduled for 12 November, time was pressing.

Hitler had already discussed his plans with his military advisers, who professed themselves profoundly surprised by his ideas for an airborne operation in conjunction with an invasion of Belgium by mechanised columns. Paratroops and glider-borne shock troops were to seize Eben Emael, the outlying fort of Liège — a strongpoint completed only in recent years and held to be one of the strongest in Europe. General Keitel, the Commander-in-Chief, had passed this information to the OKH (*Oberkommando des Heeres:* Army headquarters) and following his meeting with the Führer in the Chancellery on 27 October Student hammered out the broad details of the operation. He wrote:

'During the discussions which took place Hitler gave his views on how airborne troops should be used. His opinions were explained with clearsighted lucidity and with his own inimitable persuasiveness. I was astonished at his knowledge of what was virtually a new field — of the potential of gliders in particular. To begin with the Führer himself stressed that one had to realise that paratroops and the airborne arm was a completely new, untried and — so far as Germany was concerned — still secret weapon. The first airborne operation had to employ every resource available, and be delivered boldly at a decisive time and place. It was for this reason, Hitler said, he had refrained from using airborne troops until there were appropriate objectives.

'I told him of the paratroops' disappointment and frustration during the campaign in Poland, and of the effect on their morale. Hitler listened attentively and responded by saying "They will certainly see some action in the West!" Smiling, he added, "And it will be a *big* show!"'

Subsequently Hitler detailed what he expected of the airborne troops in the impending offensive:

1   The 7th Air Division and the 22nd Airborne Division under Generalmajor Student will seize the *Reduit National* (the chain of forts along the Belgian frontier) and hold this important line of fortifications until the arrival of the mechanised columns of the Wehrmacht.
2   Parachutists and a glider-borne force are to launch surprise attacks on Eben Emael, the bridges across the Albert Canal north of it, and the Meuse bridges near Maastricht. The aim is to facilitate the speedy passage of the 6th Army (General von Reichenau) across the Maas and Albert Canal.

General Student told Hitler that in his opinion capturing the *Reduit National* was feasible, but the other tasks were asking rather a lot. Hitler responded laconically, 'Go

21

away and sleep on it', he said 'and come back in the morning.' Student pondered on the problem and did not in fact do much sleeping on it that night. Ultimately he concluded that a surprise attack on Eben Emael could be successful — provided the preparation and execution of the operation were cloaked in secrecy. Next morning he returned to the Chancellery and told Hitler his views.

In accordance with Student's ideas, the strictest security measures were observed while the operation was planned and mounted. Complete surprise was essential, and the problem was reconciling covert operational preparations with overt technical needs — involving a myriad preparations virtually impossible to conceal. Student and Oberst Bräuer together selected the units to take part in the assault on the Albert Canal Bridges and for the capture of Eben Emael. Hauptman Koch, one of the company commanders, of the 1st Battalion FJR 1 was ordered to form the *Sturmabteilung Koch* (Koch Assault Group) and the Pioneer company of the 2nd Battalion FJR 1 under Leutnant Witzig together with Leut Kiess's Glider Commando were put under his command. The strength of the Assault Group was further increased by a draft of 500 men from the Parachute School.

D-day for the airborne operations was postponed a number of times in the ensuing months, and their form was also changed. Ultimately the objectives for operations in the Netherlands were laid down as follows:

1 Seizure of the bridges at Noerdyk, Dordrecht and Rotterdam for the passage of the 18th Army which will deal with the Belgian strongpoints on the south side of the river.
2 Occupation of The Hague and the elimination of the Dutch High Command.

Clearly the scope of the airborne offensive which Student was responsible for coordinating, preparing and directing had extended. But this was not the problem. On 3 November 1939 Hitler decided to strike north and deal with Norway before invading the West. And for the campaign in Norway he demanded a parachute battalion. Student's protestations that this would debilitate the resources available for the Netherlands and Belgian operations, were rejected. So, in order to preserve Koch's Assault Group, Major Erich Walter's 1st Battalion of the FJR 1 was assigned to the Norwegian operation. Plans for this were based on the following directive:

1 The Battalion Commander with his HQ and one rifle company would be directly responsible for seizing and securing the Oslo-Fornebu airfield for the landing of the rest of his force.
2 No 3 Company of the FJR 1, under Leut von Brandis would seize and occupy the Stavanger-Sola airfield.
3 Detachments of No 4 Company, under Hauptman Gericke, would be responsible for the capture of selected bridges and airfields in Denmark.

Operations in Norway and Denmark

In the early hours of 9 April 1940, Ju52s carrying the detachments of Walter's 1st Battalion of FJR 1 took off from airfields in North Germany and flew north. Hauptman Gericke, who was in one of the planes carrying his No 4 Company, was

The Paratroop Rifleman's badge.

conscious of the tension among the men packed into the fuselage of the narrow Ju52. Turning his head he smiled at the leader of his stick of parachutists. Then the red light above the open door of the plane flashed on indicating that they had to prepare to jump. Standing up they shuffled towards to door, and lined up behind the stick leader who positioned himself in the doorway — gripping the frame with both hands and leaning back to stop himself being swept away in the slipstream before it was time to jump. Then it was time to jump. The buzzer shrilled insistently and the stick leader released his grip on the door and leaped forward like a pike. The next man followed, then a third, then another... from other aircraft the rest of No 4 Company were also jumping, and floating down to earth. Hauptman Gericke noted with some satisfaction that there was no fire from below as the ground suddenly appeared to be soaring up to meet him. Then he landed, rolled over and detached his parachute. Three minutes later he had rallied his company and was moving towards the bridge linking the islands of Falster and Fyn (Fünen). Danish troops appeared. They had never seen German paratroop helmets before and they were caught completely off guard and gave up the bridge without a struggle. The road to Copenhagen was now open for the German mechanised column which arrived a few hours later, and Walther Gericke was subsequently awarded the Iron Cross 2nd Class for his exemplary direction of the operation.

Meanwhile, No 3 Company of Erich Walter's battalion had been dropped on the edge of the Stavanger-Sola airfield in Norway and the company commander, Leut Freiherr von Brandis, had rallied his men without much difficulty. A few shots had been fired as they floated down and when they moved in towards the airport the shooting increased. Advancing from cover to cover in a series of short dashes the paratroopers systematically overran each pocket of Norwegian resistance. By the time the first of the transport planes carrying the troops who were to relieve the paratroops touched down on the airfield and shooting had stopped, the airfield was firmly in German hands, and the Stukas and fighter aircraft supporting the paratroopers had turned their attention to the British warships off Stavanger.

No 3 Company's first operation was completely successful, but Major Walter's two companies were not so fortunate. Their objective was the Oslo-Fornebu airfield, and as the Ju52s approached the dropping zone and started to descend to the dropping altitude a radio message instructed their pilots to climb and circle. The order came from the commander of the escorting fighter wing, Obstlt Drewes. Flying in front of the formation of transports he had seen that the dropping zone was cloaked by a blanket of dense fog. This fog covered Oslo and extended over the Scharen chain of islands outside, and as there was no hope of an alternative dropping zone there was no option but to call off the drop. Turning back, the lumbering transports headed for an airfield near Aalborg in North Jutland, which had been supposedly occupied by one of Gericke's detachments after his occupation of the Falster-Fyn bridge. As eight Messerschmitt Me110s of Hauptmann Ingenhoven's I/ZG76 swept in to land, however, they were greeted with bursts of fire from the ground. Clearly the airfield had not been taken by the paratroops — or if it had, then the surrounding area was still enemy territory. In the event the situation was resolved by Ingerhoven's aircraft strafing the area while the Ju52s landed and discharged their paratroops on the runways.

24

In general the campaign had gone according to plan. About 2,000 men under General Dietl had boldly landed at Narvik on 8 April and quietly taken control of the sleepy little port. However, when British troops landed at Namsos north of Trondheim on 14 April, and at Aandalsnes to the south on the 17th, it was soon apparent that Dietl's force was in a hazardous position. In consequence the remaining uncommitted company of the 1st Battalion FJR 1 under command of Leutnant Herbert Schmidt was ordered to block the natural line of advance from Aandalsnes to Oslo. Schmidt was told that his company would be dropped in the Gudbrandsal valley near Dombaas and his task was to prevent Norwegian troops holding out north of Oslo linking up with the British invasion force.

The Ju52s carrying Schmidt's men took off in the afternoon of 17 April. Oberstleutnant Drewes was in charge of the air aspects of the operation, and under his direction the drop was made 150km in front of the German lines in the valley. Because of fog the planes had some difficulty making their approach to the dropping zone and darkness was closing in as the paratroops floated down into the deep snow. Nevertheless the combination of fog and nightfall did not guarantee protection. The transports were spotted and the enemy opend fire. Machine gun fire whipped down the valley and one Ju52 was blown apart by a direct hit from an anti-aircraft gun. The paratroops had been scattered by this action and the mode of the drop. But Schmidt landed almost on top of his company sergeant-major and, together with the aid of two other paratroopers who also landed nearby, as many men as could be rounded up were hurriedly assembled. When a count was taken there were 61 of them. Moving down to the road which ran through the valley Schmidt's depleted force came under heavy machine gun fire and Schmidt himself was wounded in the stomach and the hip. It seemed that the paratroops had dropped into the very middle of a locality defended by a Norwegian unit which was both alert and quick on the trigger. Carrying their stricken company commander with them, the paratroopers withdrew from the road to establish a defensive position on one of the slopes of the snow-covered mountains dominating the valley. Once they had dug themselves in they returned to the offensive, sending fighting patrols to seek out and clear the nearest Norwegian positions.

Fifteen Ju52s had flown Schmidt's company into action and of these eight had gone off course, or had been shot down by the Norwegians. Yet the paratroopers who had landed were not dismayed. They were in a position to intercept road and rail communications with Lillehammer in the south and they continued to fight. In the course of the next few days they inflicted many casualties on the Norwegians and harassed them continually with raids and fighting patrols. (Some of the latter penetrating up the valley clashed with British troops advancing southwards.) Schmidt continued to retain command throughout this period despite his painful and incapacitating wounds.

After four days and five nights of fighting however ammunition was running low and the 34 surviving paratroops had to surrender. For four days they had blocked a strategically important road and railway and made a material contribution to the battle for Norway, by hampering the British link up with the Norwegians long enough for the German Army to be reinforced. The gallant Schmidt received the *Ritterkreuz* for his role in the action. (Major Schmidt — as he was then — died in Brittany in June 1944, killed by a sniper's bullet.)

25

Army and Paratroop Rifleman of Air Force badge.

Later in this campaign in Norway another airborne operation had to be mounted to reinforce General Dietl's acutely threatened troops in the Narvik region. Moving troops in Northern Norway was possible only by air as the land and sea routes had been severed by the enemy. So, in the second half of May 1940 Major Walther's 1st Battalion of FJR 1 was called upon again to drop, this time near Narvik. Adverse weather conditions, which precluded all but a few transports taking off from the German base on the Norwegian airfield at Trondheim, made this perhaps the most hazardous operation of the whole campaign. And it took 12 days to get the whole battalion to its objective. Dietl's troops were almost at their last gasp when Walter's paratroops joined them. Yet the effect they had on the battle was negligible. The campaign in the West had begun and at the beginning of June the British and French began to evacuate their troops from Norway. By 8 June Walther's men were fighting in the outskirts of Narvik where they were joined by the 2nd Battalion of FJR 1 — the latter having flown in from Trondheim following a train journey from Oslo. By the time they reached Narvik however, the enemy remaining in the region had capitulated and the 2nd Battalion flew back to Germany.

The paratroops were blooded in Norway and the campaign there had served to demonstrate their immense potential; it had also uncovered some of their weaknesses and shown that heavy casualties could result from their improper employment. For Kurt Student who had been promoted to the rank of Generalleutnant on 1 January 1940 this campaign had important lessons for the impending operations by airborne troops on the Western Front.

CHAPTER 3
The Battle in the West

The Bridges across the Albert Canal

The days preceding the launching of the offensive against the West were a period of hectic activity in the Führer's Headquarters in the Reichschancellery in Berlin. On 2 May Generalleutnant Student and Generalmajor Graf von Sponeck were called to headquarters to be briefed by Hitler and told that D-day would be in four days' time, 6 May. The Führer then went on to issue specific instructions.

'I reckon that Queen Wilhelmina will stay in the Netherlands', he told the two generals. '. . . in her castle in The Hague, perhaps — or her country residence Huis ten Bosch; one or the other. As royalty she is to be treated with the greatest respect. Both of you — Student, Sponeck — will see to it personally that neither the Queen nor any of the royal family is subjected to any personal affront or suffers in any way at all in the course of the forthcoming operations.

'I can be held responsible for most things and I am not going to let anything happen to Queen Wilhelmina. She is well liked by her people and respected throughout the world . . .'

6 May came and passed like any other day, and it was 9 May before the expected directive concerning D-day for the offensive was issued. During the morning the telephone in Student's office rang: Major von Below was phoning on Hitler's orders to ascertain whether the plans and preparations for the airborne operations were complete. Having assured von Below that everything that could be done had been done, Student was told curtly 'D-day is 10 May'. So the operations could now get under way.

The Koch Assault Group of 11 officers and 427 men, standing by in the Hilden-Düsseldorf area moved to the airfields Cologne-Ostheim and Cologne-Butzweilerhof on 9 May. The Group had been divided into four assault sections, to each, allotted a special task. They would be flown to their destinations in 42 gliders which would crash-land on the objectives. The 'Steel' Assault Section, under command of Leutnant Altmann, would capture the Veldwezelt bridge across the Albert Canal and hold it for the Wehrmacht columns which would already be driving hard towards the Canal. Similarly, the 'Beton' Section, under Leutnant Schacht, was to seize the bridge near Vroenhoven and keep it open for the 4th Panzer Division: while the 'Iron' Group, commanded by Leutnant Schächter was to take the bridge near Canne and hold it for the 151st Infantry Regiment advancing from Maastricht. This last objective was a particularly hazardous one because the bridge was under the guns of the fort at Eben Emael.

But it was the objective of Leutnant Witzig's 'Granit' Assault Section which was the most hazardous and difficult of all. With two officers and 83 men — all of whom were pioneers or sappers — Witzig's job was to knock out the Eben Emael fort itself. How formidable his task was may be judged from the fact that this land fortress, completed only in 1935, was one of the strongest in Europe. Built on solid rock, the towering concrete walls of its 64 strongpoints dominated a great stretch of the Albert Canal. The strongpoints themselves bristled with a variety of weapons — field artillery pieces, anti-tank and anti-aircraft guns in the bigger bastions, machine guns in the pillboxes. Six of them were mobile armoured cupolas of 5 metres diameter with steel walls 30cm (12in) thick; at night the beams of 15 searchlights swept the area to lessen the chances of a surprise attack. The entrance to the fortress was on the reverse slopes of the hill on which Eben Emael stood; at the actual gate there was a pillbox built and camouflaged to look like a simple cottage. A water-filled moat ran round the bottom of the hill and the protection this afforded had been supplemented by masses of barbed wire, an extensive minefield and other pillboxes. Inside the fort the garrison under Major Jottrand was 1,200 strong; and the 7th Belgian Division was deployed in the vicinity of Eben Emael to give further protection if it were needed. All in all the Belgians had good reason for considering this, the outlying fort of Liège, to be impregnable.

It was still dark when the gliders carrying the Koch Group were towed off the two Cologne airfields in the early hours of 10 May 1940, and the nine carrying the men of the 'Steel' section were released over the Veldwezelt bridge at 0520. Leutnant Altmann was travelling in the leading glider and on his order the pilot dived towards the objective; the others followed. No sooner had Altmann's pilot shouted a warning 'Hold tight' than the wire bound skids of the glider struck the ground, and the men inside were thrown forward. Altmann leaped out, saw that his glider had landed some distance from the bridge, and watched as one of his other gliders carrying a party under Gefreiter Ellersiek, came to rest directly in front of a Belgian pillbox at the end of the bridge. Ellersiek had landed right on target, but as his men scrambled out of the glider they were greeted by a storm of small-arms fire. Altmann's own men were also engaging the Belgians' attention by this time, and they too came under fire. Ellersiek hurled grenades at the pillbox while one of his men placed an explosive charge at the door. Meantime Altmann had rallied his party and led them under cover along a ditch to the canal bank close to the bridge; from there two of his men were able to climb along the girders of the bridge and disconnect the demolition charges plantd there by the Belgians. The shooting continued, but at 0535 Leutnant Altmann was able to radio a message to Hauptmann Koch: 'From Assault Section Steel: Have captured objective.'

In effect this message might be considered to have been somewhat premature, since the Belgians were still in position and continuing to put up a stiff resistance. Not until a platoon of paratroops, under Leutnant Ringler, landed to reinforce Altmann did the Belgian troops give up their positions near the bridge. Withdrawing to the village of Veldwezelt they were no longer of any concern to Altmann. But two quick-firing field guns located near a slag-heap about 500 metres south-west of the bridge continued to be troublesome, and Altmann radioed a request for air support to deal with them.

Before the Stukas answering his call arrived on the scene, Altmann had unrolled and laid out the recognition parcels his men had brought with them to indicate the limit of their positions. The Stukas roared up, made a pass over the bridge and waggled their wings to show they had spotted the bomb line. Turning now, they screamed down in a vertical dive to their target, with the sirens on their wing tips howling. Bombs crashed down as the aircraft climbed again, and made off to the east. As the noise of their motors faded Altmann's men saw that the Belgian guns had been knocked out by a direct hit, and they played no further part during the rest of the battle of the bridge.

Altmann's party were supposed to be relieved at 1430, but the troops who were to take over arrived in dribs and drabs and the relief was not effected until 2130. Until then Altmann's men had to hold off several Belgian attacks on the bridge. When they were able to break off and move to Maastricht, eight of their number had been killed and 30 wounded — 14 of them severely. But they had achieved their objective and done everything they had been expected to do.

The 'Beton' Section reached the Vroenhoven bridge at 0515 — five minutes before 'Steel' went into action at Veldwezelt. The section had taken off from the Cologne-Ostheim airfield in 11 gliders, carrying five officers and 129 men. Over Maastricht, however, the aerial convoy ran into heavy anti-aircraft fire and one glider carrying Leutnant Kempas's engineer troop was compelled to make a forced landing near Hottdorf. The aircraft towing the remainder dropped their tows between the Dutch border and Maastricht, leaving the gliders to coast quietly over the enemy countryside down to their objective.

The stillness of the night was shattered by more anti-aircraft fire from the neighbourhood of the bridge and the gliders fanned out to pierce the curtain of fire beyond which the objective lay; once through this curtain they swung round and back to crash-land close to the bridge. The glider carrying Stolzewski's party was hit and stalled at a height of 15m (50ft). Three of the men in it were severely wounded, but the remainder scrambled out of the wreckage and rushed in to attack the bridge. Unteroffizier Bading's glider came down about 120 metres from a strong and fortified enemy position protecting the bridge and manned by men responsible for its demolition. Bading's men, led by Gefreiter Stenzel, raced towards the enemy post shooting several of the defenders who tried to stop them on the way. Then Stenzel, covered by fire from the rest of his party, threw himself down into a ditch which ran towards the enemy position and wormed his way forward until he was almost at the steel door leading into it. When one of the defenders opened the door to see what was going on, Stenzel threw a hand grenade inside and raced after it as soon as he heard it detonate. A rapid burst of fire disposed of the rest of the men inside the post, and Stenzel tore out the wires connecting the explosive charges on the bridge with the demolition set in the enemy post. The bridge could not now be destroyed.

But the fighting had only just begun. The Belgians in other positions along the side of the canal were putting up a fierce resistance and their strength was greatly superior

Left: Oberleutnant Walter Kiess of Sturmabteilung Koch. As a glider pilot in the assault on the Albert Canal he was awarded the *Ritterkreuz.*

Below: The limit of Rotterdam airfield. Waalhaven is on the right.

to that of the Germans. Several attempts were made to recover the bridge, but Schacht's men managed to ward off all the attacks. Much of their success can be attributed to the able support they received from a section of machine guns which was flown in at 0615 to reinforce them. Nevertheless it was touch and go on a number of occasions, and the situation was not considered secure enough to warrant Schacht's withdrawal until 2140. By then an infantry battalion had arrived to hold the bridge and some troublesome Belgian artillery had been eliminated. So Schacht, having completed his task, handed over and pulled his men back to Maastricht. His casualties amounted to seven dead and 24 wounded.

The 'Iron' Section were not so successful. Ten Ju52s took off on time from the Cologne-Butzweilerhof airfield towing the 'Iron' gliders, and headed west for the bridge at Canne. But a navigational error took them off course into Dutch territory and one of the gliders never actually got to its destination. After running through a gauntlet of heavy anti-aircraft fire near Aachen the other nine were eventually released by their tugs in the area of their objective. Gliding towards it, the pilots saw the bridge they were making for suddenly disappear in a shattering explosion; moments later it was clear that the bridge had ceased to exist. What had happened was that the forward elements of the German mechanised column making for the bridges were 20 minutes ahead of schedule. Consequently when the 'Iron' men glided in at 0535 the enemy had been forewarned. Someone in Eben Emael had pressed the remote control button to demolish the bridge at Canne, and the Belgians were ready and waiting for the invaders. Nevertheless the operation had to go on to secure the bridgehead for the columns (the 15th Infantry Regiment and the 51st Panzer Battalion) now driving fast towards the Canal from the German border.

As the gliders came in to land they had to fly through a curtain of anti-aircraft fire. One, which received a direct hit 35m (100ft) above the ground, crashed in flames, and only six of the men inside scrambled out of the burning wreckage. Others came down right in the middle of the Belgian position, and when the troops leapt out they went straight into action with grenades and machine-pistols. Leut Martin Schächter, the commander of this section, stormed up one enemy trench with some of his men. A bullet in the leg checked him momentarily, but he recovered and continued to lead the attack until he fell with a bullet in the head. Leut Joachim Meissner now took over command and pressed on with the attack. At 0550 when his men had smashed their way through to the village of Canne and Belgian resistance in the area had been all but overcome, Meissner sent a radio message back to the Koch Assault Group command post: 'From Assault Section Canne to Assault Group. Reached objective. Enemy has demolished bridge, but engineers can repair damage.'

Shortly after this message had been despatched the Belgians launched a strong counter-attack. This was broken up by the timely support of German Stukas, and the Belgians did not try again in daylight. However, from 2000 on throughout the night the bridge was subjected to a heavy bombardment, and two unsuccessful attacks had to be fought off before the arrival of the vanguard of the German columns at 2330 brought relief. Meissner's section continued to hold positions in the bridgehead until 11 May when they moved to join the rest of the group at Maastricht. By that time casualties had mounted to a total of 22 dead, and 26 wounded — high figures for the numbers involved.

The Assault on Eben Emael

It will be recalled that the objective of Koch's 'Granit' Section was the fortress of Eben Emael. When the section was ordered to stand by on 9 May 1940, the men were living in the Anti-aircraft Barracks at Hilden near Dusseldorf; Leutnant Witzig, the officer in command of the section, was a first class engineer and explosives expert. Eleven gliders had been allotted to transport the section to its objective, and the men who were to fly them were the pick of Germany's best glider pilots.

On the order to stand by the sub-section commanders collected their men and the section was driven to the Cologne-Ostheim airfield, the starting point of the operation. As they awaited the order to emplane, the story is taken up by Oberfeldwebel Peter Arent, the commander of No 3 troop.

'Having reported "all-correct" to Leutnant Witzig at 2100, I paraded my troop and addressed them as follows: "Comrades, we will be going into action tomorrow morning. We have to prove that we haven't wasted our time and that we have learned everything we were supposed to learn." Then I dismissed them, telling them to get some rest. Reveille next morning was at 0245 and we paraded in full kit ready to emplane at 0330. Leutnant Witzig then said a few words, concluding with the order *"An die Maschinen!"* (Emplane!)

'We walked over to the gliders, climbed in, and at precisely 0430 the 11 aircraft tugs took off towing us up towards the morning sky.

'Sometime later our aircraft and gliders rendezvoused with the 11 gliders of the "Iron" section which had taken off from the Cologne-Butzweilerhof airfield. And it was then that an unforeseen and wholly unanticipated accident threatened the hitherto smooth running organisation of the operation. Manoeuvring into a compact air formation the machine pulling the glider with Leutnant Witzig aboard flew across the path of one of the other aircraft, and Witzig's pilot had to bank sharply to avoid his tow rope getting entangled with that of the second glider. Unfortunately the extra stress occasioned by this evasive manoeuvre resulted in the tow rope snapping and Witzig's glider was no longer under tow. Turning back, the pilot was just able to get his glider back across the Rhine before landing. But the assault section had lost its commander. Nor did the bad luck end there, since an engine of one of the aircraft pulling No 2 Troop glider failed, and the glider had to land near Düren. Seeing these mishaps I turned to my companion, Merz, and said to him that if anything happened to me he was to take charge; Merz nodded. Meanwhile Oberfeldwebel Sapper our pilot, continued with the tuneless melody he had started to whistle when we took off... Sapper was completely unimaginative; he just carried on with his job as if nothing worried him.'

When the Ju52 tug signalled that the convoy had reached its destination, Sapper disconnected the tow rope and glided down to earth in a tight spiral. As the ground rushed up towards them, the men in the gliders could see their objective, and Peter Arent glimpsed four of the other accompanying gliders on their way down towards it. Then his machine landed — less than 50m from the fortress. Grabbing their packs of explosives his men dived through the door and raced through a hail of small-arms fire towards the concrete walls of Eben Emael. Right and left of them, men from the other gliders were also running. Merz was carrying a big satchel of explosives and Peter Arent recalled that among all the noise it was Merz's heavy breathing behind him that seemed loudest of all. Dashing through the tracer whipping across the open ground, the two men reached the armoured steel cupola which had been designated as their target. The explosive charge was planted and a great hole was blown in the side of the cupola. Followed by the rest of his troop Arent dashed into the casemate to blast its dazed inmates with a few short bursts from their machine-pistols. Resistance collapsed within minutes, Arent's troop had secured its objective and his men settled in to defend it against a counter-attack.

Outside, the battle was still raging. Of the other nine gliders which landed on the Eben Emael plateau at 0520 that morning, only two made difficult landings from which their crews were unable to make any material contribution to the assault. The pilots of the other seven put their machines down as planned and the 55 men they carried did everything that was expected of them. Seven cupolas were blown sky-high — as were two dummy cupolas — while twelve 75mm and two 120mm guns were put out of action. Much of the credit for these achievements must go to Oberfeldwebel Wenzel who assumed overall command when he learned on landing that Leutnant Witzig was not with the section. It was Wenzel who directed the battle and switched men to points where they were most needed. His first signal to Koch's headquarters was timed 0540 and read as follows: 'From Assault Group "Granit": Reached objective. Everything going to plan'.

Everything was certainly going as planned, but the greater part of Eben Emael was still in Belgian hands, and the Belgians were vigorously fighting back. Peter Arent was not allowed to rest on his laurels. On Wenzel's orders he and his party were sent to deal with the strongpoint known as No 4, where two anti-aircraft guns continued to be troublesome. Carrying 50kg (110lb) of explosives Arent and his men gingerly approached their objective, edging along the concrete walls below the fire of the Belgian machine guns chattering away in the casemates and turning the ground between the fort and the canal into a death trap. Arent had taken the main cupola of No 1 as his primary target. This cupola housed two machine guns which continued to fire right up to the time the Germans detonated their charge and blew the crews to pieces.

Wenzel, who had appreciated the significance of Strongpoint No 1, had trained as an engineer in Königsberg and he was a dedicated soldier. After the events that have been described he became known as 'the dome-cracker of Eben Emael', and but for a singular omission he might have been judged to have earned the *Ritterkreuz* several times over; this second message to Koch was timed 0835: 'Eben Emael: Enemy being repulsed. Main position occupied.'

Only five minutes before this message was tapped out a glider had landed at Eben Emael. It carried Leutnant Witzig. As soon as his pilot had successfully negotiated an abortive landing on the German side of the Rhine he had radioed a demand for another aircraft tug. A Ju52 was despatched immediately which landed in the field where Witzig's glider had come down. A successful tow and flight through the curtain of Belgian anti-aircraft fire at the border took him to his objective where he landed more or less without incident. Happy to be back with his men Witzig resumed command,

and immediately issued fresh orders for a fresh assault to overwhelm the areas of the fortress in which the Belgians were still holding out. Arent, whose party was now ensconced in the strongpoint the Germans had dubbed No 12, was told to reconnoitre Strongpoint No 3. As bursts of fire were still coming from this position it appeared that it was still held by the Belgians, but there was no indication of how strongly. Arent's patrol started out but was cut down by fire. As time passed the shooting grew more intense, and the German attackers were compelled to return and seek shelter in the casemates and bastions they had overrun.

By the late afternoon it looked as if the Belgian garrison had recovered from its initial setbacks. A series of counter-attacks were launched to try to dislodge the Germans, and Koch — back at his command post — was kept busy directing Stuka squadrons to targets which would ease the pressure on Witzig's men. When darkness precluded any more close-support sorties on targets in the Eben Emael complex, many of the defensive works had been bombed and battered into ruin. Because of the dangers of a night attack, the scattered airborne commandos concentrated and consolidated their position in a smaller perimeter. Arent was ordered to evacuate the No 12 strongpoint; before leaving he planted a 50-kilo charge which effectively smashed the defences. Strongpoints 13 and 19 were treated in a similar fashion, and captured Belgians said afterwards that the sight and sound of these positions being blown up rocked their morale. This was already low because they believed the Germans were already in control of most of the underground communication system.

Next morning a detachment of engineers from the 51st Engineer Battalion under Oberst Mikosch, reached the outskirts of Eben Emael, and Oberfeldwebel Portsteffen succeeded in breaking through the Belgian perimeter to establish contact with the airborne troops inside. Morale soared with his arrival and news that other German troops were close at hand. In the event the first fighting patrols linked up with Witzig's men about noon on 11 May and shortly afterwards Leutnant Marquand arrived at the northern approaches to the fortress at the head of a company of the 151st Infantry Regiment. Preceded by a carpet of bombs laid down by supporting Stukas, Marquand smashed his way through the Belgian perimeter. The Belgians stubbornly fought back and in the course of the action the 2nd Belgian Grenadiers suffered very heavy losses — many of them as a result of the bombing and strafing by the Stukas.

The end came suddenly. A trumpet blared, a white flag appeared over Strongpoint No 3, and a hush descended on the battlefield, as Strongpoints 17, 35 and 23 ceased firing. Moments later a man carrying a flag of truce climbed out of one of the Belgian positions, and was taken to Hauptmann Hauboldt — whose company (14/IR 151) had come up in support of Marquand. The Belgian offered to capitulate, and shortly afterwards the Belgian troops began to evacuate the casemates and positions they were still occupying. A total of about one thousand officers and men — including the commandant, Major Jottrand — surrendered. Questioned about booby-traps, Jottrand assured Oberstleutnant Mikosch that the garrison had not left any mines or explosive charges behind.

There the action ended. At 1600 on 11 May the survivors of Witzig's 'Granit' Section climbed into trucks and were driven to Maastricht. Eighty-five soldiers had gone into battle and of these six had been killed and 20 wounded. Witzig, promoted to

Hauptmann as a reward for his contribution to the success of the operation, wrote a report outlining his views on why the troops manning one of the most modern fortresses in the history of warfare had been compelled to give up. He said:

'... There are three main reasons:
a   The shattered morale of the garrison, linked to the fear that we were already inside the casemates.
b   The weakening of the fortress defences caused by the loss of a number of the defensive posts, and the apparent uncertainty attached to which posts had been lost and whether the outer defences were holding.
c   The lack of support — other than of indirect artillery support — and of reinforcement from outside. Because of this it was not possible to mount a strong counter-attack. 40 infantrymen were sent into one counter-attack; of these only 12 survived.'

Commenting on the 'Granit' operation, General Student said after the war:

'It was a deed of exemplary daring and decisive significance. A handful of paratroops, with powerful support by the Air Force, forced a passage for an army to breakthrough. I have studied the history of the last war and the battles on all fronts. But I have not been able to find anything among the host of brilliant actions — undertaken by friend or foe — that could be said to compare with the success achieved by Koch's Assault Group.'

Operations in Holland

Nevertheless the behaviour and performance of the remaining airborne units was no less courageous than that of the Koch Group. In the attack on 'Fortress Holland' there were more airborne operations, deep into Holland, well beyond the Albert Canal. ('Fortress Holland' was the name given to that vital corner of Dutch territory in which are grouped Amsterdam, Utrecht, Rotterdam and Dordrecht.) The German plan was to disrupt this vital area by launching two major airborne operations, whose aim may be described as follows:

a   Surprise landings by the 7th Air Division to seize the important river crossing inside 'Fortress Holland'.
b   An airborne assault on The Hague by the 22nd Airborne Division to annihilate Holland's political and military leaders.

Both of these operations were to be integrated in the overall plan of the 18th Army whose objective had been set as the destruction of the Dutch Armed Forces. The 9th Panzer Division was to cross the Maas river near Gennep, pierce the main line of defence on the Yssel-Maas, push across the Peel marshes, and advance via Breda across the bridges seized by the paratroops to occupy Rotterdam and The Hague. To be successful it was clear that the timing of the airborne operations would have to be carefully coordinated with the move of the armour, and that the paratroops would have to be dropped in exactly the right places. Furthermore surprise was an all-

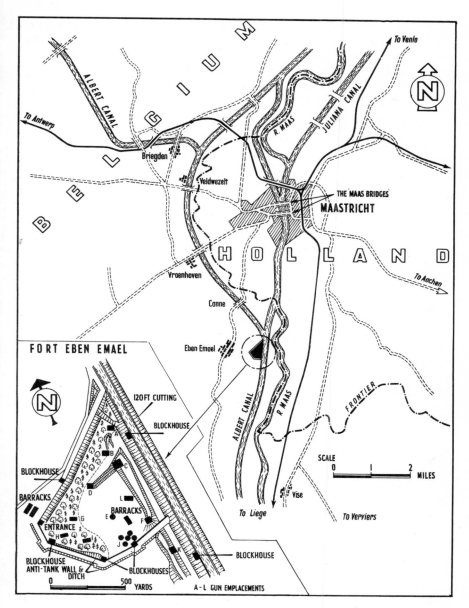

Eben Emael and the Maas Bridges.

important factor in the capture of three important pairs of bridges — at Moerdyk, Dordrecht and Rotterdam — and the airport at Waalhaven. Of these objectives the last was vital since it was proposed to fly in the 22nd Airborne Division to Waalhaven. The 1st and 2nd Battalions of Oberst Bräuer's 1st Parachute Regiment were given the task of capturing the bridges at Moerdyk and Dordrecht, while the 3rd Battalion of the same regiment, under Hauptmann Karl-Lothar Schulz was allotted the Waalhaven airport task.

'Get ready! — Keep your distances. After landing make straight for the assembly area!' Hauptmann Schulz went to the open door of the Ju52. 'One more minute, men!'

Air whistled through the plane, and then the Boschhorn signalled it was time to jump. Schulz, leading his battalion into action in the time-honoured fashion, was the first out. The bulky equipment bag and the weapons he was carrying felt heavy and he was tugged into the slipstream; the air felt as dense as a board. Then came a massive jerk as his parachute opened, and the silken canopy overhead thundered and whipped like a sail in the wind. Schulz shuddered excitedly as he peered down to see the hostile territory rushing up towards him. If the enemy were to open fire now . . . well then . . .

Above and around him the sky seemed filled with the white umbrellas carrying the rest of his battalion; in the pale light of dawn they were easily spotted and seemed terribly vulnerable. Thick clouds of smoke obscured the Rotterdam airport and as Schulz neared the ground he could hear the hiss of bullets as they swept past him. Pulling his legs up towards his torso and pressing his face into his gloved hands he landed and rolled forward. The parachute rustled and flopped down behind him and Schulz threw off the harness. He was down, and nothing had happened to him. Dashing for the cover of dead ground he raised his signal pistol and fired a flare to indicate his position. Panting with exertion, Leutnant Schuller came running up, followed by the machine gun section which immediately took up firing positions. Other detachments followed; the whole battalion had landed . . .

Three Dutch personnel carriers were now seen driving towards them. A burst of fire caused the first to pull round and overturn, and the two remaining vehicles stopped. Dutch troops stumbled out and within seconds the fire of their small arms added to the cacophony created by the stuttering of the German machine guns and machine-pistols. Leutnant Becker, commanding the 10th Company wormed his way up to where his battalion commander was, carefully taking note of the enemy positions. 'Becker', said the latter, 'your company will attack the anti-aircraft gun position on the north edge of the airfield. The 9th Company will assault the positions at the south edge. Kerfin, take your 11th across to that island in the Maas and knock out the anti-aircraft guns there. I shall take the airport control buildings; Schuller's machine gun section will come with me.'

Within a few seconds the three companies were on the way and Schulz, closely followed by Schuller's machine gunners got up and started to advance towards the airport control tower. But Schulz got no further than 20m before machine gun fire forced his party to stop and take cover in a ditch. This was a situation the paratroops had rehearsed many times, and machine gunners from Hillenbrandt's section set up their guns and went into action. Under the cover of their fire Schulz and some of the other paratroops made a dash for the nearest abandoned Belgian vehicle. Reaching it, the men piled in and one of them squeezed behind the steering wheel. Starting up the motor and slipping into gear, he drove straight for the airport buildings — spinning the wheel and forcing the vehicle into an erratic slalom as it came under small-arms fire. Most of this fire came from the airport buildings themselves, but machine guns and quick-firing cannon emplaced in positions at the corners of the airfield were turned on the vehicle as it neared the airport's nerve centre. Once inside the complex of buildings however there was cover, and as the truck slowed the paratroops jumped off and made for the control tower. Schulz himself was in the lead. Kicking open the door of what turned out to be the main office, he was confronted by a number of Dutch officers who raised their hands in surrender at the sight of the German sub-machine guns.

'Gentlemen', said Schulz, 'the airport is in German hands. You are my prisoners.'

'You are invading a neutral country', retorted a Dutch colonel who turned out to be the airport commandant.

Behind him, on a table, stood a silver plaque of a laurel wreath surrounding a centre piece made up of the figures 40.

'Is that for you?', Schulz asked.

The colonel nodded. 'Yes', he said, 'Today I am celebrating 40 years of service to my country.'

'Congratulations', said Schulz dryly, and then snapped out the question: 'Have any mines been laid on the airfield?'

'No, Hauptmann' replied the Leutnant who appeared to be the Dutch colonel's adjutant.

'Good! then you'll come with us!', Schulz responded. 'We have to secure the runways for aircraft bringing our main force.'

Driving in commandeered Dutch vehicles Schulz headed for the main runway. The rattle of small arms coming from the direction of the island in the Maas indicated that not all Dutch resistance had been overcome and that Kerfin's men were battling for the anti-aircraft gun positions there. Nevertheless Schulz considered that the situation warranted his sending the success signal, and his radio crackled out the message 'Airfield in our hands. Anti-aircraft batteries silenced. Landing feasible.'

Ten minutes later the first German troop carriers were seen approaching from the east; these were aircraft carrying units of the 22nd Airborne Division. Above them a screen of fighters hovered like hawks. 'Enemy fighters!' yelled one of the spectators suddenly, and Schulz's men watched as a flight of Hurricanes flew from the north-west towards the Ju52s. German fighters screamed down to protect their lumbering wards and the air was filled with the high pitched sounds of whining motors, and the distant crackle of machine guns as an aerial dog fight developed. Seconds later a Hurricane was seen to crash in flames, followed by a German fighter and the thud of two distant explosions signified their end.

Meantime the Ju52s had continued as if nothing untoward was happening. Sweeping over the airfield in formation, they circled and came in to land one by one. As the first plane rolled to a standstill men tumbled out, ran across the airfield, and deployed along its boundaries. An officer with them, Oberstleutnant von Choltitz, walked over to Schulz. 'My word, Schulz, I'm damned glad you made it', he announced — before going on to say how relieved he was that there had been no anti-aircraft fire to oppose the landings. It seemed he had spoken too soon, however. Hardly had he finished talking when a hitherto silent Belgian anti-aircraft battery opened up and one of the incoming planes was blown to pieces by a direct hit. Schulz ran across to the trucks which had carried his men across to the runways. 'Becker', he shouted, 'Bring your company. The fire is coming from that spit of land on the river'. Paratroops scrambled into the vehicles and drove off.

As Schulz was driving past the airport buildings, he was flagged down by the Dutch commandant he had taken prisoner less than half an hour before. 'I will order them to surrender', he said to Schulz. The German nodded curtly, the Dutch colonel climbed on to the vehicle, and they drove on towards the troublesome battery. About 200 metres from where the guns were continuing to fire salvo after salvo at the incoming German planes, the trucks stopped and the paratroops rapidly deployed for action. As they moved into positions for an assault the Dutch colonel ran forward towards the battery. Waving his hands to draw attention he shouted repeatedly 'Cease fire! Cease fire!' In the event nobody in the battery heard his order or, if they did, nobody took any notice. The guns continued to fire and the colonel was seen to stumble and fall, struck no doubt by a stray bullet.

Now it was up to the paratroops, who attacked and silenced the battery in a bloody little encounter. Waalhaven airport was completely in German hands at last, and there was nothing now to impede the landing of the troop carriers. General Student and Major G. Trettner of the Headquarters of the 7th Air Division were in one of the planes which landed soon after this. Schulz was there to greet them and to give the general a brief run down on the course of events. Meanwhile the transports were ferrying in artillery and the 3rd Battalion of the 16th Infantry Regiment. With these troops at his disposal and the build-up proceeding satisfactorily the airborne commander was confident that he was now able to exploit the successes his paratroops had attained.

Recalling this particular operation after the war, Student said: 'In their assault on prepared positions the behaviour of these men was impeccable and in accordance with the highest martial traditions. Schulz's battalion was crucial to the ultimate success of the operation.'

Turning now to the remaining operations in the Netherlands: while the 3rd Parachute Battalion of FJR 1 was fighting for the Waalhaven airport and occupying the approaches to Rotterdam, the regiment's 2nd Parachute Battalion was dropped at the northern approaches to the great Moerdyk bridge. Hauptmann Prager, the commanding officer, had persuaded the medical authorities to discharge him from the hospital where he was being treated for intestinal cancer, specifically in order to take part in the operation and to be with the men he knew so well. The battalion landed as planned and without loss, and made for the northern end of the bridge. This was defended by a pillbox and the first men who tried to rush it either became casualties to its machine guns or were effectively pinned down by their fire. However, when a properly coordinated attack was launched from two sides simultaneously by Leutnant Straehler-Pohl's 5th Company, the Dutchmen inside the pillbox gave themselves up. As soon as this happened Leutnant Cord Tietjen led his platoon in a mad rush across the road bridge. One or two Dutch soldiers tried to stop Tietjen's men en route and were shot. But the garrison sitting in the pillbox on the far side of the bridge was quickly overpowered before any of them fully realised what was happening. In

Above left: Leutnant Martin Schächter, commander of the Assault Group 'Iron' on the Albert Canal.

Above: Oberleutnant Alfred Schwarzmann, an athletics medallist in the 1936 Olympics, was FJR 1's 8 Company commander and won a *Ritterkreuz* in Holland.

Left: Oberleutnant Rudolf Witzig, commander of Assault Group 'Granit' at Eben Emael.

consequence the bridge was captured intact and Tietjen was awarded the *Ritterkreuz* for his gallantry and initiative.

The battle for the 1,400-metre long Moerdyk railway bridge was decided by other paratroops in a matter of minutes, as there was virtually no opposition. At the Killbrücken in Dordrecht, however, a tough battle developed. Leutnant von Brandis's 3rd Company had landed nearby according to plan, and Brandis had led his men in a dash to gain possession of the south end of the bridge before the enemy had recovered from the sight of parachutists dropping all around them. But the Germans were met by a hail of small-arms fire and Brandis received a fatal wound. One of the platoon commanders took over and pressed on with the attack — driving the Dutch back up the ditches they were defending on and up into the town. There, in the built-up area they met stern resistance and the paratroops suffered heavy casualties when their determination to advance at all costs led them into an ambush.

Oberst Bräuer, who had landed with the 1st Battalion near Tweede Tool saw the situation was deteriorating rapidly. The 1st Battalion (less the 3rd Company) constituted the regimental reserve, and Bräuer decided that the time had come to commit it to the battle. The battalion was ordered up to the bridge and on 10 May the road bridge was securely in German hands. But the paratroops had not been able to take the railway bridge; this had been demolished by the Dutch before the paratroops of the 1st Battalion could occupy it.

With all the principal bridges captured by the paratroops, it is now time to review the situation in the area surrounding The Hague.

The objectives of the 1st Battalion of the 2nd Parachute Regiment and a company of the 2nd Battalion (No 6 Company) attached to it, were The Hague's airfields at Valkenburg, Ypenburg and Ockenburg. Of these only the airborne assault on Valkenburg was achieved as some of the troops were dropped in the wrong zones and those who did land in the correct areas found themselves up against numerically superior enemy opposition. Heavy anti-aircraft fire over Ypenburg and Ockenburg caused many casualties among the transport planes carrying the paratroops, and these airfields were littered with the wrecks of Ju52s which had crashed in flames or tried to land when they were hit. Other planes, whose pilots assumed that the invasion schedule was going well and attempted to land were sometimes more fortunate. That carrying the artillery commander of the 22nd Airborne Division, Oberstleutnant de Boer was approaching the Ypenburg runway when the pilot suddenly realised that not only was the landing ground obstructed with wrecked aircraft but that the Dutch were still in occupation. Gunning the engine he took off again to put de Boer down at Waalhaven.

There, in the meantime, the redoubtable Hauptmann Schulz had been reinforced. The Light Airborne Anti-Aircraft Battery, under Leutnant Timm — which at that time was the only airborne AA unit in the Wehrmacht — had been flown in to Waalhaven to bolster the German air defence. (Schulz's men had in fact taken over and were manning a number of Dutch AA guns.)

Having got over the first shock of surprise the Dutch were fighting back and putting up a stern resistance. The noise of battle was everywhere, and in the confused welter of fighting in and around 'Fortress Holland' the German air assault was thrown out of gear. Apart from those transports which were able to land at Valkenburg as scheduled, the second wave of airborne troops intended for the subjugation of The Hague had to

Left: Leutnant Wolfgang Graf von Blücher was a section commander in I Battalion FJR 1. He won a *Ritterkreuz* in Holland and died on Crete 20 May 1941.

Below: Sturmabteilung Koch with Hitler. From left to right: Lt Delica, Oblt Witzig, Haupt Koch, Oblt Zierach, Lt Ringler, Lt Meissner, Oblt Kiess, Oblt Altmann and Oberarzt Dr Jäger (who received a *Ritterkreuz* on 15 May 1940 as doctor).

be set down on the motorways near Delft and Leiden or among the dunes at Katwijk. In consequence Oberst Fichte, at 22nd Airborne Division's rear headquarters back in Germany, postponed the fly-in of the third wave of airborne units. With all the paratroops committed, the capture of The Hague's airfields was now no longer feasible and General Kesselring ordered the 22nd Airborne Division to call off the operation.

But those men who had already been flown in to Holland — men of the 47th and 65th Infantry Regiments — could not be pulled out. The had to fight on with the paratroopers, and they were already having to stand up to counter-attacks which were increasing in strength and vigour as the Dutch strove desperately to eject the invaders. They were also being bombed and strafed by the Royal Air Force.

A Dutch attack on the flank of the 1st Parachute Regiment was repulsed only by Oberst Bräuer throwing in his last reserves. The Dutch were pushed back behind the Killbrücken sector. But in the late afternoon of 10 May it was learned that motorised Dutch units had overpowered the lightly held German outposts between Dordrecht and Moerdyk, and were now attacking the positions covering the Moerdyk bridge. With the situation going from bad to worse Bräuer, on the morning of 11 May sent for the commanding officer of his 3rd Battalion. 'Schulz', he said, 'get over there right away . . . take two companies. No! just take one; I need the other here. One should suffice, I think'.

Moving in captured Dutch vehicles, Schulz and his one company hurried off to the 5km-long bridge, spanning the chief estuary of the Maas (known as the *Hollandsch Diep*) separating North and South Holland, to join Hauptmann Prager whose battalion had seized it in the first phase of the operation. As Schulz's men neared the southern end of the bridge they were fired on by Dutch soldiers sheltering behind its steel pillars. Schulz rapped out an order: 'Debus and advance up the ditches on the left and right sides of the road.' The company's machine gun took up a position to give covering fire and pin down the Dutchmen who had managed to fight their way on to the bridge; meantime the rest of the paratroopes advanced in open order. Barely 50 metres from the bridge Schulz felt a sharp pain in his hand: one finger had been ripped to shreds. Schulz continued to advance, however. Breaking into a run he was within ten metres of the bridge when he was hit again. This time it was his foot, and when he tried to go on he found he could not. It was the end, so far as Schulz was concerned; together with others wounded in these operations he was taken back to the airfield and flown home to a base hospital. Meanwhile, when Schulz collapsed, his men had surged forward on to the bridge and those Dutchmen who had not been killed or surrendered had fled back towards Rotterdam.

The battle was also going well elsewhere on 11 May. The 18th German Army had pierced the Dutch main line of defence on the Yssel-Maas and were pushing rapidly ahead across the Peel marshes. The 9th Panzer Division had crossed the Maas near Gennep over the only undemolished bridge, and had swept on towards Breda. Brushing aside the French force which had come up to support the Dutch, the Panzers pushed on towards Rotterdam. During the afternoon of 12 May the divisional reconnaissance unit had linked up with the paratroops at Moerdyk and on the 13th a mechanised column rolled on to Dordrecht and Rotterdam, where fierce fighting was still going on.

General Student, who had flown in to Waalhaven on the morning of the 10th, had set up his tactical headquarters there. The following day Oberstleutnant Triebel, a liaison officer on Kesselring's staff, reported to him. The situation was confused and Triebel had been sent to get an up-to-date picture of what was happening in the forward area. He had had a rough passage from Germany; flying in a Henschel Hs126 artillery observation aircraft he had been chased by enemy fighters all the way to Waalhaven. Student handed him a handwritten summary of the situation as it appeared to him, and a brief outline of his future intentions. This report concluded laconically 'It can be assumed that when the airborne operation is over, it will have been completely successful.' This message was immediately relayed to Göring and Hitler when Kesselring reported to Berlin.

The validity of Student's prediction appeared to be confirmed on 12 May when a Leutnant commanding the leading troop of a reconnaissance unit reported to Student near the Dordrecht bridges. His tanks were the vanguard of a mechanised column of the 18th Army, and in his memoirs Student recorded the time a 'memorable moment': it was exactly 1730. The paratroops and the men of 22nd Airborne Division had done all that they had been required to do. They had occupied their objectives and held the airfields and bridges until the arrival of the main force.

But the war in Holland was not yet over, and on the morning of 13 May General Student — accompanied by his ADC and his battle adjutant — reconnoitred the situation on the outskirts of Dordrecht. The south-eastern suburbs were quiet, so Student and his companions, armed only with a carbine apiece, ventured further into the town. There they were joined by the officers commanding two of the advanced panzer units of the 9th Armoured Division, and on Student's orders the task of clearing the rest of Dordrecht began. The tanks moved in and systematically eliminated all the remaining pockets or resistance. The battle ended during the afternoon when a white flag was hoisted over the tower of Dordrecht Cathedral.

Thus by the evening of the 13th, Student was ready to move on Rotterdam. He had the paratroops and part of the 9th Panzer Division at his disposal. But the bridges between Dordrecht and Rotterdam still had to be secured, and there was a sizeable enemy force deployed north of these bridges which blocked the road to Rotterdam. Once this force had been destroyed the road to Rotterdam was open for the 18th Army.

At dawn on 14 May — the day destined to be the last of Holland's five day war — Generalleutnant Hubikki, the commander of the 9th Panzer Division, arrived at Student's tactical headquarters in Rijsoord, to be followed a little later by General Schmidt, the General Officer commanding XXXIX Corps, and Student handed over the direction of the remaining operations.

So ended the first successful airborne operation in military history. And it is a great pity that its conclusion should be marked by the tragic bombing of Rotterdam. The chapter of events which led to what has been described as a display of terrorism of the most horrible kind and on an unexampled scale, opened with the operation to clear Dordrecht. Here, if the Dutch were determined to fight on in a built-up area, Student saw his troops would sustain heavy casualties unless they had air support. He had to decide whether or not his men should be sacrificed and he opted for air support; any general would have done the same in a similar situation. But on that occasion precise targets of military significance were specified — strongpoints where the enemy continued to resist, near the Maas station and in a small sector at the northern end of the Dordrecht bridge. Moreover no incendiary bombs were used.

The fact that these air attacks proved to be decisive now undoubtedly influenced the course of events, starting on 14 May when the commandant of the Dutch troops in Rotterdam refused to heed a German demand to surrender. General Schmidt had issued an ultimatum and the Dutch response came by way of a Dutch captain who was taken to Schmidt's headquarters under a flag of truce. Schmidt thought that he had come to discuss terms, but this was not so. The ultimatum passed to the Dutch general bore no signature, the captain said, and he was not authorised to talk about capitulation until his commander had a properly authorised document. Schmidt concluded that the Dutch were merely playing for time, but he agreed to a truce and a postponement of the attack on Rotterdam planned for that afternoon while the Dutch emissary returned to consult his commander. At this stage Schmidt remembered his request for air support for the attack, and a signal was sent to Air Headquarters ordering the aircraft involved to stand by on the ground until further notice. Unfortunately when this signal filtered through to the operational airfields the bombers had already taken off.

In the early afternoon, Schmidt and Student were waiting in the forward area near the bridge for the return of the emissary with an answer from the Dutch commandant. Close by troops who were to attack Rotterdam if the answer was 'No' were standing to, awaiting the signal to move to their start lines. Suddenly there was the sound of aircraft approaching from the east, and when they got nearer they were seen to be German bombers flying in formation. 'For God's sake', Schmidt exclaimed, 'there's going to be a catastrophe!'. He and Student were soldiers of the old Prussian school — chivalrous and brought up to scrupulously respect the laws and usages of war. Yet before their very eyes the truce to which they had agreed was about to be violated. Clearly they had to stop the aircraft dropping their bombs.

'Flares!', snapped Student. Signal pistols were produced and the two generals and a number of other officers fired red illuminating flares — the agreed signal for stopping an aerial sortie. When the leading formation wheeled, turned away from Rotterdam it was clear that some of their crews had seen the flares and understood the message. In the event the leading commander had radioed the order to turn back to the two formations behind him. But it appears that the message was either not picked up or not understood, and these two units flew on to their targets.

The ghastly destruction of Rotterdam which followed is thus attributable to a sequence of unfortunate circumstances and poor communications. The fact that it was neither intentional nor even necessary at that time heightened the tragedy. All the targets which had been designated were of military importance — the idea being to pulverize the enemy points near the bridges in order to open a path for the panzers to effect a break-through. In the event some of the aircraft failed to identify their targets and many of their bombs fell in the densely populated centre of Rotterdam, the area known as the old town. Official Dutch sources say that 850 people were killed in this particular raid.

The destruction of Rotterdam, combined with the military defeat suffered by their armies, convinced the Dutch that further resistance would be useless and General Winkelman, the Dutch commander, decided to capitulate. On the German side

General Student was selected to conduct the surrender negotiations and organise the arrangements for the Dutch troops to lay down their arms. Accompanied by Hauptmann Hübner, he drove to the Dutch commander's battle headquarters, on the third floor of an apartment building in the north-west corner of the city; there the two men were joined by Oberstleutnant von Choltitz.

Addressing the Dutch officers who had gathered at the headquarters to meet him, Student said a few words to soften the blow of defeat. ' . . . Every battle has to end with victors and vanquished', he said. 'In this instance, gentlemen, you are the vanquished, but your troops have fought with great courage . . . '

The sound of shooting in the street outside made Student pause, and the Dutch officers seemed perplexed. General Student, in a greatcoat with broad white lapels denoting his rank, stepped up to one of the broad high windows in the room and looked out. And what happened next is best described in his own words:

'All of a sudden I felt a terrible blow on my forehead, as if someone had hit me with a big hammer. Then there was a strange frightening noise in my head — a rubbing, squashing, splintering of bones, and my whole skull seemed to be ringing and vibrating. I had been struck tangentially by a shot which stripped a hand-sized portion of flesh clean off the top of my skull. Had I not lived through it I would never have believed it possible for anybody to actually feel a shot in the head and remain fully conscious. In my case it was almost a slow motion experience. Momentarily I assumed that I had been mortally wounded. Then the urge to survive welled up, and I turned to grip the edge of the negotiating table. However my legs gave way and I collapsed as darkness surged over me.'

Student was taken to a Dutch hospital in Rotterdam and that night a Dutch surgeon successfully performed what might be termed a model operation. This undoubtedly saved Student's life, besides restoring his ability to speak. Professor Tönnis, the famous brain surgeon travelled to Rotterdam from Berlin a few days later and it is to him that the credit must go for Student being fit for service within nine months. Student had been awarded the *Ritterkreuz* on 12 May and on 29 May it was announced that he had been given accelerated promotion to the rank of General der Luftwaffe.

The paratroops, whose total strength was still small, had played a decisive role in the campaign in the West. Numerically they were inferior to the troops against whom they had been deployed, and many foreign military analysts have been inclined to assert — even since World War II ended — that their success could be put down to 'special circumstances'. A German 'Fifth Column' was largely the reason why the vital bridges fell into German hands so easily, they have suggested. And in broadcasts during the war authoritative Dutch sources stated that German parachutists 'fell from the skies disguised as market-women, postmen and even priests'. The final word must be that of General Student:

'So far as Germany was concerned the paratroop and airborne assault on Fortress Holland, the bridges across the Albert Canal, and Eben Emael justified the airborne force concept. Everybody sat up and took notice, including the Wehrmacht.

'During the Polish campaign nobody had much faith in the idea, and the prestige of the parachutists suffered a set back. But after the operations in the West morale soared and the paratroops became an elite corps.'

CHAPTER 4

Building of the Airborne Forces and Germany's Intermediate Aims

Operation Sealion fails to materialise

In the weeks that followed Germany's victory in the West there was a good deal of talk about an invasion of England, and rumour had it that the paratroops were to play a vital role in the initial phases of this operation. How much truth there was in the gossip and the rumours can be gleaned from reports emanating from General Student's operational headquarters.

It appears that even before the invasion of the Low Countries and the campaign in France, Kurt Student had worked out a plan for the employment of airborne troops in the first phase of an invasion of England. Their role was to be a straight-forward tactical one, with paratroops being dropped in the immediate vicinity of the bridgeheads they were to hold for a seaborne force. A period of three weeks was considered sufficient for preparations before the operation, and Student called for well-trained infantry regiments to be earmarked as air landing troops — the latter being flown in to reinforce the paratroops. Surprise was considered to be of paramount importance, and the plan assumed that the airborne assault would be launched at the most propitious time, ie when the enemy's defences were weakest. In the event this was June 1940 shortly after the British Expeditionary Force had been evacuated to England — the weeks after Dunkirk of which the military historian Captain Liddell Hart wrote later '...the armed forces available in Britain were so weak that a few divisions could easily have brushed them aside.'

When Hitler issued his directive for Operation Sealion towards the end of July, it was a good six weeks too late to take advantage of the enemy's weaknesses; the British had already recovered. Nevertheless the Führer's plan provided for the employment of an air landing division (*Luftlande*) and the 7th Air Division. These two divisions were to be set down near Folkestone to secure a bridgehead there. Thus the enemy would be engaged on two fronts.* Giant cargo gliders were developed specifically for these operations; these could carry a payload of 21 tons and were capable of transporting the PzKpfw III tank weighing 15 tons or an 88mm gun that weighed eight tons.

Meanwhile the British had learned that the main assault would be delivered in the Folkestone area and had taken energetic steps to repel it. Natural obstacles had been strengthened and a 'reception committee' assembled to greet the invaders. General Student, who had not recovered from the wound he had received in Rotterdam, and consequently was unable to advise the Führer's planning staff said later:

'Had I been there, I would have suggested to Hitler that we should launch an airborne operation to occupy the British Channel ports where the BEF disembarked. And this on the very day that it was being evacuated from the Continent. If we had done so, England's fate would have been sealed because the men who escaped from Dunkirk were at the end of their tether and the majority of them had no weapons. In Britain itself there were not enough troops to stop us.'

Student's plan was a bold one — too bold for cautious army staff officers. Indeed it was too adventurous even for Hermann Göring who, when asked for his views on the idea during his brief postwar sojourn in Nuremberg jail, replied:

'At that time I had only one paratroop division at my disposal... and I had had to build that up in secret. I could not persuade the Wehrmacht to form four airborne divisions quickly, and this was something which rebounded with a vengeance when it came to the question of dealing with Britain. For if those four airborne divisions had been available after the fall of France I would have invaded Britain at the time of Dunkirk.'

Under the threat of invasion the British began to improvise defences and to reorganise their military machine. Winston Churchill, the Prime Minister, appreciating the potential of the airborne arm demanded a British paratroop force, and within three weeks of the BEF being back in England 5,000 of them had answered the call to volunteer for paratroop training. A parachute school was set up at Ringway, an airfield near Manchester, and infantrymen were put through a quick course on how to jump. Work to develop the two gliders, the Horsa and Hamilcar was also started at this time. Meanwhile Hitler held his hand. Before giving the order which would launch the invasion he wanted air supremacy over England. But this was something which the Luftwaffe could not attain.

On 2 September 1940, whilst convalescing, General Student was summoned to an audience with Reichsmarschall Göring at the latter's house, Karinhall, and told that Operation Sealion was to be postponed. Göring then presented Student with the *Goldene Fliegerabzeichen mit Brillianten* (Golden Flying Medal with Diamants) and dismissed him with the words 'You ought not to worry so much, General; you should pay more attention to your health!'

At the end of the month Student again found himself face to face with Göring, who

---

* *Translators Note:* Which two fronts is not clear in the text. Nor in fact is it correct to say that Hitler's July plan envisaged dropping two airborne divisions near Folkestone. To secure bridgeheads for the nine seaborne divisions landing in the first wave of the invasion, 7 Flieger Div was to capture the high ground north and north-west of Folkestone and then secure crossings over the Royal Military Canal in that sector, at the same time establishing a roadblock on the Canterbury-Folkestone road. Other airborne troops were provisionally directed on the downs behind Brighton.

said to him on this occasion 'Hitler is still hoping for a negotiated peace with the British, Student. Perhaps that is the reason for his hesitating over Sealion.' Then the Reichsmarschall added, 'If we lose this war God have mercy on us!'

The Paratroops get Heavy Weapons

In the weeks that followed the fall of France the airborne potential increased. The 3rd Paratroop Infantry Regiment was raised, and a new Paratroop Assault Regiment (*Fallschirmjäger-Sturmregiment:* FJStR) was formed under the direction of Oberst Eugen Meindl. Meindl, who had trained as a mountain gunner, had commanded the 112th Mountain Artillery Regiment in Norway in May 1940 and although none of them had had any parachute training he and some of his gunners had been dropped near Narvik. Because of this he had become an airborne enthusiast, and applied for transfer to the *Fallschirmjäger*. When Meindl passed his course with flying colours Student recognised his potential as a paratroop commander and appointed him to command the embryo Parachute Assault Regiment.

The inadequacy and failings of the equipment carried by the paratroops had been all too apparent during the recent campaigns in the West. Arms containers carrying rifles had been dropped in the wrong place or could not be found, with the result paratroops had on occasions gone into action armed only with pistols, grenades and jack-knives; on other occasions the search for the arms containers had meant the loss of valuable time. Apart from this the lack of heavy weapons had proved to be a serious disadvantage when the paratroops found themselves opposed by a resolute enemy in entrenched positions.

The aim now was to make up and compensate for these disadvantages and to provide heavy weapon support and vehicles for the parachute infantry. In effect a start had been made in May 1940 when a horse-drawn parachute artillery battery had been flown into the airfield at Waalhaven.

A 'quintuplet' parachute was produced specifically for the artillery, in parallel with the development of a new lightweight gun. A parachute artillery regiment for service with the 7th Air Division was then raised and equipped with the light 3.7cm PAK anti-tank gun. But it was some time before any of these developments became effective. And time was something that was of vital concern to the paratroops because the planners were already thinking of other campaigns in which they would add to the laurels the airborne arm had already earned.

Planning for the Future

On 1 January 1941 General Student, now completely recovered, assumed command of the newly constituted Fliegerkorps XI, which included the 7th Air Division, the 22nd Airborne Division (originally the 22nd Infantry Division), and a new Parachute Assault Regiment, whose nucleus was Koch's old Assault Group. Two wings of transport aircraft and a newly formed glider wing were allotted to the formation. The Chief of Staff at Corps Headquarters was Generalmajor Schlemm and his deputy was the former chief of staff of the 7th Air Division, Oberstleutnant Trettner.

On 25 January 1941, Hitler sent for Göring to discuss matters concerning the Luftwaffe, and Student went along. The new airborne corps commander was anxious to establish that he was again fit for active service. The two men travelled by special train and on their arrival at Berchtesgaden they were taken straight to the Führer. Hitler had a great deal to say about the proposed invasion of England but Student sensed that the Führer had never really treated the invasion seriously — that all the talk and all the plans had been nothing more than a deceptive stratagem. During the course of the discussion, however, Student was told to examine the feasibility of an airborne operation against Gibralter. Hitler, it seemed, was reviewing the possibilities of driving Britain out of the Mediterranean, and in the train on the way back to Berlin Göring explained why: 'Something has caused the Führer to shy away from an invasion of England', the Reichsmarschall said, 'Anyway, we've missed the opportunity; it is too late. So the question now is how can we bring about the collapse of the British Empire. The Mediterranean and the Middle East are vital to its survival. But Italy by herself cannot kick the British out of the Mediterranean; she already needs help to defend herself'.

'Well then, we shall have to find a weak spot we can attack', Student responded, 'and it seems to me that the Suez Canal, Crete, Cyprus and Malta all come into this category of weak points.'

'All right, Student', the Reichsmarschall concluded, 'go and work out the pros and cons of an airborne assault on Gibraltar and the other places you've mentioned. It's possible that all four may be considered as suitable targets.'

From his office at Templehof in Berlin, General Student now began to follow the march of events in the Balkans with keen interest. In March the government in Belgrade which had pledged Yugoslavia's support to the Axis powers was overthrown by a military coup and the new government concluded a treaty of friendship with the Soviet Union. Infuriated by this unexpected defiance Hitler ordered the German troops in Bulgaria to deal first with Yugoslavia and then with Greece. Yugoslavia capitulated on 17 April and four days later, the Greek Army of the Epirus laid down its arms. The British Expeditionary Force of two divisions and a tank brigade which had been sent to help the Greeks retreated, and General Wavell the British Commander-in-Chief in the Middle East hastily ordered the evacuation of all British troops should take place on 24 April rather than on the 28th as planned. 54,000 British soldiers had to be embarked and shipped back to Egypt and Wavell's instructions to General Wilson, the British commander in Greece, were that the evacuation should take place from the open beaches of Attica since the Luftwaffe had made it impossible to use the Attica ports. Luftwaffe activity over the beaches however necessitated a switch to the Peleponnese, where the passage to Crete was shorter. But the route to the Peleponnese lay across the Isthmus of Corinth, and the British soon found that this had been blocked by the *Fallschirmjäger*.

On 20 April General Student and Oberst Trettner had flown to the Führer's headquarters at the Semmering, and Student had submitted that with the battle of Greece in its final phase the strategically important island of Crete should not be allowed to remain in enemy hands. His airborne corps could capture it, in one fell swoop, he claimed. Hitler was clearly interested and listened patiently while Student outlined his plan; and when the interview ended, Hitler had sanctioned the airborne invasion of Crete which Student saw as the first step in a series of such operations. First Crete, then a leap on the Suez Canal, via Cyprus. Before Crete, however, the battle for Greece presented the opportunity for another successful airborne action.

Airborne to the Corinth Canal

In March 1941, the 2nd Parachute Regiment, commanded by Oberst Alfred Sturm, moved up to the Plovdiv region of Bulgaria. From here, at the beginning of April, the 'Süssman Force' (General Süssman was now commanding the 7th Air Division) went on to occupy the island of Lemnos which the British were developing as a base for the bombing of the Rumanian Ploesti oilfields.

When, on 24 April, the British switched their embarkation from the Attica beaches to the Peleponnese, the 2nd Parachute Regiment was ordered to seize the bridge over the Corinth Canal and so block the route down which General Wilson's men were now retreating. For this task Sturm had his 1st and 2nd Battalions, one engineer company, a light field battery of artillery, and the usual supporting troops — including a signal company and a medical detachment.

On 25 April the paratroops concentrated in an assembly area at Larissa, and the Corinth operation was launched next morning. It followed a plan characteristic of the airborne operations to date: a glider-borne advance guard consisting of a strong detachment of the engineers, with a platoon of the 6th Company of the 2nd Battalion under Leutnant Hans Teusen was to make a surprise landing in the vicinity of the Corinth Canal, seize the bridge, remove any prepared demolition charges, and hold it pending the arrival of the main airborne force. This was to be dropped in two zones — that of the 1st Battalion north of the canal, and that of the 2nd Battalion south — so as to isolate the bridge.

The story starts with Teusen's operation: At 0500 his men climbed into their gliders and took off from the airfield at Larissa; two hours later they found themselves running the gauntlet of anti-aircraft fire as they came in to land near the objective, the bridge. However all but one of the gliders got through the flak; the remaining one being hit at a height of 8m (25ft) and crashing. Teusen's own glider came to rest near a couple of anti-aircraft positions at the southern end of the bridge. As he and his men scrambled out and rushed towards them, the guns were firing at gliders putting down at the other end of the bridge, and the British positions were overrun without much difficulty. Meanwhile some of the paratroops at the far end had reached the bridge, and scaled its girders, to locate and cut the wires leading from the back to demolition charges. They then went on to dismantle these charges, passing the explosive packages up from under the girders and stacking them on the road in the middle of the bridge.

Whilst this was progressing Leutnant Teusen had wormed his way up to his end of the bridge, where fire from a Bofors had forced him to take cover behind a pile of stones. Teusen had just scribbled a hurried sit-rep for his commanding officer, when he happened to look up and see von der Heyden — the special correspondent who had dropped with the paratroops — taking photographs in the middle of the bridge. As he was tearing the report from his message pad, Teusen heard the stutter of the Bofors again. Then, suddenly, there was the sound of a dull boom followed in quick succession by a thunderous crash as the centre of the bridge erupted and broke; columns of thick smoke rose as the steel frame fell into the canal. The paratroops on the bridge had been blown sky-high, but the journalist's camera was found on the shore later. Inside, the film with the exposure taken at the moment of explosion was intact. The bridge had been demolished by a Bofors shell which had detonated the explosives intended for its demolition in the first place but removed by the paratroops.

52

Hauptmann Fritz Prager who commanded II Battalion FJR 1. He was killed on 3 December 1940.

But the demolition of the bridge could not halt the progress of the operation. The second wave of paratroops dropped into the area north and south just before the bridge went up, and Hauptmann Schirmer's 6th Company, landing in a shallow depression south of the canal, was soon heavily engaged in desperate hand-to-hand combat for British positions covering their dropping zone. This took the pressure off those of Teusen's engineers who survived the explosion. Schirmer's men were steadily gaining the upper hand when Oberst Alfred Sturm contacted Schirmer to inform him he was to assume command of the 2nd Battalion as Schirmer's commanding officer had been wounded. He also told Schirmer to press on with the battle as hard as he could. The enemy was weakening, he said: 'Get after him, Schirmer. Push on as fast as you can; don't give him any respite — drive him as far as Argos and Nauplia'. And so the battle developed into the frantic pursuit which was dubbed 'The March of Schirmer's Argonauts'. Pressing hard on the heels of the enemy rearguard Schirmer's troops successfully overran Argos and Nauplia. But the highlight of the chase was the capture of the commander-in-chief of the Greek Peleponnese Army, followed by the surrender of all Greek troops in the peninsula. On 14 June 1941 Gerhard Schirmer was awarded the *Ritterkreuz* for his part in this action.

In the meantime, supported by fire from two of the anti-aircraft guns they had captured, Teusen's platoon had smashed its way into the town of Corinth. Here it was joined by Schirmer who promptly appointed Teusen commander of the advance guard of the pursuing force. 'Don't lose any time, Teusen', he said, 'Your objective is Nauplia, one of the British embarkation points'. Within minutes Teusen's men were driving south in commandeered vehicles, and just before Tolon they caught up with the enemy rearguard. Although his men were outnumbered Teusen deployed immediately for an attack, and following a short skirmish the enemy surrendered. Forty prisoners were rounded up and left under protection of two wounded paratroopers while Teusen resumed the pursuit.

He did not get far, however. Just outside Tolon his platoon came under fire from high ground on the right of the road, and Teusen himself was wounded as he was reconnoitring. Undaunted by the fact that he had clearly run up against a numerically superior enemy in a strong position, the paratroop commander sent an English-speaking NCO over to parley with the enemy. Teusen's men, the NCO told the British officer in charge, were the vanguard of a German paratroop division supported by dive-bombers whose appearance could be expected any moment. The story seems to have deluded the British, as they promptly capitulated. Thus by a single daring but foolhardy piece of deception Teusen captured a position which dominated the road south to the British embarkation area where the advance could have been delayed for hours. For this, like Schirmer, Teusen was awarded the *Ritterkreuz* on 14 June.

By the time the advance elements of the main Wehrmacht column reached the Corinth Canal on 28 April the 1st Battalion FJR2 had secured the crossing place, driven the enemy south towards the embarkation zone while the engineers were throwing another bridge across the Canal. Consequently the 5th Panzer Division was able to cross immediately. 10,500 prisoners of war were an additional indication of the success of a successful operation which postwar military historians have said would have been even more successful if it had been launched 48 hours sooner. Had it not been two days late, they have claimed, the entire British Expeditionary Force would have been cut off and would have had no option but to capitulate. This, in turn would have meant less men in Crete and consequently a lower casualty rate among the paratroops who were dropped in the subsequent operation on that island.

In retrospect, therefore, while the Corinth Canal operation may be seen as an unqualified success, there is little doubt that it had a deleterious effect on the battle for Crete. The enemy now realised that a German airborne force was not awaiting orders for operations on the Eastern Front but was probably being concentrated for an assault somewhere in the Eastern Mediterranean — an assault which would set the seal on Germany's campaign in the Balkans — possibly the capture of Crete. (Corinth, incidentally, was the first and only airborne operation mounted without the knowledge of General Student.)

Meantime, preparations for 'Operation Crete' were almost complete, and before we return to the events of 21 April, it is desirable to establish the truth in relation to the unwarranted reproach of the German attack on Crete being an incursion into neutral territory. The plain fact is that British troops had been stationed on the island since 29 October 1940 and the German assault was directed against their bases and *not* against the civil population of Crete.

CHAPTER 5
The Airborne Assault on Crete

On 21 April 1941, while General Papagos, the Commander-in-Chief of the Greek Forces, was signing in Larissa the document acknowledging Greek capitulation, a conference at the Führer's tactical headquarters on the Semmering was discussing the future of Crete. Besides General Student and his chief-of-staff Oberstleutnant Trettner, representing the airborne arm, the principal participants were the General der Luftwaffe Jeschonneck, and General Jodl, with Generalfeldmarschall Keitel of the Wehrmacht. Whether Crete or Malta should be the next objectives of an airborne operation was the most important item on the agenda.

During the course of the discussion, Student declared that in his opinion Crete was too important a base to be left in Allied hands, and he was confident that the island could be captured. Turning to Hitler he suggested that once Crete had been captured, it could serve as a springboard for an assault on the Suez Canal, and on Cyprus. This was not one of the Führer's long-matured projects but he gave his approval.

Following the decision to evacuate British troops from the Greek mainland, Operation Demon had resulted in 50,672 men being taken off. Most of them went to Crete whose defences were thus considerably strengthened. In the meantime, on the other side of the hill, the headquarters and units of Student's Fliegerkorps XI moved to Greece, while Student himself and a small group of staff officers stayed on in Berlin to finalise the invasion plan. Unfortunately the plan which was drawn up was based on a spurious intelligence appreciation supplied by Admiral Canaris head of German counter-intelligence. According to Canaris the garrison in Crete was woefully inadequate; most of the Britsh troops evacuated from Greece had been taken to Egypt and very few had been sent to Crete. This information was wrong.

The planners all agreed that there were three courses open in any assault on Crete. Those representing the Luftwaffe's Fliegerkorps IV, responsible for the supporting operation, favoured the occupation of the western half of Crete from Maleme to Canea inclusive and its capture by two divisions advancing from west to east. This, they said, would have the advantage of an overwhelming concentration of force in a limited area — ensuring local superiority even if the enemy proved stronger than expected. Furthermore Fliegerkorps VIII, responsible for the fly-in, would have an easier task.

The main disadvantage, so far as they could see, was that such an operation would necessitate difficult, and perhaps lengthy flights in a mountainous region. This could be risky because the enemy had airfields in the eastern half of the island.

Fliegerkorps XI representatives proposed the second course. They favoured a simultaneous widespread occupation of the island following drops at seven points on the island — the most important being Maleme, Canea, Rethymnon and Heraklion. The advantage of this method was that the most important localities would be occupied immediately and this would lead to the island being overrun quickly. The disadvantage was that the assault forces would be dispersed and relatively weak, and support at all points might be difficult.

The third course — a compromise, was the one that was ultimately adopted. In its final form the agreed directive read as follows:

1   The capture of Crete will be achieved by seizing the four most important strategic areas. These will be assaulted on a time scale which permits the complete support of Fliegerkorps VIII. In the morning the objectives will be Maleme and Canea in the western sector; in the afternoon Rethymnon and Heraklion will be the targets.
2   Immediately the operations on the Greek mainland are concluded the undermentioned intelligence operations will be mounted:
    a   Two squadrons of Fliegerkorps VIII will fly a series of reconnaissance missions to give continuous cover of shipping movement in the Crete area and of port activity, and to determine the strength and dispositions of the enemy air force on the island.
    One reconnaissance squadron of the Fliegerkorps XI will reconnoitre air fields, field defences, artillery positions and the dispositions of troops etc on Crete.
    b   Simultaneously, the counter-intelligence organisation, under the direction of Admiral Canaris, will try to establish the strength of the garrison on Crete by means of agents and other means.
    c   By systematic interrogation of prisoners, the 12th Army will seek the similar and confirmatory information.

As a result of these instructions the following intelligence picture emerged:

First: it became clear that Suda Bay was the most important harbour on the island. Few warships put in there but most of the commerical shipping used it. Only limited off-loading facilities existed at Rethymnon, Heraklion, in the Gulf of Mirabella and in the Bay of Mesara.

Second: Crete had two fully operational airfields, at Maleme and Heraklion, and a landing strip with limited facilities near Rethymnon. There were between 25 and 40 aircraft on each of the two airfields — mainly fighters and fighter bombers. Antiaircraft guns were deployed in strength in the Canea area, round Suda Bay, at the Maleme airfield and in the vicinity of Rethymnon and Heraklion.

Third: On the basis of reports by agents and prisoners of war, the strength of the island's garrison was estimated to be about one division plus — the indeterminable 'plus' comprising elements and units evacuated from the Greek mainland. (That this appreciation did *not* correspond with the real situation revealed later may be attributed to the fact that the British had started to build up the island's defences long before the

German campaigns in the south-east Mediterranean region. Moreover they were masters in the art of camouflage of fixed defences. Air photographs of anti-aircraft positions disclosed dummy emplacements, but the real positions were not identified. So far as the reports supplied by agents on the island were concerned, many of these were contradictory and lack of time precluded clarification of details.)

The British had resolved to defend and hold Crete. And, as they concluded that the German intention was to take the island by airborne assault, the defences had been prepared accordingly. Strongpoints, capable of all-round defence, covered the airfields and open areas which might serve as landing strips. However the German information was that the defences were weak and so the operational staff of Fliegerkorps XI decided on the following plan of attack:

The Maleme and Heraklion airfields were to be captured by one parachute regiment in the first phase of the assault; reinforcements would be then flown in. Meantime a second parachute regiment would be dropped on or near Canea, where it was believed the main garrison was deployed. One of the objectives of this assault force would be General Freyberg's headquarters. To cover the rear of the Canea force the parachute engineer battalion would be dropped at Alikianon. Finally, a fourth battle group would descend on the Rethymnon area and spread out to link up and form a continuous line with the other battle groups.

General Bernhard Freyberg had been appointed GOC of the allied troops on Crete on 30 April 1941. He and General Wavell, the Allied C-in-C in the Middle East, had decided that if the Germans did attack Crete by air and by sea the assault would be directed against one or more of four areas — Maleme, Suda Bay including the town of Canea, Rethymnon and Heraklion. Consequently the defence organised by Freyberg in the coming weeks was concentrated on these four areas and geared to an airborne assault.

The following details extracted from 'Creforce' Operational Order No 10, issued on 3 May 1941 by Freyberg's 'G' staff, outline the disposal of the garrison.

Heraklion Sector, under command of Brigadier Chappell:
14th British Infantry Brigade, and attached troops including:
7th Mediterranean Rgt; 2/4 Australian Infantry; 156 British AA Battery; 7th Australian Light AA Battery.
B Battery of the 15th Coast Artillery Regiment was deployed against seaborne landings, and two Greek infantry battalions were held in reserve.

Rethymnon Sector, under command of Brigadier Vasey:
19th Australian Brigade (2/2, 2/7, and 2/22 Australian Infantry Bns and one machine gun company). with two Greek infantry battalions in reserve.

Suda Bay Sector, under command of Major-General Weston:
A composite force to protect the supply centre of the island and the Akrotiri Peninsula — consisting of the British 151 and 234 Heavy AA Batteries with the British 120 and Australian 7th Light AA Batteries; the 2/8 Australian Infantry Bn; the Northumberland Hussars and one motorised infantry company, and the main body of the 15th Coast Artillery Regiment. One Greek infantry battalion was held in reserve.

Maleme Airfield Sector, under command of Major-General Puttick:
The 2nd New Zealand Division — with the 4th and 5th NZ Brigades and Major Oakes's battle group; one section of the 7th Australian Light AA Battery. Three Greek infantry battalions would be in reserve.

The strength of the island's garrison at this time amounted to 30,000 Empire troops and 11,000 Greek soldiers, and the British in Cairo pulled out all the stops to get reinforcements to Crete.* From the beginning of May right up to the day of the invasion, combat units continued to reach Suda Bay. The 2nd Battalion Leicesters and the 1st Argyll and Sutherland Highlanders were transferred from Egypt, and General Freyberg ordered the formation of a 10th New Zealand Brigade under Colonel Kippenberger. The 4th Brigade was commanded by Brigadier Inglis, the 5th by Brigadier Hargest; and Admiral Cunningham, Commander-in-Chief of the British Mediterranean Fleet, was made responsible for naval operations relating to the defence of Crete. The aim was to prevent seaborne landings on the Crete coast, and he tells about it himself:

'It was known that an airborne invasion was intended; but it seemed almost unbelievable that such an operation could possibly succeed against troops who had been forewarned. Moreover the airborne force would have to be reinforced by troops coming by sea, and as the convoys bringing these troops would almost certainly be destroyed by the Mediterranean Fleet, the invasion had little chance of success.'

Until 20 May, the Mediterranean Fleet did everything that was expected of it. In general these responsibilities could be considered to fall into two broad categories — keeping open the supply route to Suda Bay, and measures to counter the German attack when it was launched.

The British expected the invasion to start on 17 May and three days before that date Admiral Cunningham ordered the Mediterranean Fleet to put to sea. On 15 May Cunningham told General Wavell how he proposed to cope with the invaders:

a *Task Force C* (Rear Admiral Glennie in *Dido*) with *Kandahar, Kingston, Juno* and *Coventry* would deal with invasion forces approaching Heraklion.
b *Task Force D* (Rear Admiral Kings in *Naiad*) with *Phoebe* and two destroyers, was to stop any landings west of Rethymnon.
c *Task Force B (Gloucester* and *Fiji)* was to destroy enemy approaching the north-west coast of Crete and support Unit D.

* *Translator's Note:* None of these 'extracts' bear much resemblance to the facts and they are very misleading. For example the author gives the impression that the whole of the 2nd NZ Div *plus* two bdes was deployed in the Maleme sector: the truth is that the division only had two brigades. In the paragraph following the 'extracts' a garrison strength of 30,000 Empire and 11,000 Greek troops is quoted. In fact the combined strength of the troops deployed on Crete immediately before the invasion was, according to Wavell's despatch, 28,600. The Greek troops, who had come to Crete from the mainland were poorly armed and had very little ammunition (There is no indication of the source of the information related in these paragraphs but it would appear to have been derived from wartime German reports.)

d *Task Force A* (Vice Admiral Pridham-Whippel in *Queen Elizabeth*) with *Barham* and five destroyers was to take up a position west of Crete from where it could shield Forces B, C and D.

e *Reserve* (remaining in Alexandria): *Warspite, Valiant, Formidable, Ajax* and all other available destroyers.

f *Patrols:* Night patrols were planned as follows:
   i Force B: south from Cape Matapan on the west coast of Crete
   ii Force D: from Piraeus on the east coast down to the Kithera Channel
   iii Force C: between the island of Leros and the Kasos strait.

g On completion of their patrols all task forces were to pull back to the waters north of Crete at dawn and subsequently to the south of Crete.

h The submarine *Rorqual* was to operate in the waters around Lemnos.

i A flotilla of fast patrol boats was based on Suda Bay.

j The *Abdiel* was to lay a minefield between the island of Cephalonia (Kefallima) and Levkas (S Maura) to harass enemy traffic through the Corinth Canal.

k Air reconnaissance missions were to be flown (In the event those that were flown were inadequate.)

l The C-in-C Mediterranean was to control operations from Alexandria, but force commanders were told that they were expected to act on their own initiative against when they received information of the presence of enemy formations.

Up to 13 May Fliegerkorps VIII, on whom rested the burden of the preliminary operations, concentrated on Suda Bay and the sea approaches to the island. The attacks were directed mainly against the enemy anti-aircraft batteries and shipping, and the cruiser *York* — whose AA batteries were especially active — received a very heavy pounding. Attention was then turned on the airfields and on 19 May air reconnaissance reported only a few serviceable aircraft remained at the Maleme and Heraklion airfields. The anti-aircraft batteries on the northern and southern shores of Suda Bay were still firing however, and one of the AA batteries of the *York* remained in action. Suda Bay itself was dotted with the wrecks of burned-out vessels, and according to a report by Admiral Cunningham all but seven fighter aircraft in Crete had been wiped out. In consequence General Wavell ordered the remaining aircraft to be withdrawn and on 19 May the seven survivors took off for Egypt. The effect of this order was to deprive the British Mediterranean Fleet of air cover from 19 May.

On the same day (19 May) the Greek 1st Regiment, which had been ordered to make the incomplete airfield at Pediada-Kastelli secure, was put under command of the 5th New Zealand Brigade (Brigadier Hargest). General Freyberg had now done everything possible to organise the defences against an airborne assault. To counter a seaborne attack from the Greek mainland, he was relying on the Royal Navy.

On the other side of the hill, the Germans that day completed their preparations, and by the evening (of 19 May) they were waiting on the airfields, ready to emplane for Crete. The troops had been briefed; they knew what was expected of them, and the High Command was confident of a quick and decisive success. The tasks of the aircraft of Fliegerkorps VIII which were to support the invasion had been set out in a schedule drawn up in the most minute detail. Fighters, fighter-bombers and dive-bombers were all standing by, and waiting for the signal to attack.

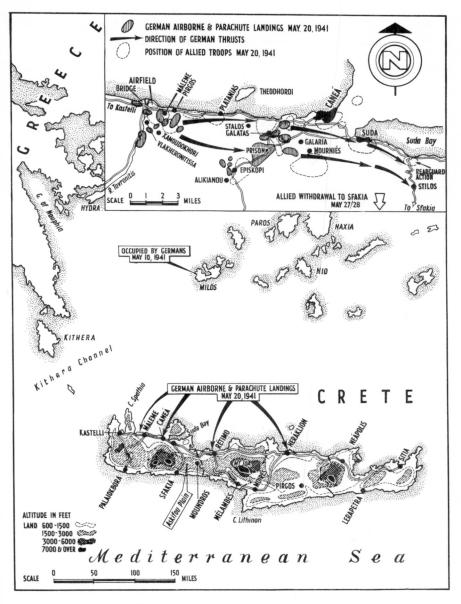

Paratroop operations on Crete.

The general plan for the airborne invasion envisaged the use of three airborne task forces — one of which had been allotted two objectives. As a simultaneous assault was not considered feasible — because it was thought that the limited air space over the objectives would be too crowded — the operation had to be carried out in two phases. Thus in the early hours of 20 May the first wave of attackers were to descend on Maleme, Canea and Suda Bay, and the transport planes would return to pick up the second wave. Phase 2, the assault on the airfields at Rethymnon and Heraklion, was thus timed to begin at 1300.

The order of battle was as follows:

PHASE 1

The Paratroop Assault Regiment (Generalmajor Meindl)

1st Battalion (Major Koch) — Glider-borne landings. Objectives the AA positions at Canea, Suda Bay and the Maleme airfield. Also responsible for the capture of Pt 107 near Maleme.

2nd Battalion (Major Stenzler) — Parachute drop east of Maleme and west of Spilia.

3rd Battalion (Major Scherber) — Parachute drop east of Maleme.

4th Battalion (Hauptmann Gericke) — Parachute drop west of the road bridge across the Tavronitis.

3rd Parachute Regiment (Oberst Heidrich)

1st Battalion (Hauptmann Freiherr von der Heydte): Parachute drop on flat ground in the vicinity of the Agya prison. Objective — to cut the Canea-Suda road.

2nd Battalion (Major Derpa): Parachute drop east of Agya prison. Objective — the Galatas Heights.

3rd Battalion (Major Heilmann): Parachute drop Galatas area. To secure the Galatas-Daratsos-Alikianon road—Canea region for subsequent occupation by the Regiment.

1st Parachute Engineer Battalion (Major Liebach) less No 3 company: Parachute *1st Parachute Engineer Battalion* (Major Liebach) Less No 3 company: Parachute drop in the area north of Alikianon.

PHASE 2

2nd Parachute Regiment (Oberst Sturm)

1st Battalion and attached troops (Major Kroh): Parachute drop on the Rethymnon airfield region.

2nd Battalion (Not deployed here)

3rd Battalion and attached troops (Hauptmann Wiedemann): Parachute drop into the area between the airfield and town of Rethymnon.

1st Parachute Regiment (Oberst Bräuer)

1st Battalion (Major Walther): Parachute drop near Gourned, east of the town and airfield of Heraklion.

2nd Battalion (Hauptmann Burckhardt): Parachute drop east of the town of Heraklion

3rd Battalion (Major Schulz): Parachute drop on the town of Heraklion.

Above: Shortly after landing on Crete. The weapons containers are unloaded.

Left: The first drink of water on the island.

63

2nd Battalion of the 2nd Parachute Regiment (Major Schirmer): Parachute drop on Heraklion to become the force reserve.

The 22nd Airborne Division, whose men had fought shoulder to shoulder with the paratroops in Holland, was not availabe to take part in the invasion of Crete — codenamed Operation Merkur. In March 1941 it had been shifted to Rumania and deployed to protect the Ploesti oilfields; to take its place in Student's Fliegerkorps XI came the 5th Mountain Division (Generalmajor Ringel). (Student had asked that Fliegerkorps VIII should also be put under his command for the invasion but this request was turned down.) During the Greek campaign the 5th Mountain Division had fought with distinction and had just marched 1,300km (930 miles) down the peninsula. Shortly after his arrival in Athens the divisional commander was handed a map of Crete and a sheaf of papers headed *Secret: Operation Merkur*. Ringel commented later:

'The first few sentences sent a cold chill down one's spine, for it was clear that the operation so laconically and soberly described would be a suicidal adventure'.

Having set up his headquarters in one of the high rise buildings on Ommonia Square in Athens, Ringel and his principal staff officers — Major Haidlen and Hauptmann Ferchl — began to translate the orders he had received into operational instructions for the issue to the units of the division. Meantime the division was concentrating near the airfields in southern Greece — on Euböa, in Attica and Böotien — from which it was to fly to an as yet unknown destination. On 14 May, when Fliegerkorps VIII concentrated the full weight and fury of its resources on the airfields in Crete the destination could no longer be considered a secret. The Mountain troops realised that they were bound for Crete.

The weather was good — hot days, blue skies and sunshine — when on 18 May, the vessels of two so-called 'light-boat' convoys were loaded with the heavy weapons of the paratroopers and men of the mountain division. It appeared that the division was to be transported to Crete in a frail armada of ships ranging from tiny trawlers to minute freighters, which had been collected in harbours in the Piraeus and on the island of Euboea. Munitions of every conceivable variety, guns, tools, vehicles, motorcycles and drums of petrol were loaded and the rest of the space was filled up with men — paratroops first and then the men of the Mountain Division. The boats were marshalled into two squadrons, with an Italian destroyer as escort — *Lupo* with the first, *Sagittario* with the second convoy. Finally in the early hours of 20 May the two convoys sailed from the Piraeus and Khalkis respectively — both heading for the island of Milos, from where they were to continue to Crete.

On board convoy number one was the 3rd Battalion of the 100th Mountain Regiment and some supporting units under command of Oberstleutnant Ehal; number two convoy carried the 2nd Battalion of the 85th Mountain Regiment under Major D. Treck.

In his book *Hurra die Gams* (Hurrah the mountain goat) General Ringel has given his views on this aspect of the invasion:

'The ferrying operation caused me far more concern than the imminent airborne move of the other units to the island. It was crazy. Anyone who had anything to do with Operation Merkur felt uneasy about it to say the least, and those who actually had to go by boat regarded it with horror. Officers and men alike all said that they would rather fly to Crete than risk going by sea.'

Everything was now ready . . . the prelude to the first airborne invasion of an island was about to begin.

CHAPTER 6
The First Day:
The Hell of Maleme

Leutnant Alfred Genz of the Parachute Assault Regiment (FJStR of Fliegerkorps XI) was given the job of knocking out an anti-aircraft battery on the southern outskirts of the Cretan capital, Canea. He and the 90 men of his company were to be landed in nine gliders and when he had completed his mission he was to try to hold the enemy position pending the arrival of the 3rd Parachute Regiment whose objective was Canea. If his men were unable to hold on, however, Genz was to break out and try to link up with the 2nd Company of the Assault Regiment which, by then, would be in action in the Akrotiri area.

On the evening of 19 May, Leutnant Genz briefed his platoon commanders: 'Toschka', he told the young subaltern who had been commissioned in the field for distinguished service in Holland where he had been an Oberfeldwebel 'You will be landed directly in front of the guns, and I am relying on you to put them out of action.' Toschka made a note on his map as Genz addressed his second platoon commander: 'Mahrenbach', he said, 'You will be put down where the road going south joins the main road along the coast, and your job will be to deal with the infantry positions shown up on the air reconnaissance photos. After that you can expect the enemy in Canea to counter attack and you must hold the crossroads.'

'What about us, Herr Oberleutnant?', Kempke the commander of the support-weapon platoon asked.

'Your platoon will be with company headquarters', Genz replied. 'One mortar and a heavy machine gun will be in the three gliders directly under my command, and we shall land near the olive grove due south of the enemy AA batteries. Air reconnaissance reports that the grove is occupied, and your job will be to keep the enemy's heads down and stop them going to the aid of the British in the gun positions ... That is all!'

The night of 19-20 May was still, clear and bright and at dawn a blood-red sun gave promise of another day of blue skies and brilliant sunshine. But activity on the airfield at Tanagra, where the 1st Parachute Assault Regiment was to emplane, also suggested that the stillness would shortly be shattered. The engines of nine Ju52s were warming up, tow ropes had been attached to the nine gliders they were to tow to Crete, as the men destined to write a page in the history books left their tents and marched across to the gliders. There was little need for the shouting of orders; every man knew exactly what he had to do. And once they had taken up their positions in the gliders the engines roared as the aircraft systematically accelerated down the runway, and towed their loads into the azure dome of the Mediterranean sky. The vanguard of the invasion was airborne; it would set foot in Crete one hour ahead of the main body of Fliegerkorps XI — at the close of the massive dive-bombing attack which had just begun.

The aircraft flew over the Peleponnese, past the island of Kithira and south towards the island where so many of the paratroops had a date with death. As they approached the coast the enemy anti-aircraft guns opened up. The intention had been to circle round, heading well to the west, and approach the landing zones from the south-east, flying in low out of the sun. But the Ju52s flew on a course which brought them to Cape Spatha, only a few miles north-west of their objective near Canea. As they flew through the flak Leutnant Genz's glider was rocked by a near miss, and he saw the two gliders to his immediate right and left break away from their tugs. There was no sign of the other gliders who were supposed to be following him, and the transport planes which were pulling them were turning back towards Greece. They had dropped their tows, and Genz realised that his glider was now also on its own. At a height of 2,200m (7,200ft) his machine was floating down towards the island through a furious light AA and machine gun barrage.

Leutnant Werner, the pilot of Genz's glider, turned in his seat and looked questioningly at his company commander. 'There is our target, Werner', snapped Genz. The pilot, gliding over olive groves and vineyards and narrowly missing a number of obstacles, held his course and landed with a crash which raised a shower of dust. Genz grabbed his machine-pistol, threw open the glider's hatch and jumped out; the first German soldier had landed on Cretan soil. As his men followed him, faces crowned by flat steel helmets suddenly materialised in front of them and there was a rattle of small-arms fire and thud of exploding grenades; a hundred metres away machine gun fire suggested another battle was in progress.

Not all the landings had gone so comparatively smoothly as that of Genz and his men. One of the enemy AA guns had scored a direct hit on the glider carrying Gefreiter Hahn's section, but the pilot had coasted through the curtain of fire to crash down on top of one of the AA positions, and the glider had ended up against the barrel of one of the guns. 'Let's get out', shouted Hahn, a tough Westphalian, as he leaped through the hatch. There was a flurry of shooting, two pistols cracked and Hahn fell to the ground mortally wounded. Gefreiter Holzmann, seeing his section commander fall, ran for cover. Diving behind the sandbagged wall of the emplacement he hurled a grenade into the gun position, and then worked his way round the wall to despatch the British gunners in the trench behind.

The glider carrying Leutnant Toschka had overflown its objective. Landing in Canea, Toschka and his men were confronted with a resolute group of enemy troops who tried to pin them down. A bloody little battle ensued, which ended when Toschka's men destroyed a couple of lorry loads of enemy soldiers. Toschka was now able to press on to his objective, the AA battery. Once there he and his men systematically worked their way up the honeycomb of trenches surrounding it —

ousting the defenders in a fierce hand-to-hand engagement, in the course of which Toschka himself was killed.

In the meantime, the two sections under command of Leutnant Genz fought their way up to the battery positions and soon after this what had represented the biggest obstacle to the airborne assault on Canea was in German hands.

'All-round defence' ordered Genz.

As his men deployed, elements of Leutnant Mahrenbach's platoon arrived on the scene. There was only a few men... so what had happened to Mahrenbach's contingent?

'There's the crossroads! Put the glider down!', shouted Leutnant Mahrenbach as he saw his objective looming up ahead. Shells were exploding all round the glider as it came in to land and the platoon commander was killed in a sudden hail of shrapnel. Oberfeldwebel Bühl, who should have taken over was wounded in the head at the same time, and all but one of the men in the glider became casualties. But the one man who escaped injury, Gefreiter Adolf Pfriemberger reached the crossroads, took up a position nearby and prepared to carry out the task allotted to his platoon. He did not have to wait long. As four truck loads of enemy troops sped down the road from Canea towards the battery, Pfriemberger raised his machine-pistol and took a careful aim. His first burst of fire struck the driver's cab of the leading truck, and it came to a halt slewed across the road. Unable to get past, the other three vehicles also had to stop. When their occupants got out and began to make for the house where his wounded comrades had taken shelter Pfriemberger nipped round from one side of the building to the other, firing burst after burst at the enemy — changing magazines as he ran. The enemy, who had attacked in company strength suffered heavy casualties and eventually gave up and retreated. Pfriemberger had fulfilled the platoon's mission — one man, on his own but supremely self-confident, had made the impossible possible.

'Look there', said one of Genz's men pointing skywards. An hour had passed since the first company had arrived in Crete and the Ju52s were returning with more gliders for a landing on the Akrotiri peninsula. 'That', responded Genz, 'is Hauptmann Altmann with No 2 Company... everything is going according to plan.'

Only a few minutes had elapsed since they had watched the descent of units of the 3rd Parachute Regiment and the morale of Leutnant Genz's men was high. The time was 0900; 34 of the men were still fighting fit and the company had accomplished its mission. The British guns were in German hands, and Genz's men were now trying to get them back into action against the enemy. Genz's mind now turned to the courses open to him. Should he attempt to establish contact with No 2 Company? To do so he would have to cross open mountainous terrain. At that moment the Gefreiter in charge of the radio reported, 'Herr Oberleutnant, a message from the 3rd Regiment: "Cannot break through to Canea. You should try to link up with us..." ' There the message had ended, and as the set was smashed by a bullet a few minutes later, it was the last that would be received.

The enemy was fighting back.

'Herr Oberleutnant, tanks are coming straight for us'...

'We'll pull back south-west through the olive groves'.

Carrying the wounded with them, Genz's men left their positions and ran back, their solitary machine gun providing covering fire until they had all reached the vineyard

Paratroops leave a
Ju52 which has
landed near Maleme
and is under fire.

Dropping on Crete.

A tented camp on
Crete.

which lay behind the battery positions. But they did not get much further — 150 metres further on the party was pinned down in an olive grove by machine gun fire. The order was given to spread out and Genz's men slithered into and along the irrigation ditches criss-crossing the plantation. Further progress was impossible. They were able to hold their ground but an attempt to fetch water from a nearby farmhouse was repulsed. All they could do was to sit and wait until it was dark.

The Fallschirmjäger-Sturmregiment

The Parachute Assault Regiment (FJStR) commanded by Generalmajor Meindl was ordered to occupy the north-eastern corner of Crete. In particular the Maleme airfield was to be captured and kept open for the fly-in of air-landed reinforcements. When Maleme had been secured, Meindl was to link up with the 'Central Force' in the Canea region.

For this task the following troops were put under command of the Parachute Assault Regiment:

3rd AA Machine Gun Battalion (*Flak MG Bataillon:* FlaMG): one section of five 2cm guns; commander Leutnant Theuerling.

1 battery 7th Parachute Artillery Abteilung (*Fallschirm Artillerie Abteilung:* FAAbt): commander Hauptmann Schram.

1 platoon 7th Field Hospital Abteilung (*Sanitäts Abteilung:* SanAbt); commander Oberst (Senior Medical Officer) Dr Sietzel.

In the afternoon of the first day the Regiment was to be further reinforced by two battalions of the 100th Mountain Artillery Regiment, and an AA battery. These would be deployed at the airfield and both would be brought in by sea. The 1st and 2nd Companies of the 1st Battalion of the Assault Regiment were detached as the 'Central Force', which had a special assignment.

In his operation order General Meindl outlined the role of the 'Western Force':

1st Battalion (HQ; 3rd and 4th Companies, each of 108 men):
Glider-borne assault at Y-hours. Objectives AA positions south of the Maleme airport. Capture of the gun positions and enemy camps in the vicinity to be followed by an assault on the airfield — method at the discretion of the commander.

3rd Battalion (reinforced by 1/3 14 Coy [one platoon of 14 Coy of the 4th Bn] and 1/2 3 FlaMG Battalion [Half of the section of 3rd LAA Battery]):
a At Y-hours plus 15 minutes one company (9th Coy Hauptmann Witzig) to parachute into the area east of the airfield — between the villages of Maleme and Kirchdorf on the edge of the airfield. Objective: support of the 1st Battalion in its assault from the east.
b The main body of the 3rd Battalion to drop into the area north and east of Maleme. Prime objective: to mop up the town and secure the river bed east of Maleme.
Subsequently, under direction of the Regimental Commander, to advance east and link up with the Central Force.

The Regimental staff battle group and elements of the 3rd Battalion — commanded by Major Braun [Meindl's principal staff officer — equating to Colonel GS in a British division], with Leutnant Schächter and Leutnant Trebes — will make a glider-borne assault at Y-hours plus 15 minutes, landing at the big bridge just west of the Maleme airport. Objectives: the bridge over the Tavronitis — its capture and the prevention of its demolition. Subsequently, support of the 1st Battalion's attack on the AA positions west of the airfield.

The remainder of the Regimental staff and the 4th Battalion: (less two platoons of 14 company, and 16 company), reinforced by a medical platoon and the rest of the 3rd FlaMG Battalion [ie the section of AA guns less those dropped with the 3rd Battalion] will drop west of the bridge at Y-hours plus 15 minutes.

Regimental Headquarters will be established at the north end of the olive grove near the bridge.

The 4th Battalion will support the 1st Battalion's attack and the Braun Group on the western edge of the airfield.

For this purpose No 16 Company (Leutnant Hoefeldt) will be dropped in the river bed 600m due south of the airfield. Objective: the tented camp which is also one of the 1st Battalion's objectives. When the camp has been captured, the road running south is to be held against a possible enemy attack from the Kandanos direction.

2nd Battalion (plus one platoon): To drop at Y-hours plus 5 minutes on the heights east of Spilia to exploit westwards and secure the road running south. This battalion will constitute the regimental reserve but it may be used in support of the attack on the airfield. In the event of the airfield being occupied with little opposition and the area around Kastelli is clear of the enemy, the 2nd Battalion will advance eastwards towards Canea.

One reinforced platoon of the 2nd Battalion (Leutnant Mürbe) will be dropped east of Kastelli to deal with the weak enemy force reported to be located in that area. If there is no opposition — or, alternatively, if the enemy is found to be in overwhelming strength — this platoon will retire through the hills to rejoin the battalion.

Now we must see how the situation developed when the Regiment landed.

At 0715 on the morning of 20 May 1941 the 1st Battalion spearheaded the invasion by 'Western Force.' With the exception of the 2nd Battalion — whose assault was delayed owing to dusty conditions on the airfield from which it was to take off, the fly-in was launched on schedule. (The 2nd Battalion, dropping at 0800 was 40 minutes late). No 3 Company of the 1st Battalion made a good landing close to the AA positions. But the gliders carrying Battalion HQ and No 4 Company crashed on the slopes of Pt 107 in the middle of an enemy locality which air reconnaisance had not revealed, and there were heavy losses.

The enemy on and around Maleme airfield was in far greater strength than German Intelligence had estimated. Moreover his positions were extremely well camouflaged and protected by barbed wire entanglements, virtually invisible in the Cretan terrain until one was almost on top of them. Automatic weapons in the enemy positions could sweep the airfield, and it was these that inflicted such heavy losses on the 1st Battalion. Within a few minutes of their landing Major Koch, the battalion commander was wounded, the company commander of No 4 Company killed and more than half of the men of the Battalion HQ and No 4 Company were casualties. The remainder were unable to achieve the company's objective. The men of No 3 Company were slightly better off, however, and they did manage to capture some of the enemy gun positions and the tented living quarters behind them. According to the War Diary of No 3 Company:

'...The strength of the 3rd LL Sturm Regiment in this action was 107: three officers, 26 NCOs and 77 other ranks. (The remainder of the company was put under command of Leutnant Osius, who was in charge of all personnel "left out of battle" (LOB)).

'12 gliders were allotted for the operation and these were sub-allotted on the basis of three per platoon.

'Objectives and tasks were as follows:

No 2 Platoon (Oberfeldwebel Arpke): To capture LAA guns on the north and north-west edge of the airfield perimeter.

No 1 Platoon (Leutnant Musyal): To knock out the heavy AA gun located about 800m distance due west from the airfield perimeter.

Company HQ and Support-Weapons Group (Leutnant von Plessen): To clear the copse on the western edge of the airfield.

No 3 Platoon (Oberfeldwebel Scheel): To knock out the enemy positions due south of the end of the airfield's south-west runway.

The quick and effective silencing of the AA guns was considered to be vital, so that the drop of the paratroop follow-up units should not be impeded.

'When all objectives had been achieved and the task completed, No 3 Company was to take up a defensive position on the western bank of the gorge, facing west. The company's right flank should rest on the sea and the left inclusive of the road running east-west from Maleme. Patrols would then be sent out to establish contact with the 4th Battalion, and to reconnoitre the immediate vicinity, and obstructions in the western sector of the airfield would be cleared away.'

No 3 Company took off from Elevis airfield at 0530 on 20 May 1941. The aerial convoy carrying the 1st Battalion was flying in formation with three gliders abreast and No 3 Company's gliders flew as Number 3, 4, 5, and 6 lines. Although there was no flak as the convoy approached the Cretan coastline, it was here that the first mishap occurred when the cable between No 3 Platoon's gliders — the one carrying the platoon commander — and the towing Ju52 snapped. All contact was lost, and Scheel's section was out of the action. But the pilot managed to put his machine down in the inhospitable mountainous terrain on the island of Antikythera. Nobody was hurt and the pilot and everyone else in the glider eventually rejoined the company on 24 May, after a long trek through the mountains and a short sea voyage. Meanwhile No 3 Company's other 11 gliders arrived at the battle zone on time, and as they floated down the crews of the planes which had towed them to their destination fired their machine guns in support of the landings.

Company HQ Group: Two gliders crashed on landing but the men involved were only slightly injured.

No 1 Platoon: All three gliders made a good landing, with the leading glider pancaking down about 300m west of its objective, the heavy AA gun. But Leutnant Musyal was severely wounded by a shot in the leg, so Feldwebel Schulz assumed command.

No 2 Platoon: This platoon's three gliders floated down in formation to land almost simultaneously and almost exactly at the pre-determined places. But the glider carrying Oberfeldwebel Arpke came down heavily and Arpke was knocked unconscious, so Feldwebel Schuster took over.

No 3 Platoon: Of the two gliders remaining to this platoon, that carrying Feldwebel Ehur's section crashed-landed about 1,000m west of the platoon objective, while the other, carrying Feldwebel Dudda's section, came down about 400m further west. Both gliders were fired on by enemy machine guns located at the southern end of the airfield.

Men of No 2 Platoon (Oberfeldwebel Arpke) were the first to reach the airfield perimeter and to attack the AA positions there. The enemy occupying these positions were dug in, and as Arpke's men advanced they came under heavy and accurate fire which caused a number of casualties. Realising that to press on with a frontal attack would be little short of suicidal Arpke ordered his men to withdraw to the river bed. Having collected them behind the bank he quickly established a defensive position facing south and east towards the airfield. Then Arpke returned to his task. Under cover of fire from the platoon's machine guns and grenade launchers a squad of his men launched another attack on the AA guns and the positions protecting them. This was completely successful; the enemy holding the centre of the airfield's western perimeter were eliminated and Feldwebel Schuster was now ordered to establish contact with No 1 Platoon and the Company HQ Group.

The three gliders carrying the Company HQ and Support Weapons Group had, in fact, landed shortly after No 2 Platoon. That of Leutnant von Plessen crashed near the coast, but the passengers were unharmed and von Plessen divided them into two squads. The first of these, under Oberfeldwebel Galla, was sent off to attack an AA gun position on the western edge of the airfield. It was completely annihilated, and the second squad was scarcely more fortunate. Leading the squad in an attack on another AA position further south, von Plessen himself was killed.

Meanwhile in accordance with their original orders the men of the other two gliders of this group had deployed to clear the copse on the west edge of the airfield. When it was found that the copse was occupied, Oberfeldwebel Gleitmann launched an attack under cover of a barrage put down by the heavy weapons of the group. Eventually, despite fierce opposition the copse was taken, as was the southernmost enemy AA position on the airfield perimeter.

No 1 Platoon (Leutnant Musyal) had more luck in its mission. When Leutnant Musyal was shot in the leg Oberfeldwebel Ellersiek took over command of the platoon, with Feldwebel Schulz as his deputy. The AA gun which was the platoon's objective turned out to be a decoy, so the platoon's efforts were directed to mopping up enemy in the buildings surrounding the dummy gun. After that the platoon pulled back to the gorge which had been designated the area where the company would concentrate once its initial objectives had been achieved.

After the setback due to the loss of one of its gliders, No 3 Platoon's luck also seemed to change. Landing near Tavronitis, the 18 men carried by the two gliders of this platoon cleared the village — taking 30 prisoners in the process — and then moved along the western perimeter of the airfield to link up with the rest of the company. A few men managed to get one of the captured AA guns back into action, and its fire was then directed towards the north side of the airfield, where Oberfeldwebel Galla's squad had been wiped out.

While all the fighting was going on among the rocks and the olives and the vines the company medical officer, Oberarzt Dr Weizel, was busy tending to men injured in the landings or wounded in the actions that followed. With the help of Gefreiter Müller, Weizel himself rescued three badly wounded men lying in the open — dragging them back to the shelter of a captured tent on a sheltered slope. At 0930 hours, however, when he was told that Leutnant Musyal and Leutnant von Plessen were casualties, Weizel took over command of No 3 Company, and ordered it to concentrate on the western edge of the airfield perimeter. Then, as soon as all the isolated groups had collected together and a rough defensive position established Weizel set about extending the area under his control. Patrols were sent out north and south and it was not long before his men had probed as far as the east-west road. By 1000 No 3 Company was dominating a strip of territory running from the bridge at the southern edge of the airfield up along the western edge and northwards back as far as the coast.

An hour later, at 1100 precisely, Leutnant Trebes with elements of No 13 Company and what remained of No 1 Platoon of No 3 Company launched an attack on the tented camp in the olive grove south of the road; the aim was to free Kahleyss's platoon which was pinned down there. The attack was completely successful and 30 more prisoners fell into German hands. But Pt 107, the ultimate objective of this assault, could not be taken, and Trebes was forced to pull back to the defensive position at the bridge from which he had started.

Finally, at 1215 Leutnant Dobke of the 4th Battalion with 15 men, arrived at No 3 Company's position and took over the northern sector on the western edge of the airfield. Dobke was all set to advance along the southern edge of the airfield capturing the AA gun position there and mopping up the trenches surrounding it. However he was forbidden to move when a report was received from Hauptmann Gericke (CO of the 4th Bn) to the effect that dive-bombers were going to strafe the northern edge of the enemy perimeter. In the event, Dobke appears to have ignored this order, and at 1300 he and his party set off towards the northern end of the airfield — taking eight prisoners with them. En route the prisoners led the group into an ambush and Dobke was killed.

By about 1400 all the wounded had been collected and No 3 Company spent the next two hours digging in. Dr Weizel reported to Hauptmann Gericke at 1500 and was told that his task was to hold his position on the western edge of the airfield. Furthermore as an enemy counter-attack could be expected during the night, it was proposed to reinforce Weizel's company with 50 men from Oberleutnant Osius's LOB Company.

At 1500 the enemy started to shell No 3 Company. However, despite a very heavy bombardment there were no casualties. At 1645 the artillery fire lifted and the company positions were attacked by enemy infantry advancing behind a medium tank.

The tank, trundling up the river bed, was stopped by a round from a 3.7mm AA gun and the infantry was dispersed by mortar fire; while the crew of the tank were taken prisoner. Between 2000 and midnight, 21 casualties — 15 of whom had been severely wounded — were evacuated to the main medical post which had been set up in Tavronitis, and the rest of the company grimly settled down in the trenches and waited for a night attack. That day, 20 May, 17 men of the company had been killed (including Leutnant von Plessen) and 27 others wounded — 19 of them seriously.

In the event no attack came that night — nor did the 50 reinforcements which had been promised.

The 3rd Battalion was dropped into a huge area in the Maleme-Pyrgos region extending from the west of Platanias to Marina, south of Maleme. Because the battalion's sub-units were scattered, this phase of the operation was wasteful. Having been dropped in the wrong place the battalion commander was unable to exert any influence on the battle. Nor were the company commanders of the 10th and 12th Companies, as many of their men came down near enemy positions and were killed or wounded during their descent or almost as soon as they touched the ground. It was the same story as that of the 1st Battalion. Only elements of the 9th Company succeeded in getting to the rendezvous where the battalion was to come under the orders of the regimental commander. And in the course of their trek to this appointed RV the company commander, Hauptmann Witzig, was wounded. Some of the stragglers of the company were picked up a few days later when the Germans gained the upper hand and the regiment overran the terrain where groups of parachutists had continued to fight or hide.

As planned, the nine gliders carrying Braun's battle group landed near the bridge west of Maleme airport. The enemy machine gun posts defending the bridge were knocked out, and Braun made contact with No 3 Company. But he could do no more, and heavy fire from enemy positions on Pt 107 eventually compelled his group to withdraw to the comparative shelter of the riverbed. Even this was not accomplished without casualties. Braun died from a shot in the head, and as Leutnant Schächter had been severely wounded when his glider crash-landed, there was only Leutnant Trebes to take over command of the survivors of the regimental staff battle group.

The remainder of the regimental staff had parachuted into action with the 4th Battalion, and nothing went wrong with their drop. Having set up the Regimental HQ this group set off for the bridge and the western sector of the airfield. Like Braun's men, the group came under fire from Pt 107 and Generalmajor Meindl was severely wounded while trying to make contact with Braun and the commanding officer of the 1st Battalion. Learning that Braun had been killed, Meindl ordered Hauptmann Gericke to assume command of the sector.

No 16 Company: The 16th Company was dropped into the correct target zone. From there it took over responsibilities for the area and exploited to a depth of about 2km south-west of the airfield. The company also attempted to link up with the 1st Battalion in the vicinity of the heavily defended enemy strongpoint at Pt 107.

2nd Battalion: The men of the 2nd Battalion came down in an area adjoining the intended dropping zone, and was under enemy fire as the battalion concentrated and moved towards its objective — the heights east of Spilia. From the heights No 6 Company went on to occupy the region west and south of the Spilia Pass.

One platoon (Platoon Mürbe) which was dropped too close to the village of Kastelli came under heavy fire from partisans and civilians as the men floated down. Many were killed and wounded before they touched ground and by the end of the day Mürbe's platoon had ceased to exist. The company lost 73 men in the course of the action, and when 26 of them — some of whom had been wounded — were captured and freed later, it was learned that the local population had behaved barbarously towards the dead and wounded.

Summing up, the situation of the FJ Sturm Regiment at the end of the first phase of the assault was as follows:

With Hauptmann Gericke in command, a polygot force of men from the 4th Battalion and No 3 Company of the 1st Battalion was about to launch an attack with a view to occupying the northern part of the airfield.

On the orders of the regimental commander, sub-units of the 2nd Battalion, under command of Major Stentzler, were preparing to seize and occupy Pt 107. Both Gericke and Stentzler were briefed personally by Generalmajor Meindl, in the middle of the day: 'Stentzler's battalion will attack the enemy flank making a wide sweep with a start line on the right of Gericke's battalion. Meantime the 4th Battalion will maintain its pressure on the enemy holding the airfield — advancing up both sides of the asphalt road running west towards Maleme.'

When the 2nd Battalion's heavy weapons were parachuted down west of the airfield during the afternoon, they were put at Gericke's disposal to support his forthcoming attack up the northern slopes of Pt 107. Meanwhile two companies of the 2nd Battalion had been working their way round Pt 107. (Men of No 7 Company had infiltrated from the south, while No 5 Company had moved in from the west.) By the evening they had occupied the southern slopes of the feature, capturing four officers and 100 other ranks in the process.

By this time the 2nd Battalion's heavy weapons had silenced the enemy guns, and what remained of the 1st Battalion now under command of Oberstabsarzt Dr Neumann (Major Koch had been wounded), was able to gain a foothold on the northern slopes of the hill. In the teeth of bitter resistance however, it was still not yet possible to occupy Pt 107 before darkness cloaked the battlefield.

That first night was considered to be a critical period and just before midnight the entire 6th Company was pulled back into reserve from their advance positions at the Spila Pass. In the event the enemy did not attack, so there was no call on the reserve and at first light on 21 May the company returned to reoccupy its old positions.

On the orders of the regimental commander, Major Stentzler assumed tactical command of the regiment in the late afternoon (of 20 May), but overall command was retained by Generalmajor Meindl.

This had been a hard fought day, during which Luftwaffe fighters and dive-bombers flew many sorties in direct support of the FJ Sturm Regiment.

Luftwaffe Operations

Every serviceable aircraft of Fliegerkorps VIII participated in the Cretan operations on 20 May — bombing, strafing or flying on fighter cover and escort duty.

As the first wave of troop carriers of Fliegerkorps XI approached their objectives, an intense air attack was launched, aimed at enemy AA guns and their teams and designed to weaken enemy resistance. Under the cover of this assault the gliders and paratroops descended. The programme of support operations planned jointly by Fliegerkorps XI and Fliegerkorps VIII may be summarised as follows:

a Dive-bomb attacks (by Stuka Geschwader 2) on the AA gun positions near the dropping zones at Maleme and Canea.
b Strafing attacks (by Jagdgeschwader 26 and 77) on the three tented camps in the area south of the Maleme-Canea road.
c Disruption of telephone lines (by fighters) on the outskirts of Ierapetra, Heraklion, Rethymnon and Canea — to upset the enemy's command communication network.
d Bombing and strafing attacks on the military installations at Heraklion and Rethymnon by units of the Italian Aegean Air Force.

The aim of these attacks was to weaken the will and strength of the garrison at the very beginning of the battle.

The actual dropping operation was supported by bombers and fighter-bombers whose task was to deal with enemy strong points, centres of resistance, and AA guns in the immediate vicinity of the dropping zones. The value of this support may be deduced from the fact that only seven of the 502 Ju52s used in the operation were lost — despite formidable enemy defensive preparations.

Apart from those of Fliegerkorps VIII, Fliegerkorps XI was allotted the following additional Luftwaffe units:

Stab Kampfgeschwader zbV   (HQ Bomber Wing)
I. Kampfgeschwader zbV 1   (1st Bomber Wing)
II. Kampfgeschwader zbV 1   (2nd Bomber Wing)
I. Luftlandegeschwader 1   (1st Transport Aircraft Wing)
Stab Kampfgruppe zbV 2   (HQ 2 Bomber Squadron)
Kampfgruppe zbV 101   (101 Bomber Squadron)
Kampfgruppe zbV 102   (102 Bomber Squadron)
Kampfgruppe zbV 105   (105 Bomber Squadron)
Stab Kampfgruppe zbV 3   (HQ 3 Bomber Squadron)
Kampfgruppe zbV 40   (HQ 40 Bomber Squadron)
Kampfgruppe zbV 60   (60 Bomber Squadron)
Kampfgruppe zbV 106   (106 Bomber Squadron)
I. Kampfgruppe zbV 172   (172 Special Duties Squadron)
(zbV: for special duties)

CHAPTER 7

Operations in the Central Region – Losses at Galatas – A Battalion ceases to exist

The role of the 3rd Parachute Regiment's advance guard fell to Major Heilmann's 3rd Battalion, which was dropped at 0700 on 20 May 1941 with orders to secure the dropping zone prior to an advance on Galatas, Canea and Suda Bay. The battalion took off before dawn and No 9 Company with the battalion commander was the first of the German invasion force to fly across the Mediterranean. British warships in Suda Bay were clearly visible as the troop carriers neared the island and were rocked by heavy anti-aircraft fire.

Mushrooms of smoke created by the bombs of the Stukas which had preceded the Ju52s were rising as the paratroops approached the dropping zone; and a vigilant fighter passed overhead, flying in from the west. Paratroops standing by the open doors of the planes, awaiting the order to jump, could hear the rattle of small-arms fire over the noise of the engines; as the planes coasted down to dropping height the sound of the shooting got louder.

New Zealanders were firing into the dropping zone — well-aimed shots which were picking off the paratroopers as they descended. There was a company of Greek infantry in the area also, but its men surrendered to the first Germans who landed. Major Heilmann jumped with the first stick and, as soon as a few men of the 9th Company had assembled, he led an assault on the nearest enemy positions. At this stage few of the paratroopers had anything more than tommy-guns, pistols and grenades. But determination made up for lack of weapons and several pockets of enemy resistance were overwhelmed before the enemy had realised what was happening. Advancing up a depression Heilmann turned a corner to see a wounded platoon paratrooper and a wounded New Zealander bandaging each other. Beyond them the ground sloped gently upwards and Heilmann spotted a party of New Zealanders sheltering among some trees. Seeking safety in audacity, the German Major strode quickly up the slope, with a lone Gefreiter stumbling along behind. For a moment or two it seemed as if Heilmann's boldness would pay off. But as he neared the top of the rise and approached the New Zealanders there was a shot followed by a scream and the Gefreiter fell. A fusillade of shots followed and as they lashed past, Heilmann dived for cover. Looking round he was able to see another group of about

Above: Feldmarschall Sperrle (front) with from left to right: Oberstleutnant Count von Carnap, Generalleutnant Peterson, Major Schulz, Leutnant von Bonin and Major Schleicher.

Below: Paratroops run to the assembly area.

20 New Zealanders coming from the direction of Galatas and making for the top of the hill by way of a sunken road on the far side. Fighting flared up on both sides of him. On his right Heilmann's adjutant was heavily engaged in a grenade duel which concluded with the destruction of an enemy machine gun post; on his left he saw the company commander of No 9 Company struck down as he was leading some of his men up the slope. The men pushed on leaving their wounded officer under an olive tree, and an Oberfeldwebel rushing up to the battle passed by without noticing him. Only when he himself came back down the hill, nursing a shattered shoulder, did he spot his company commander.

The situation was black for the paratroops when the New Zealanders coming from Galatas appeared to be winning the scramble for possession of the hill top. But at that moment a hurriedly assembled machine gun arrived on the scene, and set up where Heilmann was rendering first aid to the wounded Gefreiter.

As the first ammunition belt chattered through the machine gun, the flat helmets of the enemy vanished from the sunken road. More paratroops arrived and a senior medical officer (Oberarzt) of the 7th Medical Company set up a casualty centre barely 200m from where the 9th Company was now able to consolidate its position. For the moment all was relatively quiet. But when the company attempted to continue to advance towards Galatas the paratroops found themselves under fire coming from the rear, and they sustained heavy losses.

Bitter fighting followed, but two hours later with the sun beating down on their backs Heilmann's men were in possession of the dominating feature south of Galatas. Heilmann had also made contact with regimental headquarters. 'Hold on to the hill you've just taken', Oberst Heydrich told him. 'And get ready for an attack on Galatas.' That afternoon the enemy launched a counter-attack, and the 19th New Zealand Battalion kept up an incessant pressure — returning time and again to the assault. With no sign or sound of the Nos 10, 11 and 12 Companies of his battalion Major Heilmann had only what remained of the 9th Company and his battalion headquarters to defend the hill. But everyone of his paratroopers steadfastly refused to yield ground — which, at the end of the day, had been literally soaked with blood. Nevertheless as the sun went down the situation looked pretty desperate. An ominous sound of heavy motors and the grinding of gears could be heard coming from the direction of the enemy lines. Worse still — ammunition was running low. An attempt had been made that afternoon to drop supplies to Heilmann's hard-pressed men, but most of the containers had fallen in terrain controlled by the enemy. To cap the gloom the company commander (of No 9 Company) who had been wounded earlier in the day, died during that evening.

The situation was partially resolved by Oberst Heydrich, who was now in occupation of Agya prison. Before nightfall Heilmann was ordered to evacuate the hill his men had struggled to hold. Heydrich needed every man he could lay hands on if he was to keep the regiment together and husband his resources. It was therefore sensible for Heilmann to withdraw, leaving only a skeleton platoon to deal with any nocturnal attempts by the New Zealanders to take possession of the hill.

But what had happened to Heilmann's other three companies — the 10th, 11th and 12th? Where had they got to, and why had they not tried to report to their battalion headquarters?

Parachute tents
provide protection
from the sun.

General Student on
Crete; in the
background British
prisoners.

Paratroops and
mountain troops
meet.

The first news concerning the fate of the missing companies reached Heilmann while he was serving as one of a gun crew made up of men of the 9th Company, directing the fire of a captured field-piece at enemy positions.

According to radio reports most of No 11 Company had been dropped in the mountains, and fought through to the 1st Battalion. The company commander was not among these men, however, and it transpired that he and the section with him had landed in the correct dropping zone on the road to Gatatas. So, in accordance with his orders he and his little party set off up the road towards Galatas. En route he must have run into an ambush, because his body and those of his men were discoverd a few days later lying by the roadside in single file where they had fallen.

No 12 Company suffered a terrible fate. It ceased to exist as a fighting unit when it was dropped into a reservoir. Few of the men could throw off their heavy harnesses when they hit the water and most were drowned.

The 10th Company was dropped near Daratsos, and floated down into the middle of an enemy camp, where men were waiting for them. The paratroops fought a gallant battle against odds that were heavily weighted against them and the outcome was never really in doubt. Nevertheless one of the platoons did manage to gain control over one section of the camp for a while and the paratroops concerned were happily marching 400 prisoners away towards the Galatas road, when they were shot up by a machine gun and subjected to a shower of grenades from an enemy post dominating their path. The platoon was caught entirely by surprise and the New Zealanders were able to mop up the whole company after this. Towards the end of the action the surviving paratroops were called upon to surrender, and as they had little option, they marched — prisoners themselves now — back into the camp. During the engagement the company commander was wounded and fell, and as he was trying to get to his feet he was killed by a second shot. And his death signified the demise of No 10 Company.

Oberst Heydrich dropped near Canea with Major Derpa's 2nd Battalion, whose objective was the Galatas Heights. And Heydrich was standing next to Major Derpa during an attack on the Galatas castle when the latter was killed.

The Parachute Engineer Battalion (*Fallschirm-Pioneer Bataillon* : FP) under command of Major Liebach was dropped, as planned, into an area in the rear of the 3rd Parachute Regiment and its operations in support of the regiment were a complete success.

The operations of the 1st Battalion (of FJR 3), commanded by Hauptmann Freiherr von der Heydte, were intended to supplement those of Heilmann's 3rd Battalion. Von der Heydte's men were to be dropped near the Agya prison and their first task was to block the Alikianon-Canea road and seize the heights south of the road. With the 2nd Battalion landing north of the penitentiary, the three battalions should then be in a position to concentrate prior to closing in on the Cretan capital, Canea.

The battalion landed, more or less according to plan, near the prison. The men quickly assembled in their company groups; physical and wireless communication was established, and the battalion was ready to move. But the paratroops had hardly advanced 100m when they came under machine gun fire which compelled them to fan out and move through an olive grove. Having crossed the Cladiso river the paratroops, with men of No 2 Company in the lead, zig-zagged up the river valley. Leutnant Knocke's company advanced alongside that of Leutnant Straehler-Pohl. A building loomed up in front of them and Hauptmann von der Heydte shouted to ask if anyone was inside; there was no answer. The paratroops dashed towards the building, and somebody looked at his watch. It was 10.30 precisely — three hours after their landing on Crete, and No 2 Company had knocked out two British machine guns, and the first prisoners had been taken. (They were Greek.)

Meanwhile the men of No 1 Company had come under fire and were floundering around in difficult terrain. With the road on their left and the deep channel of the Cladiso on their right their progress was hampered by a couple of enemy machine guns. Minutes passed, during which von der Heydte was joined by No 4 Company commander, and the two men crawled forward to direct the fire of the mortars when they opened up. But they were spotted by the enemy and a torrent of small-arms fire from the nearby olive grove occupied by the enemy sent them squirming back.

The two mortars with No 4 Company now opened fire and the British responded with an artillery concentration on the area where the paratroops were sheltering. There was no question of going forward or back, and the number of casualties began to mount.

When eventually there was a lull in the bombardment Hauptmann von der Heydte crawled forward once more. This time he observed some of the enemy near the building and he called for rapid fire from his mortars. Bombs straddled the building and when four salvoes had been fired there was no sign of the enemy.

Just then a message which had been handed along the line of paratroops was passed to von der Heydte: 'No 4 Company commander has been seriously wounded', it read. Von der Heydte had barely had time to absorb this when he was handed a second message telling him that the commander of his 2nd Company had also been wounded. Then the British artillery re-commenced their bombardment. 'Direct hit on the building, Herr Hauptmann' reported the Gefreiter in charge of the mortars. 'We must establish contact with the 3rd Battalion, Herr Hauptmann', the adjutant insisted. Suddenly a British tank appeared, but this was despatched at 50m with a shot from a rocket-launcher (*Panzerbüchse*).

While all this was going on, Leutnant Hagel reported to the battalion commander. Hagel, a sturdy Bavarian, ex-ranker, and a man of exceptional daring had fought his way through the British lines with a platoon of No 2 Company. With a feeling of relief Hauptmann von der Heydte handed over responsibility for the sector to Hagel and started back for his battalion headquarters accompanied by his adjutant and a runner. On arrival he found a number of messages and reports awaiting him. A fighting patrol had reconnoitred to Peribolia and seen enemy positions south-east of this village, and No 3 Company was digging in on a hill surmounted by medieval ruins which had been captured. From this hill a thickly wooded and rocky ravine ran eastwards down to the coast near Canea. And Greek troops deployed in the valley had been taken by No 3 Company.

A hundred metres behind von der Heydte's battalion headquarters, Oberarzt Dr Petritsch had set up a regimental aid post; his deputy, the other battalion medical officer, had gone off to one of the companies. Petritsch was operating on one of the casualities in an improvised theatre camouflaged by foliage when the battalion commander visited the regimental aid post in the middle of the day. Twelve gravely wounded men waited for the surgeon's attention; there had been many more casualties, but most of the lightly wounded who needed attention had been taken to the field hospital which had been set up near the Agya prison.

Von der Heydte went from one casualty to the next, saying a few comforting words to each. Among them was a wounded British soldier who had been carried back with some of the German casualties. On learning that the officer who had come to see him was the commanding officer of one of the paratroop battalions, this man said, 'Sir, the war is over for me. I hope it will soon be over for you and your men too.' .'

By the afternoon it appeared that the enemy had consolidated his grip on the plain of Canea, and there now seemed little hope of the battalion breaking through to the town. Moreover when warning signal flares were seen fired from the positions where No 2 and 3 Companies had dug in, it was clear that the enemy were not going to be content to sit and wait for the paratroops to make the next move. The British were attacking and the impetus of their advance carried them up to No 1 Company's positions where a desperate hand-to-hand struggle ensued. With casualties mounting and ammunition running out the outlook for the battalion looked grim indeed. Then suddenly the attack stopped.

Later in the afternoon radio contact was made with the 3rd Battalion, and Regimental Headquarters at Agya prison issued fresh orders: the paratroops would resume the offensive. The 3rd Battalion would advance up the Canea Alikianon road; the 2nd Battalion would constitute a mobile reserve to be deployed as and when the Regimental Commander thought fit; the engineers would be responsible for securing the northern and western flanks of the reservoir; and the 1st Battalion would dig in on the right (east) of the Cladiso.

With these orders to Hauptmann von der Heydte came the news that the divisional commander, Generalleutnant Süssman, had been killed. He had been in a glider which had crashed on the rocky island of Aegina following a mishap involving a Heinkel He 111. Oberst Heydrich assumed command of the division, but retained control of his own regiment. In von der Heydte's own battalion the company commander of No 4 Company had died of his wounds in the course of the afternoon.

As darkness fell the shooting in the 1st Battalion's area tapered off until silence reigned. Battalion Headquarters was then moved into a ravine flanked by vineyards through which one of the tributaries of the Cladiso flowed.

The first day on Crete was over for the 1st Battalion FJR 3.

CHAPTER 8

A King Escapes – Death of
a Divisional Commander –
Dive Bombers Intervene –
Starting for Rethymnon

The descent of the paratroops of the 3rd Regiment, and the subsequent storming of the grim grey buildings of Agya Prison by Oberst Heydrich's men was watched by King George II of Greece and his Prime Minister from the windows of the monarch's country house near the Alikianon road. From his bedroom King George had a grandstand view of the spectacle. He had seen the paratroops falling out of the skies — some of them in his grounds, only 100m from the house; seen them detach their parachutes when they were down; and he had seen them grab their weapons and race towards where the sound of battle indicated the presence of their comrades. Everything had seemed to happen very quickly and it was the very speed of the German operation which made it possible for the Greek king to escape. Ten minutes after the realisation of what was happening he and the Prime Minister, accompanied by a few Greek officers, left the house and fled on foot to Alikianon. Nobody took any notice of the fugitives. The air was filled with the thunder of low-flying Ju52s; the ground as far as Galatas and Canea was quivering under the shock and blast of bombs.

The royal party tramped over winding trails through the mountains south towards the coast for 70 hours. In so far as this was the first time that a crowned head of state had to undergo the same sort of hardships and fatigue as the troops in this new third-dimensional warfare, the flight set a record. It took the king and his entourage two days and two nights to walk across the island. But eventually they reached the little fishing village of Roumeli where on 24 May the Greek Sovereign boarded the British destroyer which took him to Egypt.

From Cairo the king then broadcast to the population of Crete calling for malicious partisan warfare, for massacres and murder — an appeal which ignored the fact that Greece had signed the Hague Convention condemning partisan warfare.

The Second Wave

Towards noon on 20 May the staff at Fliegerkorps XI in Athens waited anxiously for some reassuring news from Crete. Neither the Chief of Staff, Generalmajor Schlemm, nor the Chief of Operations, Oberst Trettner, had any idea of how the German invaders were progressing and the Intelligence Officer Hauptmann Mors had not been able to build up a coherent picture from the enemy point of view. As the time passed and there were still no reports from the island General Student decided to act, and Oberst Snowadzki was sent off in a Ju52 with orders to land on Malema airfield — organise a flying control unit and prepare for the fly-in of the first line units of the 5th Mountain Division. Snowadzki returned sooner than expected, and his report was pretty dismal. In short Maleme airfield was still in enemy hands and there was no question of aircraft landing there.

Snowadzki's plane had in fact managed to put down on the airfield and had been lucky to get away. As the pilot was taxying back down the runway he had realised that the airfield was still occupied by the British; gunning the engine he had taken off again under fire. A second Ju52, carrying the men who were to operate the airfield control, was coming in to land, but it roared away when the pilot saw what happened to the first aircraft.

Following Snowadzki's return to Athens there was a reappraisal of the situation. Viewed from the HQ of Fliegerkorps XI the situation did not look good. Only seven out of the 502 transport aircraft used to fly in the first wave of invaders had been lost, and arrangements had been made for the returning Ju52s to be refuelled as soon as they got back to their base airfields. On the original schedule the second wave should have taken off at 1030, and so far as availability of aircraft was concerned there was no reason why it could not do so at that time. But nobody knew what was happening on the ground; the chief signals officer, Oberstleutant Dr Weyland had failed to contact both 'Western Force' and 'Central Force'. Despite persistent calls his radio operators had failed to get any response from Crete.

A second disturbing factor stemmed from the fact that the refuelling arrangements had gone awry. As there were no proper refuelling facilities at the forward landing strips at which the transport aircraft were based for this operation, the fuel had to be hand-pumped from barrels. And this had taken far longer than expected. A third factor was the disruption of communications — caused by saboteurs cutting telephone lines between the two Fliegerkorps' HQs and the airfields.

Despite the delays and the pitiful scarcity of news from the island it was decided to continue with the bombardment programme scheduled as a prelude to the launching of the second wave. Thus it was that about 1515 the air over Rethymnon and Heraklion was rent with the screams of the dive-bomber 'Jericho' sirens and the ground shook with exploding bombs. But the paratroops who should have dropped after the bombs were sitting on the airfields in Greece.

The first radio message from the island was picked up by Fliegerkorps XI HQ shortly before the Stukas began their dive-bomb attack on Rethymnon. Oberst Heydrich reported that he had taken Castle Hill but the force at his disposal was not strong enough to attempt an assault on Canea. In his view the capture of this town, the Cretan capital and the enemy's communication centre, was vital. But to do so he would need reinforcements and so he was asking for FJR 2 (Oberst Sturm) to be dropped in his sector.

It was impossible to comply with Heydrich's request. The 2nd Regiment, which had been briefed for a drop in the Rethymnon area was already airborne and as it was well on the way to Crete it was not possible to divert it to Canea. The troops did not have maps of that area, nor did the aircrews who were to fly them there have the requisite navigational information. In spite of the lack of information it had been decided to adhere to the original programme and the aircraft carrying the 2nd Regiment started to take off at 1330. The destination was Rethymnon, and as the 2nd Battalion (Hauptmann Schirmer) had been allocated to the 'Eastern Force' (Heraklion) the regiment had only two battalions.

The regiment's objectives had been defined as the airfield and town of Rethymnon. The 1st Battalion, under Major Kroh with No 2 company of the 7th Paratroop Machine Gun Battalion (*Fallschirm MG Bataillon: FMG*) and one platoon of AA machine guns from the FlaMG Battalion, followed by a platoon from each of No 13 and 14 Paratroop Companies of the regiment as reinforcements — was to drop on both sides of the airfield; capture it; remove any obstacles on the runways, and repair them as necessary to allow more troops to be flown in.

'Kroh Force' started to take off at 1330 from the airfield at Megara, and 15 minutes after the dive-bombers had started to soften up the defences, the first of Kroh's paratroops were spilled out over Crete. A heavy pall of dust over the dropping zones delayed the drop and it was an hour before this particular drop was complete. No 4 Company and the Battalion Headquarters group were the first to jump, and they landed in the right area. But machine gun and small-arms fire cracked through the din of bombs and exploding shells as they floated down, and many paratroopers were killed in the air — their parachutes depositing only inert clumsy bodies on the ground. When the survivors assembled about 800m east of the airfield perimeter they found that the company commander Hauptmann Morawetz and all the other officers of No 4 Company had been cut down by the enemy fire.

No 3 Company, which followed No 4 Company to the ground, was dropped about 7km east of the designated dropping zone. Coming down on rocky ground west of Pt 217 many of these men were injured when they hit the ground.

No 1 Company landed close to where the survivors of No 4 Company were concentrating and they too ran into heavy fire. As they ran to recover their weapons containers more of them were picked off by enemy riflemen and by the time they were ready for action their numbers had been decimated. Once the two companies had assembled however they moved boldly forward towards the airfield and were within 600m of the perimeter when they were pinned down by fire.

Although he and No 3 Company came down too far east, Major Kroh was in a better situation than his No 1 and 4 Companies. No 3 Company and the machine gun section was formed up near an olive oil mill and Leutnant von Roon was put in charge of it.

Von Roon's force started to advance towards the airfield about 1700 and 15 minutes later it struck the road running east of the vineyard adjoining the airfield. Heavy fire indicated that the vineyard was occupied by the enemy, and von Roon decided that his best chance of getting the airfield lay in shock tactics. It had been a hot day and the sun was still beating down, but the paratroopers were urged to get on as fast as they could move. By 1800 with the aid of a medium mortar, the men of No 3 Company had succeeded in overrunning the northern slope of the vineyard and holding on there despite enemy efforts to dislodge them. (This was the same vineyard on whose southern slopes No 1 and No 4 Companies were pinned down.)

Major Kroh now issued orders for a combined attack on the remaining enemy positions and when this went in an hour and a half later it was completely successful. There was a short brisk action, most of the enemy withdrew and at 1930 the whole of the vineyard was in German hands.

It was dark when the assault on the airfield was resumed. Supported by a captured LAA gun, a combat group led by von Roon moved up to the perimeter of the airfield and worked its way along it. There was some hard and bloody fighting but the enemy were gradually forced back in both directions. At the south end of the airfield, however, they were entrenched in well-camouflaged strong points and von Roon could get no further, so his men dug in for the night.

It was at this stage of the battle that Major Kroh took stock of the situation. On the debit side his battalion group had so far suffered 400 casualties — dead, wounded and missing. On the credit side his men had achieved a partial success. Next morning it would be seen whether they could exploit their gains, capture the airfield and hold it against the counter-attack which would almost certainly be launched against them.

The aircraft carrying 'Wiedemann Force' — comprising the 3rd Battalion (FJR 3), the 1st Machine Gun Company of the 7th Battalion, a section of the field artillery, and a section of LAA — started to take off from Megara airfield about 1400. Over Crete it had to fly through heavy anti-aircraft barrage.

The buzzers (*Boschhörner*) in the Ju52s sounded at 1620 and by 1630 the last of the paratroops had been dropped beside the Platanias bridge. They landed on both sides of the bridge on rough ground covered with undergrowth in which it was difficult to locate those weapons containers which had survived the drop. (Some containers hit by enemy AA fire were destroyed on their way down. Three Ju52s which also received hits managed to make emergency landings, their pilots setting the machines down more or less unscathed.)

As soon as he had collected his force together Hauptmann Wiedemann set off on the road to Rethymnon. He himself marched at the head of No 9 Company; behind him marched elements of No 11 Company, the anti-tank guns, the AA guns, and 105mm field-pieces of the 2nd Section FAAbt 7 (Fallschirm Artillerie Abteilung) the first resistance was met east of Rethymnon when the paratroops ran into defensive positions manned by Greek troops, who showed little stomach for a fight. Brushing aside their opposition, Wiedemann's men continued their advance to the eastern outskirts of the town. Here they were brought to a halt by small-arms fire from the town, and artillery fire from the hills to the south where the British had established defensive positions dominating the sector running from the road to the coast.

At 1800 the enemy moved against Wiedemann — with an attack from the south against the German flank. The paratroopers fought for an hour, before Wiedemann ordered them to break off the engagement. This was completed successfully and by 2000 the Wiedemann Force was back at the village of Peribolia, having carried the wounded with it. There they settled down in hedgehog formation and prepared to stand against the enemy who had been coming up behind them.

'Schulz Force' — consisting of the HQ of 7th Machine Gun Battalion, and the regimental signal platoon, the 2nd Battalion of FJR 2, and a platoon from each of the 13th and 14th Companies — was ordered to clear the area west of Rethymnon airfield. After this it would become the Regimental reserve, to be used as and when required. This force took off from Tabagra airfield at 1330, and over Rethymnon the leading aircraft flew into heavy anti-aircraft fire. One Ju52 carrying men of No 13 Company crashed in flames and because of the fierce AA barrage No 2 Company was unable to jump. By 1550, however, most of the force had parachuted down into the assigned dropping zone west of Rethymnon airfield.

It was some time before Major Schulz managed to assemble the scattered groups of his force, and when he set off for the map reference of Regimental HQ there were still quite a number of men missing. On arrival at the supposed location of Regimental HQ, he found some stragglers from No 1 Company and the Regimental Adjutant who told Schulz that the rest of the regimental staff had been dropped in the wrong place, quite far away. Next day it transpired that the regimental signal platoon had landed 8km too far east but had managed to join up with the 1st Battalion. And the rest of the regimental staff, jumping into enemy-occupied territory, had suffered terrible casualties even before they touched down. Oberst Sturm, 52 years old and the oldest paratrooper in the corps, was among those listed as missing. (In fact he had been captured and was freed 10 days later. It appears that he had dropped with 10 other men in an area outside the killing zone in which the rest of his staff had met their fate. But he had been forced to give himself up during the evening of the second day, when his party's ammunition ran out after several hours of fighting.)

Assuming command of the regiment, Major Schulz moved with his force in a westerly direction and during the night of 21 May he reached the Wiedemann Force near the Platanias bridge.

CHAPTER 9

The Battle for
Heraklion – A Long Night

Oberst Bruno Bräuer's 1st Parachute Regiment (FJR 1 of the 7th Fliegerdivision) group, whose attached troops included the 2nd Battalion of FJR 2, the 1st FlaMG Battalion, and No 2 unit SanAbt 7, was scheduled to drop in the second phase of the operation, starting at 15.15. Its objectives were the town and airfield at Heraklion; when these had been captured the airfield was to be held open for the fly-in of reinforcements. Tasks were allotted as follows:

Bräuer's 2nd Parachute Battalion (of FJR 1), with artillery, mortar and air support was to capture the airfield, while his 3rd Battalion (of FJR 1) occupied the town — moving in from the west and southwest. Meantime the 1st Battalion (of FJR 1) was to seize the signal station near Gournes (8km east of the airfield) and exploit eastwards; and the 2nd Battalion (of FJR 2), which would be dropped in a zone west of that of Bräuer's 3rd Battalion, would secure the west flank of the operation.

To be successful one of the prime requisites of this operation was that *all* the units should be dropped on their correct zones simultaneously, and at 1515 precisely when the preliminary air strike was scheduled to end. In the event the take-off of the various groups of transport aircraft was delayed by up to three and a half hours, and as the telephone lines between the airfields on the Greek mainland had been cut the officers commanding the different groups had no opportunity to discuss the delays or agree on a new zero hour. The result was the different units started the operation in the wrong tactical sequence and reached their dropping zones not in massed formation but in dribs and drabs by flights and squadrons up to two hours late. The preliminary bombardment by aircraft of Fliegerkorps VIII timed to finish at 1500 had forced the enemy to take cover, but it had not destroyed him. And because of their limited range, the Luftwaffe bombers could remain in the target area only until 1615. So those of the paratroop units which were dropped after that time — which was most of them — were deprived of a good deal of the air support they might otherwise have expected. Finally, because some of the Ju52 transports participating in the first phase of the operation were not available for the second phase, the fly-in of Bräuer's regimental group carried 600 men less than had been planned.

Heraklion was one place where the enemy had gone to considerable trouble to

Paratroops in
Heraklion.

Greek girls admire
the paratroops' tents.

The Mayor of
Heraklion with Major
Schulz.

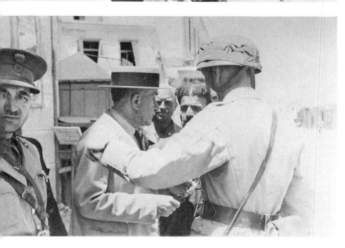

Right: Oberst Bruno Bräuer, the regimental commander of FJR 1 (right) talking to Major Schulz, CO of III Battalion FJR 1.

Below: Discussing the progress of the battle; Oberst Bräuer is in the centre.

prepare defences against an airborne assault. Taking advantage of the chalky terrain which was rich in caves, an intricate and comprehensive network of inter-communicating trenches had been dug from which the fire of the defenders could sweep not only the airfield and environs but also command those sheltered areas likely to be selected as paratroop dropping zones. Consequently the transport planes carrying the 2nd Battalion of FJR 1 — whose plan was to capture the airfield in a simultaneous assault from two sides — ran into heavy anti-aircraft and machine gun fire during their run in. Several planes crashed in flames and, because the nature of the terrain as well as the intense fire compelled the drop to be made at an altitude of 200m (600ft), many of the paratroops were killed or wounded on their way down.

At the eastern limits of this battalion's dropping zone, the group commanded by Hauptmann Burckhardt never had a chance to follow the plan of attack. Leutnants Hermann and Platow, the respective company commanders of Nos 5 and 8 Companies, and other junior officers rallied the men who were still fit to fight after landing, and advanced up the sloping field which bordered the airfield. Armed only with pistols and grenades, they were annihilated before they had advanced more than a few metres. Later the bodies of Leutnant Platow and several officers were found in the field.

Leutnant Hermann, who had been hit in the head and temporarily blinded while still in his parachute, carried on as long as he could. Supported by his Oberfeldwebel on one side and a Gefreiter on the other he stumbled forward at the head of his men until he collapsed. This left only Hauptmann Burckhardt who managed to collect 60 or 70 of the survivors at the foot of Pt 182 at nightfall.

Under the command of Hauptmann Dunz, the 6th and 7th Companies of 2nd Battalion, and a machine gun detachment (of FlaMG Battalion 7) dropped near the western edge of the airfield perimeter, and within 20 minutes this force had ceased to exist. Those paratroops who were not killed or wounded by the AA and machine gun fire during their descent, or picked off by riflemen, were wiped out when several light and medium tanks rolled into the dropping zones. Only three men of No 6 Company and two of the machine gun detachment got away. Jumping into the sea and swimming along the coast, they eventually reached regimental headquarters to report the course of the battle. In this action alone 12 officers and 300 men of the 2nd Battalion were killed and 8 officers and 100 others wounded.

Only No 3 Company of the 2nd Battalion FJR 1 made its drop on schedule in the Gournes area, but Battalion Headquarters and Nos 1 and 2 Companies followed after a three hour delay. (Because of the late hour the take-off of No 4 Company was cancelled and this company was subsequently deployed elsewhere.) However, these drops were made without enemy interference, and despite the fact that No 2 Company — which was supposed to land 2km west of Gournes — was dropped 5km (3 miles) too far to the east and was two hours late joining up with the rest — the battalion went on to occupy the radio station.

Oberst Bräuer, dropping with his regimental staff, into the area east of Gournes about 1840 had no idea of the true situation. Assuming that it had already been occupied by his 2nd Battalion, he set off for the airfield, protected only by a platoon of the 1st Battalion under the command of Leutnant Graf Blücher. Disillusionment came

Karl-Lothar Schulz in
Heraklion;
Oberleutnant Kerfin
on the left.

A road through the
Cretan mountains.

Major Schulz and
Oberst Bräuer in front
of a strongpoint near
Heraklion.

94

General Student at the command post of the 5th Mountain Division; Generalmajor Ringel is on the far left.

Generaloberst Löhr in the command post of a Luftwaffe formation that was transferred to Canea, after the battle, for operations against Egypt.

General Student with Generalmajor Ringel.

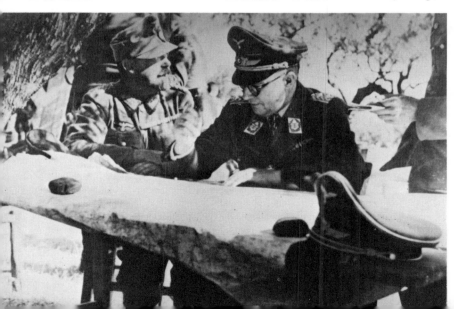

at 2340 when Blücher's leading scouts reached the slope at the eastern edge of the airfield perimeter and came under fire from what were clearly strongly held enemy positions. During the night Graf Blücher with a platoon of No 2 Company eventually captured the dominating feature on the eastern edge of the airfield. Meantime regimental tactical headquarters was established on a feature north of the road, 2km east of the airfield.

The 2nd Battalion of FJR 2 — less its No 5 and 6 Companies, which were left behind on the mainland because there were insufficient Ju52s to transport them — was supposed to follow Bräuer's 3rd Battalion (of FJR 1) and be dropped *after* the 3rd Battalion. In the event they arrived over the dropping zone before the 3rd Battalion, jumped without undue enemy interference and set about their task of exploiting west and south of the DZ in order to secure the Regiment's flanks.

Meanwhile the 3rd Battalion with the artillery, mortar and machine gun detachments which moved with it, had been dropped 2km west and south of Heraklion. During the descent the paratroops were fired on from positions in the hills on the town's walls and even by men in some of the houses. It was almost 1800 before the dropping zone was free of enemy and the paratroops had suffered heavy casualties in the clearance operation. Among those killed was No 9 Company commander, Leutnant Singer.

During the night Oberst Bräuer did his best to concentrate his widely dispersed units for a concerted attack on the airfield next morning. After such a grim and desperate struggle, the Germans on Crete welcomed the onset of darkness. At that particular stage of the battle the situation was critical and from the invaders' viewpoint the outcome rested on a razor's edge. General Student seriously considered giving up the operation, but discarded the idea because it would have meant abandoning 7,000 paratroops already on the island.

Since the afternoon a stream of radio messages had flowed in to Student's battle headquarters in Athens, and nearly all of them had been calls for help. Against all expectations the attackers had failed to get control of any of those areas in which Crete's airfields were sited. And possession of at least one airfield was vital to the build-up of the invasion force on Crete. So General Student decided to compensate for the failures by concentrating all his available resources and every available reserve at Maleme. Once Maleme airport was firmly in German hands the mountain division could be flown in, and the tide of battle would be turned.

The staff at Fliegerkorps XI HQ knew that this was the only course open, or their general would never have decided to risk everything in such a prodigal fashion. Justifying his action Student himself said later:

'It was not an easy decision to take. The airfield at Maleme — which, viewed from an aircraft, looked like a little red tennis court — was very small, and the English had used it only as a strip for light aircraft; that was a fact. Relying on this single tiny airfield as the base for an airborne operation employing 500 heavy transport planes — with all the unforeseen hazards attached to such an operation — was analogous to staking everything on a single card. But there was no alternative; Maleme was to become the centre of gravity of the operation.'

The first night on Crete was a nerve-wracking experience for the 7,000 paratroops faced

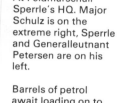

At Feldmarschall
Sperrle's HQ. Major
Schulz is on the
extreme right, Sperrle
and Generalleutnant
Petersen are on his
left.

Barrels of petrol
await loading on to
Ju52s at an airfield in
Serbia.

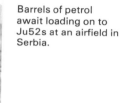

Loading the 'Auntie
Ju's' with petrol for
the forces on Crete.

Right: Reporting at the Führer's HQ. Major Schulz is second on the left.

Below: Heraklion a year later.

by a vastly numerically superior force of 43,000. What would happen if the enemy now launched a counter-offensive? If he were to put in a determined attack, throwing in everything he had, the paratroops were as good as lost. So what happened?

A copy of the operation orders issued by the 3rd Parachute Regiment had fallen in General Freyberg's hands during the day. Besides detailing the objectives and tasks of the 3rd Regiment, these orders also contained a broad outline of other aspects of the invasion. It seems however that Freyberg failed to make the proper deductions from the Germans plans. But this was not all, for other unfavourable factors also came into play. For communication the units defending the island relied mainly on telephones and, when many of the lines were cut by the bombing there was no way of getting information to and from some of the areas under attack. Radio might have been adequate substitute, but the garrison was short of radio sets. Consequently Freyberg's HQ never received much of the vital information which might have enabled him to influence the battle at critical stages. Ultimately this was the reason for the loss of Maleme — so important to the fly-in of German reinforcements, since General Freyberg did not order a counter-attack until it was too late.

If the island was to be held at all counter-attacks were imperative, and it is fair to admit that the British commanders were well aware of this. Indeed, a massive counter-offensive had been a regular feature of the exercises in which the garrison had participated prior to the invasion. And the British tanks in Crete were intended to play a decisive role in these counter-attacks, driving the invaders into the sea or crushing them into the ground. When the paratroops landed, however, all this seems to have been forgotten. The few local counter-attacks which were staged had varying degrees of success, but for the most part the defenders preferred to stay where they were. As an example: about 1000 on 20 May the commander of C Company of the regiment (C/22 Coy) on the edge of Maleme airfield requested a counter-attack by the battalion reserve company; but the battalion commander refused. Only at 1700 when the Germans had consolidated their positions in the area, did one company of Fusiliers supported by two infantry tanks, try to recover the ground they had lost to the paratroops. By then it was too late, and the counter-attack which would almost certainly have succeeded seven hours earlier was held, and the British repulsed with heavy casualties. What is more the defeat caused the battalion commander in question to withdraw from the positions he was still holding. And this, in turn, led to the loss of Maleme airfield next day.

During the night only limited counter-attacks were staged at all the critical points on Crete, and the enemy lost the one opportunity he had of sweeping the paratroops off the island.

CHAPTER 10

The Second Day:
The Decision at Maleme

By the evening of 20 May the commander of Fliegerkorps XI had concluded that the enemy resistance on Crete was stiffer than had been expected. The speedy capture of an airfield to allow the fly-in of reinforcements would decide whether the Germans won or lost the Battle of Crete. And, as things were, that airfield would have to be Maleme. Having come to this conclusion, Student ordered his staff in Athens to concentrate all their effort and all available resources on the capture of Maleme airfield.

Good radio communications had been established with the paratroop groups at Maleme, Canea and Heraklion fairly soon after the invasion and this continued until the end of the operation. Only between Rethymnon and Athens did no radio link exist. This was because the main radio equipment accompanying the Rethymnon force was damaged in the drop, and two substitute sets parachuted in later were also damaged. (An attempt to deliver a third radio set in a Fieseler Storch also proved fruitless — the crew being captured when the aircraft landed on Rethymnon airfield.) Over those links which were operating General Student was able to glean enough information for a rough appreciation of what would be necessary for the capture of Maleme. Nevertheless Student wanted to be sure, and during the night he sent for Hauptmann Kleye. The latter, a well-known dare-devil pilot on the staff of Fliegerkorps XI, duly reported, and was told that he was required to fly to Maleme, land there, see what the situation was, and try to establish contact with the Parachute Assault Regiment.

Kleye made his own arrangements: he had to, since the rest of Fliegerkorps XI staff was too involved in the logistics of Student's new plan. And at dawn on 21 May Kleye touched down in a field 3km west of Maleme. The situation he found had not changed during the night; that was all to the good — in the darkness the enemy had missed the one big opportunity open to him. An hour later six Ju52 successfully landed where Kleye had put down, unloaded a very welcome consignment of ammunition, took off again and returned to mainland Greece — all without incident. But the question was where and when would the mountain troops arrive? The survival of the gallant paratroops on Crete depended on them.

In the early hours of the morning of 21 May, the 1st Battalion of the Parachute Assault Regiment, under the command of Oberarzt Dr Neumann, launched an attack on Pt 107 at the northern edge of Maleme airfield. The attack was a success; following a brisk fight the enemy defences around the objective were over-run, Pt 107 was occupied, and only a few isolated enemy positions on the edge of the escarpment overlooking the airfield continued to hold out when the battle was over. Meanwhile, when the fight for Pt 107 was at its height Hauptmann Gericke was handed an order transmitted from Fliegerkorps XI HQ:

'Maleme airfield *must* be captured on 21 May', he read, 'You will attack at 1300. More paratroops, dropped in the enemy's rear at Maleme and Pyrgos in support of your operation, will participate in the battle for the airfield. Two additional paratroop companies will be dropped as Assault Regiment reinforcements, and these will also be used to secure the airfield. Commencing 1400, fighter aircraft will strike at targets in Maleme, and direct air support will be available from then on.'

When two of the captured British AA guns on Pt 107 were found to be intact, some of Neumann's paratroops quickly got them into action — firing at enemy positions on the hills overlooking the airfield from which the enemy was shooting down into the narrow strip occupied by men of the 4th Battalion. Meantime the battle continued in a desultory fashion as the paratroops endeavoured to exploit their gains by dislodging the enemy from the positions in their immediate vicinity. Shortly after noon the dull reverberation of an aircraft engine caused the paratroops to look expectantly up through the midday haze towards the sky. Minutes later a plane could be seen approaching:

'A Ju52 Herr Hauptmann', one of the men shouted.
'Then, there'll be others', Gericke called back.

But there was only one plane. Skimming the tops of the olive tres and flashing recognition signals a solitary Ju52 was clearly heading for the airfield. Enemy machine guns started to hammer as it approached; but the aircraft did not seem to be hit. Side-slipping to lose height, the pilot touched down safely on boiling hot sand, and almost before his machine had rolled to a halt its doors had been thrown open and paratroops were leaping out. Crates of ammunition were then unloaded and there was a cry from one of the crew 'Fetch the seriously wounded'; whilst this was being organised the pilot, Leutnant von Koenitz, left his cockpit and stolled nonchalantly over to Hauptman Gericke. Von Koenitz was the first pilot to attempt a landing on the airfield — and get away with it.

The wounded were loaded into the plane, among them Generalmajor Meindl; von Koenitz took off and the men on the ground watched until the plane disappeared towards the north.

The termination of this interlude was marked by the crump of mortar bombs and the crash of shells. Apart from a sector on its western edge the whole airfield was under bombardment and the runway was being churned up by the explosions. Just as Student had promised the air strike started at 1400 and three Messerschmitt Me110s flew over the airfield — roaring over the German positions at tree-top height.

'Tackle the British battery . . . the one across there! They are firing on the airfield all the time', cackled the radio. The Mes climbed steeply, banked and turned to dive on the enemy positions their guns blazing. Three times they repeated this manoeuvre, risking enemy fire to strafe and hit; and when they turned away and flew off back to the mainland the enemy positions were silent.

At 0530 on the second morning the men of No 3 Company of the Parachute Assault Regiment were standing to, awaiting the expected enemy counter-attack. At 0900 the company's positions were shelled, but, surprisingly, there was no counter-attack — surprisingly because if the British had launched an attack at that time there is little doubt it would have been successful.

Early in the afternoon the paratroops staged their own counter move against the field artillery which was still pounding the airfield. Two captured 40mm AA guns were got into action to shoot up the troublesome enemy battery. The battery ceased firing but it had not been knocked out, and about 1600 when the mountan troops started to arrive, its guns opened up again to lay down a barrage along the western side of the airfield. During this bombardment No 3 Company helped to organise the landings mustering the mountain troops as they deplaned and recovering wounded men and equipment from the flaming wrecks of the big troop-carriers smashed by the British artillery.

At 2000 Oberarzt Dr Weizel reported to Hauptmann Gericke to be told by the latter that his company, reinforced by a platoon of mountain troops (*Gebirgsjäger: GJ*) would move to the coast near the airfield and stop enemy troops landing there. Weizel's paratroopers and the mountain troops moved off about 2100 took up positions near the beach, and waited for boats bringing more of the enemy to Maleme. None came, but gun flashes indicated that a great and violent action was in progress at sea.

When dawn broke on the second day the area into which the 3rd Battalion of the Parachute Assault Regiment (FJStR) had been dropped presented a scene of desolation and death. Olive trees were shrouded with the white silk of countless parachute canopies their twisted harness cords looking like giant spiders' webs. Corpses still dangled from the branches in some of these harnesses, and the ground was strewn with other gruesome remains. Turned out pockets indicated that Cretan partisans had been at this place of carnage during the night. 580 paratroops had jumped into this area and of these 250 are known to have leaped straight to their deaths and 115 others were wounded either in the descent or shortly after they reached the ground; of the remainder, 135 were subsequently posted missing and only 80 managed to get through to other units during the course of the operation.

At 1400 precisely Stukas screamed down on Maleme and the air was again rent with unearthly howls as they sent their bombs crashing down on Cretan soil. Yellow arrows, indicating the direction of the enemy positions had been laid out prior to this strike and with the earth erupting all around the enemy ceased fire. The village of Maleme, still occupied by the enemy, was repeatedly struck, and as the Stukas turned away the paratroops advanced to take possession of the smoking ruins. But the enemy was still showing fight, and when the Germans reached the outskirts of Maleme, they found they had to fight for every ruined house.

At 1500 more Ju52s filled the skies above Crete, flying in over the 3rd Battalion's dropping zone to drop still more paratroops into the hell below. These men, the last two companies of the regiment, under command of Hauptmann Schmitz were pitched

Above: Me110s over Crete.

Below: The Luftwaffe was always quick to help the paratroops.

straight into the battle. But they were not enough to turn the tide. If the invasion was to succeed the vital question was when would the promised reinforcements arrive?

Oberst Ramcke Intervenes

On 19 May Oberst Bernhard Hermann Ramcke and his adjutant, Hauptmann Vogel, had arrived at Topolia airfield, 40km (25 miles) south of Athens. Ramcke had been charged with the overall responsibility for the despatch of the parachute units and organising the arrangements to fly in those units of the 5th Mountain Division which were to be air-landed in Crete. Thus it was that the night of the 20th/21st he was occupied with the loading and marshalling of planes for the mountain troops who were scheduled to take off next morning. At this juncture air-landing troops and heavy weapons were accorded priority over parachutists. Some paratroops sub-units — including Leutnant Kubitz and Vosshage's companies — which had not so far been committed to the invasion awaited the order to emplane, but there were not enough Ju52s for them as well as the mountain division. When these men were all counted up Ramcke found that he had a force of 550 trained men whose presence on Crete would certainly count a great deal. Consequently, when Ramcke reported to Fliegerkorps XI HQ that he had formed a reserve paratroop force, 550 strong, orders for its move to Crete were not long forthcoming. Ramcke Force was to have priority over the mountain troops, and some of the latter who were already sitting in the giant troop-carriers had to deplane as the Ju52s concerned had been re-allotted to the move of Ramcke's men. Other aircraft, into which the mountain division's heavy weapons had been loaded, were also hurriedly unloaded. Ramcke Force was to be dropped west of Maleme during the afternoon to help clear the airfield, and when the planes took off on this mission Ramcke himself had been so busy with the arrangements for the move that he almost forgot his parachute; in the event he was handed one as he climbed aboard his plane.

Almost exactly six hours after Hauptmann Schmitz's two companies had floated down on Crete Ramcke Force took off. Oberst Ramcke was standing by the open door awaiting the signal to jump, when his Ju52 flew over the mountain ridge behind Maleme and the pilot throttled back his engines; close behind the force commander stood Leutnant Reil, his newly appointed adjutant. The drop went according to plan; indeed it could not have gone better, since Ramcke's group landed almost on top of the Parachute Assault Regiment's HQ. And no sooner had Ramcke pressed the device to release his parachute, than the Regiment's signal officer. Leutnant Göttsche ran across to greet him. 'Good to see you, Herr Oberst', Göttsche said. 'We need a commander! General Meindl has been badly wounded and was evacuated in the first plane to land. The CO of the 3rd Battalion has been killed; Major Koch of the 1st Battalion has been seriously wounded and Major Braun from the Staff has also been killed. Many of our other officers are dead; we've had terrible casualties.'

'What is the situation regarding Maleme?' Ramcke asked.

'We've managed to capture the actual airfield', Göttsche replied. 'And Hauptmann Gericke has deployed every man in his battalion on both sides of the coast road east of the airfield. They've dug in, and struggling to hold the enemy off. Major Stenzler, who is acting as regimental commander, is with his battalion on the south-east edge of the airfield near Pt 107. The mountain troops have just started to arrive. But the airfield is

Above left: Major Walter Koch after being wounded on Crete.

Above right: Oberst Alfred Sturm commanding FJR 2; he won a *Ritterkreuz* for Crete.

Below: Maleme airfield.

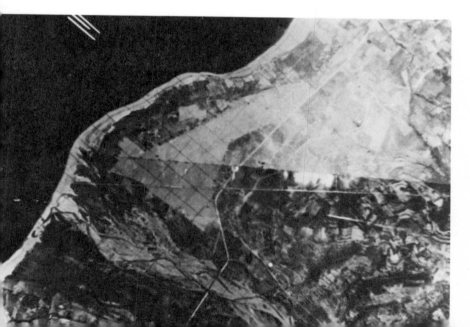

still under fire and many of the aircraft have been shot up as they came in to land; quite a number have been destroyed.'

It was a shatteringly accurate report, but Ramcke was undaunted. Within 15 minutes of touching down on Cretan soil he had assumed command of the Assault Regiment and the collection of miscellaneous other units fighting in the Western Sector.

Seen from the German side the situation around Maleme at 1815 on 21 May looked as follows:

The 2nd Battalion was dug in on the southern slopes of Pt 107, with outposts on the top of the hill. The 4th Battalion — and several groups of men from the 1st and 2nd Battalions which had joined it — was deployed across the adjacent north-eastern slope of the same hill (Pt 107) and still battling for possession of Maleme. The first company of mountain troops to land had been sent up to reinforce Gericke's force and one platoon of this unit had reached a point approximately half way between Maleme village and the coast. No 16 Company (of the paratroops — part of the 4th Battalion FJStR), reinforced by a group of mountain troops from the 100th Regiment (Oberst Utz) was advancing up the secondary road leading to the south Mulete area.

No 6 Company, with another detachment of mountain troops, was advancing west towards Kastelli in the bottleneck west of Spilia, with a view to establishing contact with Mürbe's platoon which had dropped near Kastelli. Hauptmann Schmitz's group which had parachuted into an area west of Maleme about 1500 and concentrated near the regimental headquarters, had been ordered to push on towards Maleme to support the 4th Battalion in the operations around Pt 107.

Oberst Ramcke's first orders ran as follows:

'Kiebitz company with anti-tank artillery (PAK) will move forward and come under the orders of Hauptmann Gericke. The company will attack up the axis of the coast-road; the attack will continue after dark and be pressed regardless of cost, with a view to diverting enemy artillery and mortar fire, which is now being directed to the airfield. Klein's company will join Stenzler's force. Hauptmann Schmitz's force, less the guns already deployed, will remain at my disposal.'

After nightfall on this second day of the invasion, the commanders of the different sectors were called to Oberst Ramcke's HQ, and Ramcke issued his orders for the operations which were to start at dawn on 22 May. Oberst Utz, Major Stenzler, Hauptmann Gericke and Hauptmann Schmitz were told that the aim was 'for every available man to advance east, to link up with Heidrich Force at Canea.' Meanwhile, down on the shore near Maleme sentries had been posted with shore lights to signal and guide in the expected seaborne convoy. In charge of these sentries was a naval officer, Kapitän-Leutnant Bartels, who had flown in with one of the Ju52s.

The Mountain Troops Arrive

Tense and apprehensive, Oberst Utz's 100th Mountain Regiment had been sitting around on Tanagra airfield since first light on 21 May; and when the order to get ready to emplane was given it was almost 1500.

Knocked out Ju52s
on the edge of
Maleme airfield.

Canea after the
assault.

Sunk British ships in
Suda Bay.

107

Men of the 3rd Battalion of the 100th Mountain Regiment (GJR) were the first to scramble into the Ju52s, whose fuselages had been turned into ovens by the boiling hot sun. The doors were slammed shut, the engines roared, and the planes took off. Beyond the island of Milos they flew over the flotilla of tiny ships carrying more of the Mountain Division to Crete. Until the mountains of Crete appeared on the horizon they flew low over the sea. Climbing then, they droned on past the peninsula of Cape Spatha, on towards the reddish square General Student said likened to a tennis court — Maleme. That was where they were to land!

The first Ju52 nosed down in a steep curve, and the ground seemed to rush up to meet it; its wheels touched down; there were a few bumps; and finally with a jolt, the plane came to rest. The plane's door was pushed open, and suddenly the air was filled with the sounds of battle. The chattering of machine guns was interspersed with the crump of falling mortar bombs. There was a hideous crash as a blazing Ju52 landed in a mass of flames. Another transport following it in was luckier. No sooner had it rolled to a halt than the mountain troops were out and taking cover. Other Ju52s followed into the arena of flaming wrecks and dead and dying men. Some were destroyed; some got down. Field and anti-tank guns were unloaded, so too were motorcycles, boxes of medical supplies, signal sets, tinned food, barrels of water. In the middle of it all the battalion commander was wounded, and he was carted away from the fiery heel of the landing strip.

At the height of the landing operation RAF Hurricanes suddenly appeared — one of them following a Ju52 as it steadied for a landing, and destroying it before it could get down. But it was the Hurricane's final victory, a vigilant Me109 from the fighter umbrella over Maleme swooped down to rake the British fighter with its guns, and the Hurricane blew up in a rosette of flame.

For the mountain troops Maleme was the fiery, deadly overture to the drama of the battle for Crete. From heaven they descended into hell. As planes landed, and one machine after another crashed or was smashed to pieces, it became progressively more difficult for those behind to get down safely and the pilots had to negotiate a course between the wrecks. Within a matter of hours Maleme became one huge aircraft cemetery; by nightfall on 21 May the landing strip was lined with the wrecks of 20 smashed and burned out Ju52s, and the airfield was still in the line of British artillery fire.

The message 'The mountain troops have arrived' was passed along their line by the weary paratroopers. One of the first air-landed companies moved up to support Hauptmann Gericke's 4th Battalion on the south and south-eastern sectors of the airfield perimeter. A second company was ordered by Oberst Utz to move as rapidly as possible to the Cape Spatha peninsula, where the two seaborne convoys were expected to disembark, and sweep it clear of enemy. Utz himself, with the two remaining companies of the 3rd Battalion, moved up the Anoskeli and Episkopi roads, determined to block the advance of enemy forces from Palaochora.

By the late afternoon (of this second day of the invasion) the Parachute Assault Regiment had established a continuous line sealing off the whole coastal area. From the coast in the north this line ran past the eastern edge of Maleme village south to the eastern slopes of Pt 107, and south again as far as Mariana. In this line the following troops were deployed:

Above: Reichsmarschall Göring decorates Feldwebel Erich Schuster with the *Ritterkreuz* for heroism on Crete.

Below: A glider waiting to take off for Crete.

In the north: The 4th Battalion, now called 'Gericke Force'. Next to it were the remnants of the 1st and 3rd Battalions under Oberstabsarzt Dr Neumann who had assumed command of them when Major Koch (CO of the 1st Battalion) had been wounded and Major Scherber (CO of the 3rd Battalion) killed. Further south the 2nd Battalion, commanded by Major Stenzler, was deployed. (See Appendix: Deployment of the Paratroop Assault Regiment on 20 May 1941.)

Behind this forward line stood the 2nd Battalion of GJR 101 whose commanding Officer, Major Friedmann, had been seriously wounded as he was leaving his Ju52.

It was on this day, 21 May that the British Prime Minister, Winston Churchill, said:

'The island is being defended to the last man. British troops have been on Crete since November 1940 and at least two complete Greek divisions escaped to the island from the mainland. The fact that the Germans are endeavouring to capture an airfield, and so open the way to the fly-in of further troops represents the real danger in this situation'.

While Churchill was actually speaking these words, the airfield had already been taken, and the fly-in of the mountain division was finally to turn the tide in favour of the Germans. Meanwhile the *Daily Telegraph* published on 21 May was forecasting a German defeat:

'Hitler is playing for high stakes; it is not just Crete that he is after. But his grandiose plan can only be successful if the Luftwaffe has resolved the secret of air power versus sea power. Some of Hitler's advisers believe that air-superiority is the more important and cite the conquest of Norway in support of their theory. Hitler may be trying for a similar success with Crete. But in Crete he will not have the advantage of the treachery that paved the way for his troops in Norway, a country without arms, and only a narrow gulf to cross. This time he is faced with superior naval strength, an air force superior to his own in both men and machines, and seasoned troops who have already shown that they can hold their own against the Nazi élite.'

The Times went further: 'A German defeat at this time', the paper pontificated, 'would be a terrible blow to German prestige.'
But the final word must be credited to Winston Churchill, who at the end of his speech said: 'The battle for Crete has become one of the most difficult actions in the war'.

During the first two days on Crete the Parachute Medical Section (SanAbt) of Fliegerkorps XI, under command of Oberstabsarzt Dr Berg, had to cope with an unprecedented number of casualties. Medical personnel, doctors and orderlies alike, were kept continually busy throughout the whole period — collecting and evacuating the wounded from the forward areas and giving them treatment. Those primarily concerned were under command of Oberstabsarzt Dr Neumann, Oberarzt Dr Weizel and Oberarzt Dr Malison.

On the evening of 20 May, however, Neumann radioed Fliegerkorps XI HQ in Athens asking for more medical personnel and supplies. General Student responded with a Field Ambulance unit under command of Oberarzrt Dr Hartmann, which was

Above: A glider that came down near Maleme on 20 May 1941.

Below: British troops surrendering at Maleme.

dropped on Crete next day. Taking off at 1300 on 21 May the unit was supposed to be dropped in the Parachute Assault Regiment's area between Maleme and Platanias. In the event they jumped in the dropping zone of Nos 5 and 6 Companies (of the 2nd Battalion FJStR) their sticks were widely dispersed, and they were shot up as they came down. So many men were killed or wounded and so much equipment was lost the unit virtually ceased to exist. Dr Hartmann — who jumped with a group which included a couple of medical sergeants, Sieber and Geisburger — landed in the middle of a British position at Platanias. Most of his group were picked off while they were still in their parachutes, and the men who did manage to escape the flying bullets found themselves under attack before they could even get to their weapons containers. With seven other men Dr Hartmann managed to find shelter in a ditch, and to hold off the enemy with pistols and hand grenades for two and a half hours. At the end of that time only Hartmann and Sergeant Sieber were still alive. Sieber, the sole survivor takes up the story:

'The Oberarzt had only two rounds left in his 08 Lüger pistol and he said to me: Sieber, two more cartridges, then we're finished! Dr Hartmann then stood up and fired his last two rounds at the enemy. He was then struck by a shot in the head, and collapsed dead beside me.

'I still had two hand grenades and when I had thrown them some British soldiers charged up to our position and I was captured. After that I was taken to Canea where my wounds were attended to.'

Thus it was that the medical personnel and supplies failed to reach the men in the Western sector who needed them so urgently.

In the Eastern sector No 2 Medical Company, with Oberarzt Dr Langemayer and Oberarzt Dr Kirsch dropped near Heraklion with Schulz's battalion, the 3rd Battalion of FJR 1. Despite being wounded in the chest as he floated down, Dr Kirsch — a surgeon who had specialised on jaws — operated on men with facial injuries. Men of Fliegerkorps XI who fought in Crete had good cause to be grateful for the dedication of Dr Kirsch and others of the Parachute Field Ambulance and many of them owe their lives to 'the boys with the blue facings.'

The Fate of the Seaborne Convoys

The first convoy carrying the seaborne reinforcements to Crete consisted of 30 small craft — mostly fishing cutters and motorboats. Having embarked the 3rd Battalion of the 100th Mountain Regiment the convoy had sailed from Piraeus in the early hours of 20 May. The second convoy, carrying the 2nd Battalion of the 85th Mountain Regiment packed into a similar number of small boats, sailed from Euboa, while a third convoy was being marshalled in Piraeus.

The two loaded convoys met in Milos, the port of the island with the same name, at noon on 21 May, and No 1 Convoy — which had arrived six hours before No 2 — put to sea again. The Italian destroyer *Lupo* was escorting it to its destination, Crete, and at 2250 the convoy was nearing Cape Spatha when an alert was sounded. Searchlights suddenly lit the scene and seconds later all hell broke loose. British warships had found the convoy in the darkness and turned their pom-poms and heavier guns on to the little boats — often at point-blank range. The Italian escort ship came under fire of a battleship and although the *Lupo* returned the fire it did not stand a chance. Dodging and twisting, while trying to lay a smoke screen to cover the convoy, the *Lupo* was hit 19 times and sank outright. More and more of the little boats followed it to the bottom of the sea, as the British destroyers and cruisers cruised back and forth, ramming, sinking, killing. Men swimming in the water called hysterically for help.

On the shores of Cape Spatha Kapitän-Leutnant Bartels and those who were to meet the seaborne troops when they landed had a grandstand view of the disaster. They could see the gun-flashes as the cruisers and battleships fired broadsides, and flames rising from some of the wooden ships that had caught fire. They knew that nobody could escape this hell; No 1 Convoy had ceased to exist.

No 2 Convoy's turn came a few hours later when the naval task force intercepted it. As with the first convoy the Italian escort, the destroyer *Sagitario,* had no hope of protecting the little boats. But it did succeed in laying a smoke screen, as a result of which only a few craft were lost. And the enemy lingered too long over his prey. At daybreak Stukas arrived on the scene, and in the action which followed, one destroyer and two cruisers were sunk, and two battleships and two cruisers were damaged.

That same morning 100 mountain troops, survivors from the two convoys, swimming or paddling rubber dinghies, managed to reach Crete. But the sea kept 300 soldiers of the 3rd Battalion GJR 100, including the battalion commander Oberst Ehal, and the battalion could no longer be counted a fighting unit.

The end of this most unfortunate chapter in the battle for Crete came on 23 May when three rubber dinghies carrying a Leutnant and 51 soldiers were paddled ashore. It was a happy end to the worst phase of the battle.

CHAPTER 11

The Days Preceding
Victory

Into Canea with the Paratroop Assault Regiment

Almost immediately after the destruction of the seaborne convoys the enemy launched a new offensive in the vital Maleme sector. His aim was to smash through Gericke Force to recapture the airfield, and his first attack was directed against the Kiebitz Company. (It will be recalled that the latter, with a section of anti-tank artillery, had been sent to reinforce Gericke on the evening of 21 May.) The attack was supported by tanks, two of which were knocked out and the attackers repulsed.

Soon after this action, in the early hours of 22 May, Oberst Ramcke, the new regimental commander, called Major Stenzler and Hauptmann Schmidt to Gericke's command post in the forward area and issued fresh orders. Stenzler's battalion was to take over some of the ground Gericke had won, and consolidate his position, until such time as he could be relieved by units of the 100th Mountain Regiment. Schmidt's troops would take over more of Gericke's position and dig in between Gericke and Stenzler; this should strengthen the line still further.

During the afternoon (22 May) other groups of paratroops drifted in to swell the numbers of Ramcke's force. One group, Hagele Company — men of the 2nd Parachute Regiment — which had dropped the day before near Pyrgos, arrived at Gericke's sector after fighting their way through the enemy positions. Some of the medical personnel, including Oberarzt Dr Ruge and Oberarzt Dr Gogolka also found their way to the regimental HQ (FJStR HQ) and reported for duty. (Gogolka was head of the field ambulance unit, and he was accompanied by Drs Müller and Sachs). Needless to say the medical men went to work straight away, tending the wounded.

The fact that German troops were in action on Crete had not so far been publicised either in an official Wehrmacht communiqué or on the radio. But some people, who — contrary to regulations — tuned in to the BBC on 22 May heard the British Prime Minister's speech admitting that the Germans had captured an airfield in Crete and were landing more troops on the island. At the end of this speech Churchill had appealed to the Allied Forces fighting in Crete: 'A violent and bitter battle is in progress. And I should like the men who are fighting there to know that they are engaged in what may prove to be one of the most decisive battles in the Mediterranean area.'

More of the 5th Mountain Division flew in to Maleme during the morning of 22 May despite the fact that British artillery continued to shell the airfield. Inevitably there were casualties and when the sun went down that evening the wrecks of no less than 134 German aircraft as well as a number of enemy aircraft littered the edge of the runway. One of the planes which got down safely carried the divisional commander Generalmajor Ringel. Nobody could hold him back on the mainland once his troops were on Crete, and when he landed he assumed command of the whole Western Sector of operations. The Stukas were active throughout the day, and in one massive strike during the afternoon they succeeded in silencing the enemy batteries at Modion. It was these guns which had been covering Maleme, and after this aircraft were able to land and operate from Maleme airfield without hindrance.

That the situation was changing became apparent in the early hours of 23 May when Hauptmann Gericke spotted enemy movement. From the vantage point of his battle HQ, it appeared that the enemy was retiring. He decided to advance. On his right flank, Stenzler and Schmitz followed suit, and from ravine to ravine and hill to hill the paratroops moved up in pursuit, giving the enemy no rest and smashing his resistance whenever he attempted to stand and fight. With support provided by the paratroop field artillery all the main features as far west as Platanias were captured, and once again Leutnant Horst Trebes, leading one of Gericke's platoons, distinguished himself by his ruthless exploitation of the situation. That evening Oberst Ramcke issued his orders for the following day:

'Dig in during the night and hold on. The advance will be resumed tomorrow morning (24 May) with the 5th Mountain Division moving to encircle Agya Marina. At first light fighting patrols will reconnoitre the 4th Battalion area, and individual Battalion commanders will be briefed by me personally on the ground.'

When this order had gone out the wiry little Oberst went forward to where the German front line faced the main enemy defences covering (west of) Canea. Ramcke did not consider that these positions could be taken until the mountain divisions had secured Pt 259 and was threatening Agya. That afternoon, however, the paratroops had systematically knocked out a number of enemy machine gun posts in the enemy line. With the sun in their eyes, the enemy had been unable to take any effective countermeasures against the 3.7cm PAK and captured 3.7inch AA gun which were emplaced to fire over open sights, or to cope with the paratroop flame throwers. Consequently when Ramcke's men advanced on the morning of 24 May they met little opposition. Only rearguards remained to defend what had been a formidable defensive line.

Having dealt with the enemy rearguard, Gericke's men took up the pursuit, capturing Platanias and advancing via Agya Marina as far as the hills south-east of Stahana-Canea. Here the contact was established with the Paratroop Engineer Company under Leutnant Griesinger, and this secured Gericke's right flank. Griesinger's company was attached to Major Heilmann's 3rd Battalion (of FJR 3), which was part of the Canea Force. As units of the latter had worked their way southwest to the reservoir 4 miles from Canea, the German line now extended via Utz Force (mountain troops of GJR 100) all the way to Canea. In fading light Gericke set up his command post 500m east of Agya Marina, and gave the order to dig in for the night.

Next morning, 24 May, General Student arrived and from then on the direction of the battle came under his direct control. Ramcke briefed him in the forward area, and Student approved the plans his subordinate had drawn up for the following day. Then in a brief ceremony punctuated by British mortar bombs falling nearby, the General decorated several of the paratroops — handing out clasps to the Iron Crosses which most of them were already wearing.

No news of what was happening in Crete had reached the German public by midday on 24 May, although a British communiqué from Cairo had declared that a German airborne force had been overpowered at Rethymnon and Heraklion. At lunch time on 25 May, however, people in Germany listened attentively to their radio when the announcer read the following statement:

'The High Command of the German Army reports that German paratroops and other airborne troops have been in action against the British forces on the island of Crete since the early hours of 20 May. Following a series of air strikes by fighters, bombers and dive-bombers of the Luftwaffe, our airborne forces landed to capture certain strategically important points on the island. Following their reinforcement by units of the Wehrmacht, the German troops have gone on the offensive, and the western half of the island is already firmly in their hands.

'The Luftwaffe has smashed an attempt by the British Mediterranean Fleet to intervene in the battle for Crete, and has driven it from the seas north if the island. In the course of this action many enemy warships have been sunk or damaged, and the Luftwaffe now has complete air superiority over the whole battle zone. All operations are successfully continuing according to plan.'

Shortly before dawn on 25 May, Oberst Ramcke moved his tactical headquarters from Agya Marina to Stalos, and issued warning orders for an attack by the 2nd Battalion on the right and the 4th Battalion on the left. The objective was the range of hills north of Galatas and H-hour was set at 1600. The 1st Battalion (FJStR) under Leutnant Stolz — located behind the 2nd Battalion on the right — was in reserve; Schmitz Force, also behind the two forward battalions, was positioned on the inter-battalion boundary between them; and the right flank of the 2nd Battalion was protected by the 5th Mountain Division. A heavy air-strike was to precede the attack and this commenced mid-morning, and continued until 1635 when the last Stukas turned and flew back to the mainland. H-hour had been put back and at 1700 precisely the paratroops and men of the mountain division stormed forward; the battle for Galatas had begun.

Stenzler's men, flushing snipers from the olive groves, overrunning enemy machine gun nests, and capturing a large number of New Zealanders in the process, steadily advanced from one feature to another. Seeing that the mountain unit on his right was held up, Stenzler detached one of his own paratroop companies under Leutnant Barmethler to smash the opposition, and so facilitate the advance of the mountain

Above: The bridge over the Tavronitis, near Maleme.

Left: Oberst Ramcke in Canea.

117

division. Once the way was clear Gericke Force and elements of a support unit composed of captured vehicles, some armoured, came up to reinforce Stenzler, and after a series of bitter hand-to-hand struggles, the paratroops seized the range of hills near Koljenvithra. In the course of one of these struggles four of the paratroopers were killed by shots fired at a range of five yards by New Zealanders who had displayed a white flag. With these hills in German hands, the enemy had lost the last defensive natural bulwark west of Canea.

On 26 May Ramcke Force prepared for a final assault on Canea and the attack, launched the next day, was completely successful. The British hospital on the Apostoloi peninsula was among the enemy installations that fell to Gericke Force, and the German paratroops who had been wounded and taken to this hospital were freed.

Two troops of parachute artillery were now rushed forward to take up a position due west of Mauroutrixas near Oberst Ramcke's tactical headquarters among some ancient ruins on top of a hill. From here they were able to fire across the front and cover an advance by both Ramcke and Utz Forces. A final attack on Canea was planned, in which the troops under command of Oberst Heidrich would attack from the south, while Utz Force advanced from the south-west and Ramcke Force moved in from the west.

Ramcke Force was then deployed as follows: by arrangement between the respective force commanders the Stenzler Group, on the right flank of Ramcke Force between the 2nd Battalion (FJStR) and Utz Force, was operating beyond the Ramcke/Utz Force boundary. Stenzler's line of advance had been defined as Charania-Parigoria, west of Canea. Gericke's Group (mainly 4th Battalion) whose objective was the last height occupied by the enemy before Canea — was to make a filleting attack up both sides of the main road.

The Schmitz Group, with all the available anti-tank guns (PAK) was to be responsible for providing the Gericke Group with anti-tank protection, and was deployed on Gericke's right flank. And Schramm, commanding the paratroop field artillery, was ordered to neutralise the enemy positions on the hilltops west of Canea. The 1st Parachute Battalion (Leutnant Stolz), Ramcke's reserve, was to move behind and to the right of the 2nd Battalion.

Preceded by a screen of fighting patrols the 2nd and 4th Battalions started to advance in the early hours of 27 May. The enemy had already been worn down by the pressure exerted by the 5th Mountain Division, and — as seen through British eyes — the situation is best described in Winston Churchill's words. On 26 May the British Prime Minister, addressing the House of Commons said:

'A battle of indescribable ferocity for Canea is now raging; similar battles are being waged on a smaller scale for Rethymnon and Heraklion. General Freyberg has received reinforcements by way of men and material; more will follow'

At this point the Prime Minister was interrupted by applause. He continued:

'At this moment, while I am speaking, the success of their gallant resistance is in the balance. But whichever way the battle goes, the defence of Crete, which must be seen as an Eyptian outpost, will take its place in the annals of the British Army and the Royal Navy.'

Left: Canea looked like this on 26 May after it fell.

Below: Oberst Ramcke decorates paratroops for heroism at Canea.

Into Canea

In the early hours of 27 May, the patrols reconnoitring in front of Gericke and Stenzler's battalions reported that the enemy positions before Canea were still occupied in strength. One of the 2nd Battalion's patrols, under Hauptfeldwebel Barnabas succeeded in penetrating the enemy line to raid machine gun posts and strongpoints. The success and audacity of this particular patrol was apparent when a swastika flag was seen fluttering over one of the enemy-occupied features at 0634. That patrols had managed to get so far undoubtedly had an effect on enemy morale, for when the mountain troops launched their attack at 1000 they met little resistance. Stenzler's men achieved their objective without much trouble and Gericke Force, which had been steadily working its way forward to the western slopes of the hills east of Mauroutrixas, rapidly overran the heights on the west of the town.

Having achieved the objectives the operation was supposed to end at this point, to allow for regrouping and reorganisation. But it continued with paratroops and men of the mountain division advancing shoulder to shoulder. Schmitz's Group in vehicles drove straight on into the town centre and at 1615 a swastika flag was hoisted over the red spire of the church there. Meantime Oberst Heidrich's force advanced towards the suburbs on the southern outskirts of the town. A fighting patrol of the 1st Battalion under Leutnant Krüger, sent ahead by Hauptmann von der Heydte, occupied a signal centre and then went on to hoist the Reich battle flag over the mosque near the harbour.

Gericke's troops reached the north-western limits of the town about 1700. The enemy had withdrawn towards Suda and the Akrotiri peninsula, and when Gericke arrived some of Hauptmann Schmitz's men (*Panzerjäger*) were ringing the church bells. Some time later two German paratroopers drove up to a road block, where they were confronted by an English major who introduced himself as the commandant of the prisoner-of-war camp. Walking up to a barricaded gate, he rang a bell. The gate was opened by a sentry and the major went into the guard room and told the men on duty there that Canea had fallen; minutes later 300 captured paratroops were free again.

The night 27/28 May passed quietly, and on the morning of 28 May a signal from Fliegerkorps XI instructed Oberst Ramcke to assume command of the whole Western Sector. Another signal ordered the immediate withdrawal of the mountain troops and their transfer by forced march to Rethymnon. Later in the day Oberst Ramcke issued a situation report which included details of the losses sustained by the Parachute Assault Regiment from the start of the invasion up to the evening of 27 May. From the FJStR alone 749 soldiers had been killed or were missing. In his report Ramcke said:

'The Parachute Assault Regiment and attached units has completed the mission to which it was assigned. Maleme airport was captured on 21 May after heavy fighting which resulted in many casualties. In subsequent actions the Regiment exploited east, and secured ground as far as the village of Maleme. Between the evening of 21 May and the morning of 23 May several strong counter-attacks, launched from an easterly direction were repulsed.

'When the Regiment occupied the Cretan capital, Canea, its men — fighting side by side with troops of the 5th Mountain Division — advanced up both sides of the coast road. The success of this extremely difficult and hazardous operation may be attributed to our unshakeable faith in ultimate victory. Despite the heavy losses, especially of officers, the high standard of training and aggressive spirit shown by everybody from the most senior officer down to the youngest and latest-joined paratrooper, ensured that the Regiment was triumphant.

Ramcke'

Yet the victory was not complete. What had happened at Rethymnon where, on the evening of the second day, the outcome of the battle was balanced on a razor's edge?

The Battle of Rethymnon

In the early morning of 21 May Kroh Force of the 2nd Parachute Regiment was preparing to assault Rethymnon airfield. At 0400 however, becore the operation began, the enemy attacked the German positions on the airfield perimeter. The attack was repulsed but it upset the paratroops' arrangements, and five hours later the enemy returned to the attack. This time Kroh Force was outflanked, and a commanding feature in a vineyard the paratroops had captured the day before had to be abandoned. Having suffered heavy casualties Kroh's men withdrew to the olive-oil factory, about 1,800m (2,000 yards) east of the airfield and due east of the coast village of Stavromeus. Here in the oil factory and houses the paratroops established a defensive position, and with one anti-tank gun and anti-aircraft gun settled down to await the enemy.

They did not have long to wait. In the course of the next few hours, the 19th Australian Brigade attacked again and again. And again and again the attackers were thrown back. Moreover when he learned that the enemy had captured a group of 56 paratroopers Major Kroh led a fighting patrol to recover the prisoners before they were whisked off to the enemy rear. His action was a complete success. Meantime Leutnant von Roon had set up a supply centre 7km (4 miles) east of the oil factory, and as the capture of Rethymnon seemed out of their reach at this time, this supply centre turned out to be of inestimable value.

When Oberst Sturm was reported missing, Major Schulz assumed command of the 2nd Parachute Regiment. However, as the regiment was split into two groups, Schulz, with Hauptmann Wiedemann's group (mainly 3rd Battalion FJR 2) east of Peribolia, was unable to exert much control over the other group since his only communication was by radio. In effect, therefore, Schulz took over from Wiedemann who had deployed his men in a defensive ring in the rocky terrain around Perigolia. No 9 Company — less one platoon — was occupying a line running up from the beach to the road leading to Rethymnon airfield; No 11 Company was positioned between the road and a feature known as Chapel Height, which was occupied by the remaining platoon of No 9 Company; No 14 Company, dug in and facing south, continued the line which was completed on the eastern side by a section of the Parachute Artillery Regiment, and elements of the 7th Machine Gun Battalion and 7th AA Battalion. Wiedemann's positions were bombarded by the enemy artillery throughout 21 May, and any paratrooper daring to show a finger above cover in daylight immediately drew the fire of Australian snipers and Greek partisans. Nor was morale improved when some of the bombs dropped by German aircraft striking at nearby targets fell among the paratroops. But a successful supply drop, which replenished their food supplies that afternoon, helped to restore the men's spirits. And when the Australians attacked, first the south and south-east sides of the perimeter about 1600 and later, towards midnight, Chapel Height, they were repulsed with heavy losses.

It was Kroh's Forces' turn to be attacked next. On the morning of 22 May the 1st Australian Battalion, supported by one battalion of the 4th Greek Brigade and a couple of tanks advanced towards Kroh's positions. The enemy got to within grenade-throwing distance but when the tanks were knocked out the attack fizzled out. Soon afterwards the enemy turned his attentions back to Wiedemann's positions but a series of attempts to capture Chapel Height came to nothing — mainly because of the resistance offered by Leutnant Kühl's platoon.

At 0600 on the morning of 23 May a heavy artillery concentration descended on the oil factory and the surrounding area occupied by Kroh Force. When it lifted half an hour later Australian infantry were seen moving towards the German defences. This attack was repulsed and for a time all was quiet. In the lull, Leutnant von Roon, who with other sticks of paratroops had been dropped wide of their intended dropping zones, arrived at the position — accompanied by a scratch force of paratroop stragglers he had collected en route to the German lines. With these men von Roon went on to occupy some houses at a bend in the road 400m south-east of the factory. This strengthened the defences of the Kroh 'box', and von Roon went on to exploit the situation by occupying the tiny village of Kimari — driving out the British and Greek units which were there.

Once again the enemy returned to Wiedemann. Peribolia and Chapel Height were subjected to a prolonged artillery bombardment during the afternoon and at 1600 the enemy infantry was to advance. But this time the paratroops had called for massive air support and signs had been laid out indicating the bomb-line. Consequently when Stukas, heavy bombers and fighter aircraft roared in to bomb and strafe in front of this line the enemy infantry decided there was no use going on. Another welcome feature of this air strike came with the dropping of re-supply containers which were recovered without difficulty.

Despite the successes of the defenders in repulsing every enemy attack so far, and the replenishment of stocks of food and ammunition, the situation of both groups of paratroops was becoming increasingly critical. Wiedemann and Kroh Forces were both encircled, both had suffered heavy losses, and all the men who were still able to fight were well nigh exhausted. But giving up the struggle was out of the question, since the two groups were holding down 6,700 Allied soldiers who — if Kroh and Wiedemann surrendered — would be released for deployment elsewhere in the German Western sector, or against the Germans at Heraklion. So, when 25 May dawned, the paratroops faced another day during which they knew they had to hold on to the last man and the last round. And for Kroh's men the situation looked desperate when the inevitable attack came, supported by two tanks. However this attack was no more successful than the previous ones. Kimari village, seized by von Roon the day before, was lost, and 252 paratroopers wounded in the battle were captured and sent back to the British hospital in Adhele. But the main positions held and when Kroh ordered a counter-attack some of the lost ground was re-taken.

Wiedemann Force in and around Peribolia was in similar straits. The enemy overran some of the German positions only to be ousted from them by a counter-attack by men led by Leutnant Molsen. The enemy had heavy casualties in this attack and from now on he made no further attempt to assault in this particular sector. Nevertheless Wiedemann Force was attacked on the 25th and again on the 26th, and the second action very nearly resulted in the paratroop positions being completely overrun. Advancing from the south-east, up the road and across the Platania river, the enemy infantry was supported by two tanks. It was not until one of these tanks was a blazing inferno and the other compelled to reverse after several hits, that the attackers decided to give up. In this gruelling fight the paratroop company commanders, Leutnants Paul, Pabst and Bergmann together with Hauptmann Wiedemann constantly encouraged their men and set examples deserving the highest praise. Leutnant Molsen, who led a counter-attack, also deserves special mention.

During the night 25/26 May, Kroh's men destroyed their defences before attempting to break through the enemy lines to reach Heraklion. Leaving 17 seriously wounded men in the care of a medical orderly, the 250 remaining paratroops left their positions at 0200 and marched west towards Heraklion. On the way they were joined by several isolated groups of paratroops from an assortment of units and during a halt Hauptmann Kroh took the opportunity to reorganise his column into four companies:

1 Company: commander Leutnant Schindler. Made up of the remnants of the old No 1 and No 4 Companies.
2 Company: commander Leutnant Keserberg. From elements of the Regimental Signal Section.
3 Company: commander Leutnant von Roon. From survivors of Nos 3 and 13 Companies.
Heavy Weapons Company: commander Leutnant Marr. With light AA gun, 1 light PAK, 1 heavy machine gun, 3 heavy mortars: made up of personnel from No 2 Section the 7th FlaMG Battalion.

The order to leave their positions near Rethymnon and break through to the German enclave at Heraklion had come from HQ Fliegerkorps XI, and it was something as a surprise to Kroh Force when the order was revoked that evening (26 May). The whole of the 2nd Parachute Regiment [which included Kroh Force and Wiedemann Force] was instructed now to stand fast in its present positions. This, the order went on to say was to 'pin down the enemy'. So Kroh halted and established a defensive position which he extended the next day (27 May) by occupying the small town of Prinos and some of the prominent features in its vicinity. The paratroops met little opposition, being faced by Greek troops and Cretan partisans.

In Wiedemann's area on 27 May a battle raged all day, with the enemy assaulting the eastern edge of the German perimeter. Following an artillery bombardment four enemy tanks moved up as enemy infantry advanced towards the paratroops' positions. Thorbecke's guns from No 2 Section FAAbt 7 went into action and two of the tanks were knocked out almost immediately — one by the guns, the other by daring paratroopers with slabs of explosive. A third tank was subsequently hit by the anti-tank guns but only after the gunners themselves had suffered casualties. Meantime concentrated machine gun fire had effectively broken up the enemy infantry. But the enemy kept up the pressure and during the evening and on the morning of 28 May several more attacks were launched by Australian units against Chapel Height. All of them were driven back — no mean feat when the fact that the enemy had a numerical superiority of ten to one, and the advantage of considerably more heavy weapon support than the paratroopers. It was, of course, inevitable that this superiority would succeed eventually and in the early hours of the morning (28 May) the enemy managed to open a gap in the German defences between the No 9 and No 14 Companies. Pouring through this gap the enemy overran the hospital and penetrated into Perigolia. It did not seem that Wiedemann's group could hold out much longer. But it was then that Major Schulz, the acting regimental commander, made a significant contribution to the action. With his staff and every man he could collect, Schulz led a counter-attack which halted the Australians and drove them back along the way they had come. Unfortunately some of the enemy that had penetrated into Peribolia could not be winkled out and the action itself was especially costly — Hauptmann Wiedemann and Leutnant Paul being wounded, Leutnant Pabst, Leutnant Begemann and Leutnant Molsen being killed. At the end of the day the whole of Weidemann Force had only three officers fit to fight — Major Schulz and Leutnants Klitzing and Kühl.

But the men's morale remained high.

The two Communiqués

On 28 May 1941 the German Army High Command issued the following communiqué.

'Operations on the island of Crete in which mountain troops, paratroops and other airborne units are cooperating, are progressing well. Despite difficult terrain and stiff resistance German mountain troops succeeded yesterday in smashing their way through British troops and Cretan partisans. In a daring attack they drove the enemy from their positions, captured the capital Canea, and pursued defeated enemy forces south of Suda Bay. Among the many men who have been captured is the Greek naval commander of Crete.'

In Cairo on the same day General Wavell's HQ also issued a communiqué :

'Crete: The German forces have been reinforced by other airborne units, and are being supported by aerial bombardments of steadily increasing intensity. The Germans have launched more heavy attacks on our forces in Canea. Our troops are fighting with great determination, but have had to make further withdrawals to more favourable positions.'

At dawn on 28 May, Major Kroh decided to return to the offensive — to try to recover some of the ground his men had been forced to give up on 26 May, and to advance west towards Rethymnon airfield. In the event Greek troops halted his advance on Prinos. However, on the morning of 29 May, Ju52s flew over his positions to drop ammunition and food, and fighting patrols probing forwards towards Kimari reported that it was only lightly held. When the place was assaulted at 1730 the enemy, caught off his guard, offered little resistance and No 2 Company continued on into Prinos whose houses were quickly cleared in a short brisk engagement. The enemy, it seems, had pulled back towards the oil factory, which Major Kroh resolved to attack at 0630 the following morning, 30 May.

Everything went as planned and next morning the men of Kroh force started to advance towards their objective. A surprise came as they rounded a bend in the road, and the leading scouts stumbled over motorcycles and a couple of anti-tank guns came into view. Next minute they were surrounded by cheering men in field grey — infantrymen of the 85th Mountain Regiment and motorcyclists of the 55th Mountain Battalion. These mountain troops had already seized the olive oil mill and captured 1,200 Australians. The tide had turned, and Kroh Force still had a strength of nine officers and 448 men apart from 34 wounded — many of whom subsequently died in the field hospitals. But those who had managed to escape being wounded were now safe.

So much for Kroh Force; what of the Wiedemann Force?

Going back in time to dawn on 29 May, most of the Australians who had penetrated the Wiedemann defences and evaded capture or death in houses of Peribolia had succeeded in slipping away during the night. So Peribolia was free of the enemy once more.

During the morning (of 29 May) another attempt was made to dislodge the Germans from Chapel Height and to break into Peribolia. A ding-dong battle ensued in which the enemy was gaining the upper hand and Major Schulz feared the worst when, suddenly at noon, the sound of gunfire and the rattle of machine guns was heard coming from a westerly direction.

'Those are German machine guns', an Unteroffizer yelled. He was right; a few minutes later German Verey lights soaring into the sky over on the western flank conveyed the message Schulz's men had been hoping for ... 'We are here!'

In less than an hour a section of motorcyclist riflemen rode through to Peribolia and behind them came mountain troops and a section of parachute field artillery. The guns deployed and went into action immediately, laying down a barrage on the Australian positions. Australian artillery fired back and a duel developed which lasted all day and well into the early morning of 30 May. Finally at 0700, fresh troops of the 5th Mountain Division moved to their start lines preparatory to an attack. Two German tanks, which had been ferried across to Crete from the mainland moved with them and when the attack went in the enemy pulled out in confusion, and what he had intended as an orderly withdrawal rapidly turned into fully-fledged flight. By 1100 more than a thousand Australians had surrendered, and the Peribolia battle was over. The relieving force had come in the nick of time, for it is very doubtful whether the paratroops could have held on much longer. The had stood up to an enemy with a six to one numerical superiority. And that *without* heavy weapons.

With Peribolia secure the mobile units piled into transports and made for Heraklion as fast as their vehicles would carry them. Oberst Bräuer was in trouble there and we must now see how his men of the 1st Parachute Regiment had fared.

In the early morning of 21 May the paratroops of the 3rd Battalion of FJR 1, under command of Major Karl-Lothar Schulz, were concentrating for an attack on Heraklion. When the two groups — under Leutnants von der Schulenburg and Becker — which were to encircle the town and assault it from the beach, moved off at 1430, Major Schulz ordered his two battalion mortars to open fire. Heraklion was a medieval walled town and the fire was concentrated on the approaches to the West Gate, which Schulz had reason to believe was mined. When the mortar bombs did not detonate any mines, Schulz decided there were none after all. Enemy machine guns were now firing from positions on the wall, so Schulz ordered the mortars to switch their fire to the strong points near the gate. A few high explosive rounds had the desired effect and the major shouted: 'Fire smoke!'. A glance at his watch had shown him that the time was approaching when his other groups would be converging on the town, and this was to be a co-ordinated attack. With smoke now swirling around the West Gate Schulz gave the order to advance, and all his men doubled forward. A brisk engagement around the gate was decided by hand grenades and machine-pistols. Then the paratroops were moving up the streets towards the town centre; as they advanced bursts of machine gun fire coming from the direction of the harbour indicated that Schulenburg and Becker's groups were also making progress. By first light Schulz's men had fought their way through to the market place. But nine hours had elapsed before the houses had been cleared of enemy, and the hot sun was blazing down when the shooting stopped and the paratroops were able to take stock of the situation. They had attained their objective, and casualties were not heavy. But ammunition was running low and Schulz had no reserves.

Having been turfed out of his hiding place the mayor of Heraklion was taken to Schulz; and a surrender document was drawn up to be signed by both sides. All resistance had not been quelled, but the town had been formally handed over to the Germans. A fresh outburst of firing soon suggested, however, that not everybody was aware that the town had been surrendered. Schulz himself, with one of his reserve platoons, rushed off towards the noise of the shooting. That the fight had flared up was quickly confirmed when he met Leutnant Becker, whose company was falling back towards the town centre. 'What's the matter, Becker?' Schulz asked.

'We're under attack', Becker replied, 'By a sizeable British force — and the British do not seem to recognise the fact that the town has capitulated'.

Let's get back to the Citadel', snapped Schulz.

With Schulz and Becker leading and the noise of battle swelling, the paratroops ran back to the Citadel, where Schulz learned that the enemy had cut off Schulenburg's group. Luckily Schulenburg and his party were able to fight their way through and rejoin Schulz before the enemy ring tightened, and some of the encircling troops were themselves cut off. Like Schulenburg's men, however, they managed to slip away.

At this point Schulz's first concern was to concentrate his battalion, and the various groups which had been despatched to mop up the town were hurriedly called in. Messengers were sent to the groups at the East and South Gates of the town telling them to get back to the citadel. But collecting his men at the town's ancient fortress did not resolve the problem of how he was to cope with what were clearly vastly superior enemy forces. If he was to save his battalion, it was obvious that he could not hold on to the town. Heraklion had been occupied at considerable cost in men, material and effort, but there was no alternative it had to be given up.

Leaving a small rearguard at the West Gate the paratroopers withdrew in good order and took up positions in the open country outside the town. Before he left Major Schulz sought out and spoke to the mayor: 'The Stukas will be here soon ... they'll certainly bomb the citadel and anywhere else where they think the enemy are located, so you'd best tell the townsfolk to clear out of the area straight away, if you want to avoid unnecessary sacrifice.'

As Schulz had predicted, the Stukas duly arrived, and for a breathless 10 minutes that afternoon the air around Heraklion resounded with the high-pitched whine of aircraft engines, the scream of falling bombs, and the crash of explosions. Two of the planes were shot down, but the raid left parts of the citadel battered to ruins. So ended Schulz battalion's second day on Crete.

Going back in time again Oberst Bräuer, who had dropped with the 1st Battalion of FJR 1, ordered Major Walther to get his battalion together as quickly as possible and make for Heraklion airfield — the Regiment's second objective. Assembling the battalion in the dark was not the easiest of tasks in itself, and while the different groups were sorting themselves out a platoon of No 1 Company was discovered to be missing. Commanded by Leutnant Lindenberg, this platoon had gone off on its own — completely against orders. In the event Lindenberg had led his men up into the hills south of Gourned, where they were ambushed by Greek troops and annihilated.

Bräuer, impatient to push on to the objective under the cover of darkness, prevailed on Walther to move before his battalion was complete. The regimental commander believed that it was better to accept some disorganisation rather than risk a move in daylight across a plain enfiladed by enemy machine guns on the airfield perimeter. The result was that no properly coordinated attack was possible, and when Leutnant Graf Blücher's No 2 Company tried to assault the eastern edge of the airfield it soon found itself in trouble.

The company progressed slowly in the face of strong enemy resistance from carefully camouflaged field works. When dawn broke the paratroops found themselves shelled by nine field guns, mortared by an unknown number of mortars, and in the direct line of fire of numerous machine guns. Elements of the 2nd Battalion, under Hauptmann Burckhardt came up to support the attack, but as neither the 1st nor the 2nd Battalion had any heavy weapons the paratroops had little hope of success. When the attack ground to a halt, as was inevitable, the enemy struck back with a counter-attack supported by tanks. Under Wolfgang Graf von Blücher the paratroops shooting from holes they had scraped in the rocky soil did their best to hold the ground they had taken. But Blücher was killed and silence descended on the battlefield shortly after midday. The attack had failed and during the afternoon the remainder of the 1st Battalion pulled back to the western slopes of the hills 2km south of the airfield and settled into a defensive position.

So ended a difficult day for the 1st Regiment. It had battled with an enemy force of 8,024 men, but it had failed to secure its objective, the airfield which was needed for the landing of reinforcements.

For the paratroops at Heraklion 22 May was to be another disastrous day — a day of hard fighting and bitter decisions. During the morning a British emissary under the protection of a white flag, approached the locality of the 3rd Battalion. He brought a message from the commander of the enemy troops in the Heraklion sector, which Karl-Lothar Schulz read out to his men:

'German Paratroopers!
You have fought bravely. But it is senseless to fight on. You are the only remaining group on the island, which has not so far been destroyed. Further resistance is hopeless. As much as I appreciate your courage I must ask you to surrender; you will be well treated.'

Karl-Lothar Schulz scribbled his answer on a message pad and handed it to the emissary: 'The German Army', he wrote, 'has been ordered to occupy Crete. It will obey this order.'

Shortly after this interlude the 3rd Battalion signal officer established radio contact with Regimental HQ, and Oberst Bräuer told Major Schulz to leave part of his battalion in its present position to make sure that the road to the west was cut. The capture of Heraklion, the colonel said, had been postponed. Concentrating the regiment, so that its combined strength could be used in a decisive strike, now had priority. So — taking a route which would avoid the town — Schulz was to move the main body of his battalion to Pt 491 and knock out the enemy artillery which was shelling the regiment from somewhere on this hill.

Leaving the wounded behind to block the road, Major Schulz moved off as soon as it was dark, and by dawn the battalion was sheltering in a ravine at the foot of the hill which was their objective. They were out of sight of the enemy and they had halted only because Schulz had appreciated that Pt 409 could only be taken in a night attack.

Meantime the regimental medical officer Dr Carl Langemeyer had set up a dressing station in the mountain village of Tselikakä. Apart from men of Schulz's battalion, paratroopers from other units also received treatment at this post. Casualties of the Schirmer group — men of FJR 2 who had been seconded to FJR 1 for this operation and who had been skirmishing all day with partisans — were among the first to turn up. In common with all the other medical units, Langemeyer's staff performed miracles.

After dark it took the men of the 3rd Battalion three hours to work their way quietly up the hill (Pt 491). Having arrived near the top they sprayed the enemy positions with short bursts of automatic fire and then charged in. The British gunners, taken completely by surprise, were overwhelmed, and as soon as guards had been posted over the captured weapons the paratroopers slumped to the ground and slept. They were exhausted and when a reconnaissance patrol sent out by Oberst Bräuer reached the position, the only man awake was Leutnant von der Schulenburg. Schulenburg, who had taken over guard duty, returned with the patrol to report to the regimental commander: 'Schulz Battalion has captured Pt 491, in accordance with your orders. The battalion is now asleep!'

In the course of 24 May Oberst Bräuer completed the reorganisation of his regiment, concentrating most of the units near the south-eastern limits of Heraklion. South-west of the town the detachment of the 3rd Battalion which Schulz had left to block the Pyrgos-Timbaktion road remained in position; this detachment had been reinforced by the elements of Schirmer's group of the 2nd Battalion of FJR 2 which had fought their way through the partisans.

25 May was a Sunday, which Bräuer's men had good reason to remember. Two battalions of British troops, coming from the south, were seen advancing towards their positions near Heraklion when a squadron of Ju52s flew overhead. The British columns — anticipating an air strike — left the road and the men scattered and dived for cover into the ditches at the side. But it was men not bombs that fell from the planes: Vogel's battalion had arrived to reinforce Bräuer.

The paratroopers were sniped at on the way down, but when they reached the ground they rallied, and charged the enemy. Many of the latter, disorganised by their dash for cover, were surrounded and shot down before they had time to recover. So far as the FJR was concerned the situation had undergone a radical change for the better with the arrival of, and aggressive display by Vogel's men. From now on the enemy never regained the initiative.

On 26 May the 2nd Battalion of FJR 2 went on to occupy Pt 296 — a hill which dominated Heraklion airfield. The British launched a counter-attack but this was repulsed by paratroops under the command of Hauptmann Schirmer.

The situation was now ripe for an attack on Heraklion. Bräuer's strength had been augmented by Vogel's battalion and on the morning of 27 May a single Ju52 flew over his positions to crash land with a field gun and its crew — not on the airfield — but on top of a hill. Bomb-line indicators had been spread out to show the pilot where he was to touch down, and the successful accomplishment of his mission was a tribute to his superb handling of the plane.

The gun went into action straight away, opened fire and everything seemed set for the assault on Heraklion. In the event the attack never materialised. During the morning units of the 5th Mountain Division reached the Damasta plateau overlooking the plain of Heraklion, from where the dazzling white buildings of old King Minos's legendary port shimmering in the heat haze below were plainly visible.

News of the approach of the mountain troops had preceded them; so too had demoralising reports of Allied defeats elsewhere on the island. As a result the enemy abandoned Heraklion and when Bräuer's patrols probed the defences they found they were opposed by only a weak rearguard. This was soon dealt with, and when men of the 5th Mountain Division arrived, the paratroops were already in possession of both town and airfield. Oberst Bruno Bräuer himself, one of the German paratroop pioneers, was not there to greet them; he had gone to report to General Student.

The mountains troops did not halt at Heraklion, but pushed on to Neapolis and from there to the Gulf of Mirabella. They met no opposition but as darkness closed in the motorcyclists ahead of the main column hurriedly abandoned their machines and dived for cover when they saw a couple of tanks on the road ahead. Minutes later they realised that the tanks were Italian — ferried over from Rhodes the day before.

The pursuit was also taken up by FJR 1, and when the enemy tried to stand at the mountain pass near Imwros, Oberst Utz's 100th Regiment and the ubiquitous Stukas were called in. While the dive-bombers rained destruction on the British positions, Utz's men moved round to outflank and encircle them. The end came near Sfakia Lutro when more than 10,000 British and 2,000 Greek soldiers laid down their arms.

129

The battle for Crete was over and on 30 May the German Army High Command issued the following communiqué:

'The campaign to occupy the British base on Crete, which began on 20 May with a massive airborne operation, is now nearing its conclusion. Enemy resistance has been overcome everywhere. Mountain and paratroop formations operating in exceptionally difficult conditions on the western side of the island have defeated and dispersed the enemy. A paratroop force, encircled by a numerically superior enemy force at Rethymnon has now been relieved. These paratroops who were besieged for eight days offered a gallant resistance and more than held their own.

'Our forces are now pursuing the remnants of the British garrison which is in disorderly flight towards the south coast of the island, where the survivors are embarking to avoid further fighting.'

General Wavell's HQ in Cairo also issued a communiqué that day:

'Crete: More German reinforcements were air-lifted to Crete on Thursday, and air strikes by the Luftwaffe continued throughout the day. Our troops having inflicted heavy casualties on the Germans, are now occupying new positions.'

On 31 May the German Army issued another communiqué:

'Our mountain troops on Crete, who are continuing to pursue the beaten enemy eastwards, have established contact with paratroops near Heraklion'.

And on 1 June came the final announcement:

'On Crete British and Greek pockets of resistance in the southern region are being mopped up. Italian forces landed on the island on 29 May and have established their headquarters at Ierapetra. In the course of the recent operations a company of mountain troops under command of Oberleutnant Walter is reported to have fought with exceptional valour and distinction.'

A communiqué was also issued by the British War Office on 1 June, and this read as follows:

'Following 12 days of some of the most gruelling fighting of the war, it has been decided to withdraw our forces from Crete. Although our troops have inflicted heavy casualties on the enemy, who has suffered great losses in men and aircraft, it has become obvious that our land and naval forces could not continue to defend Crete indefinitely with only the resources available in North Africa. 15,000 men have already been evacuated and arrived in Egypt; more are expected to follow, but it must be admitted that we have suffered heavy losses.'

Winston Churchill, pondering on the lessons of Crete, had already demanded that the strength of the British parachute force should be expanded from 500 to 5,000 men. He

130

had recognised the significance and potential of airborne troops, and appreciated their future in any Allied return to the continent of Europe.

The Americans had also been watching the campaign in Crete, and they too had drawn their conclusions. In May 1940 General Marshall, the Chief of Staff of the US Army, had appointed Major William C. Lee (who was later to command the 101st US Airborne Division) to be responsible for airborne development in the US. Crete served to boost interest in airborne matters and the training of American paratroops forged ahead after this. From a mere 48 men in September 1940 the American airborne force rapidly grew to become a division, and finally to two divisions.

On the German side reaction to the campaign in Crete was rather more subdued, and General Student said later:

'I find it very difficult to write about the battle for Crete. For me, the commander of the German airborne forces, the very name Crete conjures up bitter memories. I miscalculated when I proposed the operation, and my mistakes caused not only the loss of very many paratroops — whom I looked upon as my sons — but in the long run led to the demise of the German airborne arm which I had created.'

German losses on Crete were:
Army: Dead, wounded and missing: 51 officers, 1,172 men.
Air Force: Dead, wounded and missing: 297 officers, 4,464 men.
New Zealand historians put the number of British Army's casualties, in dead, wounded and missing, at 15,743 all ranks.
The Royal Navy's recorded losses were 2,011 all ranks.

CHAPTER 12

Interlude:
Between Campaigns

Crete was the End

As the campaign in Crete ended in victory, the operations of the new airborne weapon could be judged a success. But it was the paratroopers' swan song.

On 19 July 1941, when the Russian campaign was barely a month old, the men who had been awarded the *Ritterkreuze* for their valour in Crete, paraded before the Führer at his headquarters in Rastenburg. Before he stepped out to pin the medals on the recipients, Hitler turned to General Student and said:

'Crete has shown that the day of the paratroops is over. Paratroops are a weapon of surprise, and the surprise factor has been overplayed.'

Student had more to say about this comment after the war:

'Hitler spoke in most appreciative terms about the way the paratroops had fought . . . Over the next few months when the call came for paratroops to fight on the ground, I was to realise the deeper significance of his words.'

The enemy viewpoint was best expressed by the British military historian, Major-General Fuller, who wrote:

'Of all the operations during World War II, the airborne assault on Crete rates first place for audacity. Neither before nor after was anything similar attempted. The invaders came not by land or sea but by air, and their operations did not depend on land communications. The most remarkable feature of this campaign was the use of aircraft to move an army, making it completely independent of roads, railways and arduous cross-country marches.

'Next to the battle of Cambrai in 1917 — the first ever tank battle in the history of warfare — the invasion of Crete brought the most important revolution in tactics. The fact that the invasion was successful can be attributed to (a) the astounding organisational ability possessed by the Germans and (b) the equally astounding lack of imagination displayed by the British.'

Crete was intended to serve as a starting point for new and bigger operations. It was meant to be the springboard for operations which would take the Germans to Cairo, to

Iraq and to the Baku oilfields. But the start of the campaign in Russia turned Crete into a backwater. From then on the victory which had cost so dear was seen only as a successful conclusion to the Balkan campaign. The daring and ambitious dream was ended. Operation Mercur, as the invasion of Crete was called, was forgotten in the stupefying magnitude of events unfolding on the eastern front, and it was relegated into limbo. Nevertheless in the annals of military history the invasion of Crete deserves its place as the first occasion when the invaders descended from the skies.

The Russian Campaign

In the opening stages of the campaign in Russia paratroops were dropped near Bogdanow. A company of the Brandenburg Regiment was employed in this operation, and more of the Luftwaffe paratroops were involved. Air reconnaissance prior to the operation had elicited the fact that the bridges over the Dvina were guarded by Soviet troops and the aim was to make a surprise landing, seize these bridges across the Dvina and hold them pending the arrival of German armoured formations.

At about 1500 on 25 June 1941 the first of two Ju52s carrying a section of Brandenburg commandos approached the bridges at an altitude of 55m (180ft). A storm of heavy machine gun fire struck the plane and the pilot was wounded; seconds later the wireless operator collapsed over his radio, having also been hit. The men jumped before the plane had reached the designated dropping zone. But as 14 T-34 tanks were positioned around the dropping zone, it was just as well that they jumped when the did.

The second Ju52, whose pilot was following the first, but some way behind, was confused by the actions of the first aircraft, and he turned away. Circling, he made a second approach to drop his paratroops into the right area. Jumping straight into a hail of bullets, those who survived the drop found they had plunged into a fierce fire fight with Soviet tanks and infantry. Leutnant Lex, the commando leader, and four other soldiers were killed; 16 others were wounded, but the 14 survivors captured the bridge and held it until a German armoured column reached it 24 hours later. So Lex's unit achieved its purpose.

Despite this early success no more airborne operations were mounted throughout the entire campaign on the Eastern front. Only when Breslau was encircled in the spring of 1945, were paratroops dropped to reinforce the men who were cut off. This may be attributed to the salutary effect of Crete. The Führer's original Directive No 21 — covering Operation Barbarossa — included a paragraph which clearly indicated that paratroops were to be employed. 'The Soviet railways must be cut, vital bottlenecks such as river crossings will have to be seized by paratroops . . .' (*Section III (Conduct of Operations); Sub-section B.)*

But this directive was written on 18 December 1940, and five months later nobody wanted to take any notice of this paragraph.

The paratroops returned in triumph to Brunswick and Stendal, and what was left of the 1st Parachute Regiment took part in manoeuvres round Wildflecken, 34km (20 miles) east of Fulda before it settled down in Stendal to reorganise and refit. Towards the end of September 1941 the 7th Air Division was told to warn some of its units for service in Russia as straightforward infantry. And from Stendal the men of the 1st

Parachute Regiment moved via Königsberg to Tossno; they were to be deployed around Leningrad, where the 424th Infantry Regiment of the 126th Infantry Division had seized Schlüsselburg on 8 September 1941.

Bruno Bräuer, now a Generalmajor, quickly showed that his regiment could fight in the bitter cold of a Russian winter as well as they had under the hot sun on Crete. Major Schulz's 3rd Battalion (of FJR 1) took part in several crucial battles — slicing into Russian formations and cutting them to pieces. Only on one occasion did the Russians manage to stand up to the paratroops. This occurred at Petrushino, where, because of the terrain, a single battalion could be deployed in an attack. When all the paratroop battalions volunteered for the task, it was decided to give it to Major Stenzler's 2nd Battalion FJStR, and the attack took place on the night of 18/19 October. With little fire support available the attack turned into a bloody hand-to-hand struggle and the Russians fought stubbornly for every inch of the ground. They yielded eventually and when dawn broke their positions had been captured. But the paratroops had paid a heavy price. A key position blocking the road to Tossno had been taken but Stenzler's battalion had virtually ceased to exist. All the officers had been killed — Major Stenzler himself dying from a wound in the eye.

This battle and his own experience caused Major Schulz to compare the qualities of the Red Army soldier with his own men. The Russian was tough and hard, but man for man he was no match for the German paratroops.

In the event the paratroops were pulled out of the fighting in Russia in the middle of January and sent back to Germany — the 3rd Battalion being the last to go. Then, after staging at Gardelegen, Grossborn and Stendal, where the battalions were brought up to strength, the 1st Parachute Regiment moved to the Avignon area.

Other Deployments in Russia
Apart from FJR 1, the rest of the 7th Air Division — comprising the FJR 3, the Parachute Engineer Battalion (FP Battalion), some of the Parachute Artillery (FAAbt 7), most of the attached armoured units (*Panzerjägerabteilung*) and No 7 Medical Section (SanAbt 7) — was airlifted to Leningrad. Generalmajor Petersen, the new divisional commander and his staff — who were more or less superfluous at this time because the individual paratroop units were under command of Wehrmacht formations — chafed at their own inactivity. However the division was concentrated under Petersen in the middle of October, and redeployed on the Neva. Divisional HQ was established in a dug-out, and the principal staff officers were Oberstleutnant i.G Graf von Uxküll (Operations) Leutnant Tappen (Intelligence) and Oberstleutnant von Carnap (Adjutant).

During the next few weeks the paratroops on the Neva were constantly in action, repulsing 146 Soviet attacks in 46 days, knocking out 41 tanks, taking 3,400 prisoners and shooting down five Soviet aircraft with small-arms fire. For their successes however there was a heavy price to pay, and these weeks before Leningrad were a hell in which 3,000 of them perished or were wounded.

The 2nd Parachute Regiment fared worse than the 1st and 3rd Regiments. Transferred to the Stalino region and reinforced by *Panzerjägers* and a machine gun company at the end of November 1941, the 2nd Regiment was deployed at the Mius and involved in some bitter fighting under arctic conditions. Around Voroschilovka,

Left: Troops from a company of the Parachute Machine Gun Battalion in position on the Mius in Russia.

Below: The arrival of parcels from home was always a day to remember; here by FJR 1.

Bottom: Many paratroops remained in Russia.

Ivanovka and Petropavlovka there was particularly hard fighting in which Schirmer's and Pietzonka's battalions distinguished themselves. The Soviet offensive starting 23 January near Voroschilovka, the edge of which was blunted by the paratroops, deserves special mention.

In Petropavlovka the paratroops were told that they were to be sent home, but one of the most severe winters in Russian history had run its course before the vehicles carried them back to Germany. It was snowing when the first trucks left on 18 March 1942, and it was still snowing five days later when the 1st Battalion arrived in Stalino. There they stayed for five more days before finally entraining on 28 March for home. The train took them — via Dnjepropetrovsk and Fastov — first to Kiev, and on 2 April on again north-west to Gomel. It was then that the paratroops began to wonder about their destination. They did not have long to wait for an answer. On Easter Sunday, 4 April 1942, their train rolled through Krasnovardeisk, and they detrained at Tossno. The men of FJR 2 were bound for the swampy hell of the Wolchov, and here in a murderous climate they stayed and fought until mid-summer. Pietzonka's battalion was in the forefront of the fighting. Time and time again he had to send out patrols into the woods and the swamps, and time and time again the enemy tried to overwhelm his positions by sudden surprise attacks.

Eventually the enemy was cleared out of the Wolchov sector and the paratroops were again looking forward to returning home to Germany. Companies were pulled out of the forward areas at the end of June and when FJR 2 had concentrated, it moved back to Germany.

Meantime the bulk of the Parachute Assault Regiment — less two of its battalions which had been detached to serve with the 1st and 2nd Regiments — had been sent up to Schaikovka during December 1941, under command of Major Koch, and deployed around the airfield there. The regimental headquarter staff was transferred by air to Juchnov on 15 January 1942, where it was to resume its proper function as the headquarters of a fighting formation. Generalmajor Meindl, fully recovered from his wounds, had been given command of a scratch force consisting of the 4th SS Regiment, an air force construction battalion, an AA battery and one skeleton infantry battalion of the Wehrmacht, which had suffered heavy losses in the recent fighting. (The men of the Mölders fighter-bomber squadron were also attached to the force for a while, and deployed in defence of the airfield). With his old staff — blooded in Crete — to administer it, Meindl's force provided a useful reserve.

The Russians did not attempt to attack in this sector until the middle of February, contenting themselves with sniping the paratroopers and sporadic raids on their positions. But the situation was clearly deteriorating when partisans blew up the railway installations at Kossnaki and reports were received of enemy units at Issnoski. Finally, when a Soviet motorised column drove through the gap between the Fourth Army and the Fourth Panzer Group, General Meindl was ordered to take every man he could muster, block the Russian advance and destroy the Red Army formations involved.

The dynamic Meindl lost no time blocking the enemy spearhead and then trying to throw a ring of steel around the enemy salient; unfortunately he did not have enough men to surround the Russians completely, and a sector on the east had to be left open. Consequently many of the enemy were able to get away, but Meindl had forestalled a

Christmas 1942 with
the boys in the front
line.

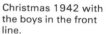

Oberstleutnant
Schulz decorates
paratroop heroes in
Russia, winter
1942/43.

Briefing battalion
commanders at Karl-
Lothar Schulz's battle
HQ in Russia; from
left to right: Schulz,
Gröschke,
Polschewski and
Count von der
Schulenburg.

breakthrough and the German line was re-established when his troops joined hands with the 20th Panzer Division on the road to Gshatsk.

In another engagement near Yokhnov more enemy were severely mauled when Meindl Force went to the relief of a German field hospital almost completely surrounded by the enemy. The MO in charge of the field hospital was none other than Dr Neumann, the regimental medical officer who had been awarded the *Ritterkreuz* for his service on Crete. Here in Russia Neumann had found himself faced with a situation in which it was impossible to guarantee the safety and care of 2,000 or so of the wounded in his charge. With Russian tanks sitting on the road to the nearest airfield at Roslavl from which casualties could be flown back to Germany, the prospects for these 2,000 men seemed grim indeed. It was then that Neumann thought of General von Richthofen — an old friend since the days of the war in Spain — and a radio message was sent to the General at HQ Fliegerkorps VIII:

'About 2,000 soldiers are condemned to death at Yukhnov', the message ran, 'unless they can be evacuated by air at once. These men have fought well, given their best, and risked their lives more than once. Their efforts deserve our gratitude and we can show our appreciation by flying them out of the Soviet ring now closing round us. If they stay here their deaths are a certainty.'

General von Richthofen responded immediately. Between 60 and 72 Ju52s landed on two consecutive days on an improvised strip in the middle of the surrounded pocket, and over a thousand of the more seriously injured casualties were flown to safety. That was the end of the air lift, but Stabsarzt Dr Neumann breathed a sigh of relief. Subsequently the remaining wounded were evacuated by road in a convoy commanded by Neumann himself, when the route to Roslavl was opened by an operation by Meindl's men supported by squadrons of Me109s under command of Major Morhahn. For his work and achievements with the wounded at Yukhnov Dr Neumann was promoted Oberfeldarzt.

By this time the Paratroop Assault Regiment had been reduced to a few understrength groups. The 4th Battalion under command of Major Gericke had been disbanded, the 2nd Battalion under Major Stenzler had been annihilated at Petrushino, and Major Koch's 1st Battalion had sustained very heavy casualties in the fighting near Schaikovka and Yukhnov in the central sector.

The employment of paratroops in a ground role in Russia deprived General Student of the greater part of his specialist force. The 7th Air Division, stationed in Normandy, had been reconstituted and brought up to a strength of 21,000 and every man had undergone parachute training. But as soon as the remnants of the Assault Regiment and the 2nd Parachute Regiment returned from Russia, this division — now under command of Generalmajor Heidrich — was sent to Russia and deployed in the Smolensk region.

The 1st Parachute Regiment which was sent to Vitebsk, was now under command of Karl-Lothar Schulz, who had been promoted to Oberstleutnant and taken over in Avignon. Major von der Schulenburg was commanding the 1st Battalion, Major Gröschke the 2nd, and Hauptmann Becker the 3rd; the regimental adjutant was Hauptmann Kerfin.

Dated 3 March 1942 this is a card from Generalmajor Lanz to the Zimmermann *Fallschirmjäger Kompanie* who had been attached to the Lanz Group in Russia, commending them for their fighting ability and comradely help.

On return to Hildesheim after the attack on Crete. In front with the white cap, Major Walther Koch.

Return of the FJStR to Hildesheim after the battle for Crete. From the left: Oberfeldwebel Festerling, Oberfeldwebel Schelling, an unknown Feldwebel, Oberfeldwebel Reisinger and Oberfeldwebel Herter all from I Battalion FJStR.

139

Around Vyazma and south-east of Smolensk partisans directed by General Belov were causing so much trouble that the German High Command in Russia decided they must be dealt with without further delay. Split into little combat groups 1st Parachute Regiment was sent to hunt down the partisan units and the war in this area degenerated into a series of minor actions between the paratroops and a vicious enemy who rarely stayed to fight and who took refuge in the forest when the first snow of winter started to fall. By December 1942, however, the partisans had been driven out of the area, and in January 1943 the regiment was redeployed around Orel.

Several attempts by the enemy to break through the German line in the Duchovtschina region were frustrated by the regiment. On one occasion when the Russians had penetrated the 12th Panzer Division area and a tank regiment was surrounded, Schulz's men smashed a gap in the Soviet ring, so enabling the panzers to break out. A similar operation on another occasion near Alexaiyevka resulted in some of the most bitter night fighting the division had experienced. Counter-attacking in the darkness, Karl-Lothar Schulz led his paratroops deep into the enemy positions to destroy the deadly Stalin-organs (rocket-launchers) which had been so effective against the German positions. Standing beside his regimental commander in this action, Horst Kerfin was killed.

When, finally, the heavy losses the regiment had suffered led to it being relieved, General Rudolf Schmidt, the GOC of the 2nd Panzer Army sent a handwritten letter to the regimental commander expressing his appreciation of the regiment:

'Dear Schulz,

I want to express my appreciation and gratitude and to say how proud I have been to have your paratroops under my command. On several occasions you have prevented the enemy effecting a mass break-through and destroyed those elements which did get through. Indeed, your paratroops have been the saviours of Orel; without them the 2nd Panzer Army would have had far heavier casualties.

Yours gratefully,
Generaloberst Schmidt'.

This letter marked the end of employment of paratroops in Russia, where — in the toughest of battles and the worst ever climatic conditions — they had shown that they were not just 'fair-weather soldiers'. Their era was over in this theatre because they never recovered from the losses they had sustained.

But now it is time to turn back and look at events in Germany.

CHAPTER 13

New Plans and Paratroops in Africa

Expansion and Extension of the Paratroop Force

It was the spring of 1942 before General Student was able to do anything about expanding the paratroop arm. Individual units returning from Russia had been reduced to mere cadres, and what remained of von der Heydte's battalion after a winter in Russia became a training unit at Döberitz-Elsgrund. Apart from the normal daylight parachute jumping practice, dropping by night was practised; and the technique of men jumping with their weapons as distinct from the latter being parachuted down separately in containers was adopted.

Additionally, trials with the new type of 'dive' glider (*Sturzlastensegler*) started in May. This glider had been developed for a specific operation. An invasion of Malta was being planned and it was proposed that a battalion under von der Heydte should be crash-landed *six hours before* the dropping of the main invasion force of paratroops. The aim was to knock out the British AA defences.... But let us look at this enterprise.

Plan for an Invasion of Malta

The implication of Hitler's comments on the future of paratroops was not lost on General Student but this did not prevent him planning more airborne operations. In Student's view the lessons of Crete had not been exploited and he was convinced that paratroops still had a tremendous untapped potential.

In April 1942 a signal from Rome took Student to Generalfeldmarschall Albert Kesselring's headquarters to meet his erstwhile subordinate Generalmajor Ramcke, now acting as an adviser to the new Italian Parachute Division 'Folgore'. An airborne invasion of Malta by a joint German-Italian force had been proposed, and Ramcke had been told to plan the operation in conjunction with Student. The plans were to be drawn up by the Germans but the Italian Commander-in-Chief, General Count Cavallo, was to be primarily responsible for their execution.

In simple terms the plan that was eventually agreed envisaged an operation in four phases:

1 A glider-borne assault by a battalion-sized force led by von der Heydte would

141

neutralise the main AA defences on the island. An advance guard of parachute troops (under General Student's personal command) would then be dropped to seize the heights south of Valetta. This bridgehead would be extended to include the airfield and town of Valetta.

2 The way should then be open for the main seaborne invasion force to land south of Valetta. Once ashore this force — in cooperation with the paratroops and other air-landed troops flown in to reinforce them — would go on to invest the whole island.

3 To divert attention from the main operation a feint attack would be staged against the Bay of Marsa Scirocco.

4 The Italian Navy was to be responsible for the safe passage of the seaborne force to Malta, and Luftflotte 2 supported by units of the Italian Air Force would provide air support for the airborne operation. This air support was to include massive strikes on the airfields and AA positions before H-hour, and the destruction of the enemy air force of Malta before the operation was launched.

In essence the planners visualised the deployment of a task force far more powerful than the force used to invade Crete, and a rapid surprise stroke which would deliver Malta into German hands and avoid any of the long drawn-out fighting such as had occurred on Crete. Twelve Me321 *Gigants* were to be allotted for the transport of heavy weapons and light tanks; Sicily was to be the assembly and embarkation point for the seaborne element; and the headquarters of Fliegerkorps II where Luftwaffe General Lörzer would direct the air side of the strike and coordinate the support of the Italian Air Force, would also be on Sicily. With Mussolini enthusiastic to the point that he had even agreed to his precious battleships participating in the operation, the chances of success looked good.

The airborne element included the Italian Folgore Division whose training in Viterbo and Tarquini was being supervised by Generalmajor Ramcke. The morale of the Folgore was said to be good, and Ramcke had a high opinion of its commander General Frattini. There was also the German 7th Air Division, soon to be brought up to strength, the Italian air-landing Superba Division and four well-equipped Italian infantry divisions.

All seemed set for the operation to be launched in the near future and preparations were going ahead when a telegram summoned General Student to the Führer's HQ. And when he arrived there the Chief of the Luftwaffe General Staff, General Jeschonnek, took him aside: 'You'll have a difficult time with the Führer tomorrow, Herr Student', Jeschonnek said. 'General Crüwell of the Afrika Korps has been here this morning and they discussed the morale of the Italians. Crüwell does not think much to Italian troops . . . so you may well find the Malta operation is in danger'.

Next day General Student presented the plan for Operation Hercules to a large and critical audience including Hitler. The latter asked a string of questions but when the presentation was over he pronounced the plan to be a good one.

'In principle', said the Führer, 'the operation is feasible. *But'* and now he dropped his verbal bombshell — 'although I have no doubt that your airborne troops will get a foothold and your bridgehead be more or less a certainty, I'll guarantee that as soon as the invasion starts the whole of the British Mediterranean Fleet will converge on Malta. And then you'll see what the Italians will do! As soon as ever the radio messages start

Above left: With Colt and camera into Tunisia — General Patton.

Above centre: Posters like this were stuck up by the maquis; it reads: *TRUTH — These photographs were taken by an Allied reporter nine hours after the first landings in Normandy.* The men of FJR 6 have added their own comments: (top) *Enemy propaganda* (middle) *All lies!!!!* (bottom) *Victory will be ours!*

Above right: In the Tunisian bridgehead: Generaloberst von Arnim (in front) C-i-C 5th Panzerarmee and General Gustav von Vaerst, commander of the DAK.

Below: 44km to Tunis. Many paratroops saw this sign.

to arrive reporting British warships are on their way from Alexandria or Gibraltar, the whole lot of them — battleships and all — will run back to their harbours. So you'll have no reinforcements coming by sea and you'll find yourself on the island — alone with just the paratroops.'

'General Kesselring has provided for that sort of situation', replied Student. 'If the British do send their fleet out they'll suffer worse than they did at Crete — where you will remember von Richthofen's aircraft sent a sizeable portion of the Alexandria-based squadron to the bottom of the sea. Malta is well within the range of the Luftwaffe; indeed the distance between Sicily and Malta is much less than the distances between Greece and Crete. Furthermore the British fleet has to travel twice as far from the eastern end of the Mediterranean than it had to get to Crete. So you may well find that Malta becomes the Royal Navy's graveyard.'

Hitler was not convinced. And he was not prepared to sanction the invasion, even when Student assured him that the airborne troops would be able to take Malta on their own when the Luftwaffe had finished bombing the place. In the end he ruled that: 'The invasion of Malta will not be attempted in 1942'.

Because of this high level decision an operation which might have given the conduct of the war in the Mediterranean an entirely new aspect, was never launched.

Ramcke's Brigade in Africa

While in Italy, Generalmajor Ramcke was ordered to raise a paratroop brigade for service in Africa. As the Malta operation had been postponed, von der Heydte's training unit and Kroh's battalion were destined to become the nucleus of the new brigade. Following an attack on the Gaza line on 26 May men of the Afrika Korps captured Tobruk on 20 June. It had taken them a year to get within striking distance of this fortress port and less than 24 hours to capture it.

From Tobruk the Afrika Korps swept on into Egypt to capture Mersa Matruh before being forced to halt just short of El Alamein. The tables had turned, and the enemy grew stronger daily, as fresh divisions were brought in from Syria, India and Iraq. Erwin Rommel, newly promoted Generalfeldmarschall, consequent on his victory at Tobruk, asked for another armoured division, but was sent only an infantry division — the 164th Infantry Division, which had been garrisoning Crete. However he was also promised a brigade of paratroopers under command of Generalmajor Ramcke.

Ramcke flew to Africa ahead of his troops, and when his He111 landed on the airstrip serving Air Command Africa, the date was 31 July. He was met by a duty officer who told him: 'The Herr Feldmarschall wants to see you at 1000 tomorrow morning.' Ramcke duly reported and told Rommel that his brigade group — 2,000 paratroop infantry plus an artillery battery and an anti-tank battalion — was on its way. 'Thank you, Ramcke', said the Feldmarschall, 'I am glad to have you over here. You already know what is going on and what is expected of you. Get your men here as soon as possible. In the meantime have a good look round; this theatre is brim-full of problems.'

That Rommel had not understated the position became clear when Ramcke made a brief reconnaissance of the forward areas and gained an insight into some of the difficulties associated with positional warfare in the Western Desert. Next morning as

Ramcke flew back to Athens Major Kroh's 1st Battalion was deplaning in Africa — the Air Transport Commander Mediterranean and his staff had quickly resolved the problems that surrounded the move of the brigade to Africa. The 2nd Battalion, under Major Friedrich Freiherr von der Heydte followed on the heels of the 1st; then Major Hübner's 3rd and the Parachute Training Battalion under Major Burckhardt. When the Parachute Artillery battery under Major Fenski arrived, the brigade was complete and the order of battle in Africa read as follows:

Ramcke's Parachute Brigade in Africa
Commander: Generalmajor Ramcke
Operations: Hauptmann Schacht, later Major Kroh
Adjutant: Oberleutnant Wetter
Brigade Medical Officer: Stabsarzt Dr Cohrs
Interpreter: Sonderführer Wesselow
FAAbt (artillery): Major Feiski
Panzerjäger Company (anti-tank): Oberleutnant Hassender
FJ Pioneer Company (engineers): Oberleutnant Tietjen
1st Battalion: Major Koch
2nd Battalion: Major von der Heydte
3rd Battalion: Major Hübner
FJ Lehr Battalion (training unit): Major Burckhardt

Kroh's battalion and that of von der Heydte, the first to set foot in Africa, were sent up to take over from units of the Afrika Korps at Ruweisat and Deir el Shein. Digging in on the edge of the wadis, the paratroops slung their groundsheets over their weapon pits to protect them from the sun, and covered the groundsheets with sand to camouflage their positions. Hot sun and artillery fire by day and enemy air raids by night combined to make life difficult enough. Fighting patrols of Gurkhas and Indian troops which attacked the positions regularly at night made it even harder. Anyone found asleep by these patrols was liable to have his throat cut.

The Italian Folgore Division which had also been sent to reinforce the Afrika Korps was deployed near Ramcke's battalions, and these Italians were first rate troops. Whenever the enemy attacked he was driven back, and on 30 August Rommel issued an Order of the Day, which was read out to all the paratroops:

'Soldiers! The Army in Africa has been reinforced by fresh divisions and a new offensive will be launched today. My aim is the complete destruction of the enemy forces, and I am expecting every soldier under my command to give of his best in the decisive days which are to come.

(Signed): The Commander-in-Chief
Rommel, Generalfeldmarschall'.

At a commanding officers' conference at Ramcke's HQ, the brigade commander explained the plan of attack:

'We shall attack in the following manner:
'Assembly area and Brigade tactical HQ are here in Fort Kattara. Von der Heydte's

Top and above: The Luftwaffe supported the paratroops by day . . .

Right and above right: . . . and at night was still there.

146

Below left: Major Hans Jungwirth, commanding I Battalion FJR 5.

Below centre: The first paratroops march into Tunis.

Below right: American and British prisoners of war in Tunisia.

battalion will assault the Ruweisat Ridge; while a task force consisting of Hübner and Burckhardt's battalions, two battalions from the Folgore Division under command of Colonel Camosso, and the heavy weapons of the brigade will constitute a special task force under my command. This force — Ramcke Force — will advance east from Bab el Kattara (The Quattara Depression). Once we have broken through the enemy crust we shall then turn north and continue the advance to the line Deir el Ankar and Deir el Munassib. Here we shall dig in.

'Major Boeckmann, CO of 187 Artillery Regiment will be in support. On our northern flank the Trieste Division, under command of my old friend General Count Ferrari Orsi, and on the southern flank the 164th Light Division will be advancing with us. Our immediate objective is 14km (9 miles) from the assembly area here, and intelligence reports that the ground we have to cross is thickly mined.'

Shortly before the conference took place there had been some changes in commanders: Major Kroh had ceased to be the CO of the 1st Battalion when he became the Brigade Operations Officer in place of Hauptmann Schacht, who had contracted amoebic dysentry. Kroh's place was taken by Hauptmann Schwaiger, and Leutnant Wetter of the 135th AA Regiment took over as brigade adjutant.

An open staff car driven by Oberfeldwebel Börner, carried Generalmajor Ramcke to his brigade's start line on the evening of 30 August 1942, and the operation started on schedule at 2200. The assault company of the brigade under command of Leutnant Wagner, moved off down a corridor, which had been cleared of mines; the second company followed close behind. In the moonlight the paratroopers appeared to be stooping as they advanced. Then the enemy artillery opened up and Ramcke ordered his gunners to respond. The attack which Generalfeldmarschall Rommel hoped would end with the encirclement and destruction of the British Eight Army at Alamein had begun in earnest. The 15th Panzer and the 90th Light Divisions would sweep on via Cairo to Suez just as soon as the jaws of Rommel's pincers closed around Alamein while the 21st Panzer Division occupied Alexandria. To start with, however, the two armoured divisions were essential components of the pincers and the 90th Light Division with the XXth Italian Corps constituted the pivotal hinge of the encirclement.

The Afrika Korps had been regrouped for the attack and moved south during the nights of 29 and 30 August. The northern flank of the *Panzerarmee (Panzerarmee Afrika* was the official title for all Axis forces in Africa from 30 January 1942. Ramcke's Parachute Brigade, the Afrika Korps and the Italian division were all separate parts of the *Panzerarmee.)* was denuded of troops, and in the middle of a sea of dummy positions Ramcke's paratroops now were the only worthwhile fighting formation. Their task was to engage the enemy's attention on their sector of the front during the move of the armoured divisions.

Wagner's company and that of Knacke which followed, formed the spearhead of the advance by Ramcke Force. As they moved cautiously out of the lane which had been cleared of mines and entered unexplored terrain, mortar bombs exploding round them detonated every now and then with a great flash. These bombs had set off some of the mines in the ground which the paratroops had to traverse.

'Knock out the enemy mortars, the anti-tank and machine gun positions', Ramcke

DIE HEIMAT RUFT !

EURE LIEBEN, EURE HEIMAT, EUER VOLK - SIE RUFEN EUCH ZU : GENUG DEUT- SCHES BLUT IST SCHON GEFLOSSEN !

Wollt Ihr doch sterben, deutsche Landser ? Sterben fuer einen Fuehrer, der Euch nach Afrika schickte, und dabei ganz genau wusste, Ihr kaemet nie zurueck ? Fuer einen Fuehrer, der Euch jetzt hier im Stiche laesst, und nur, wie bei Stalingrad, den Befehl gibt, auch der letzte Man soll fallen?

Nur fuer den Fuehrer koennt Ihr fallen ! Nicht fuer das Vaterland ! Denn das Gebot des Vaterlandes an jeden jungen Deutschen lautet :

LEBT FUER DEUTSCHLANDS ZUKUNFT !

Lebt also ! Wir wollen Euch nicht das Leben nehmen !

Streckt die Waffen und kommt zu uns ! Der einzige Weg in die Heimat fuehrt ueber die Gefangenschaft ! Nach Kriegsende kehren die Gefangenen nach Deutschland zurueck, und sehen die Lieben in der Heimat wieder.

Kommt also zu uns ! Ihr braucht keinen Passierschein mitzubringen. Bringt diesen Zettel, wenn es geht ! Notwendig ist es aber nicht.

LANDSER, IHR SEID STUR ! IHR HABT EUCH TAPFER GESCHLAGEN. IHR HABT EURE PFLICHT GETAN. JETZT ABER MUESST IHR WAEHLEN : DER TOD, ODER DIE GEFANGENSCHAFT ! FUER EINE SCHON VERLORENE SACHE FALLEN : ODER FUER EINE BESSERE ZUKUNFT LEBEN !

IHR HABT DIE WAHL !

Above left: Leaflet dropped in Tunisia at the end of April 1943. The main headings read: *Home is calling! Live for Germany's future! You have got the choice!*

Above right: Captured Americans and British.

Below: The paratroops march into Tunis.

ordered his gunners, after a prolonged view of the battle front through powerful night-vision glasses. The gunners opened fire and within minutes a violent counter-bombardment duel was raging. By this time Ramcke's leading infantry was approaching the British defences and with the brigade commander leading — as was customary in the paratroop formations — the first assault wave charged into the forward positions.

By dawn Ramcke's Force had fought its way through to Wadi Deir el Ankar and were within striking distance of the objective. But the sudden detonation of mines which blew the leading scouts to pieces brought the advance to a halt; the paratroops had walked into an unknown minefield.

'Get the mine detectors up here!', ordered Ramcke. 'Kroh, get a message to the 164th Light. Tell them to send us some more engineers. If we don't look out we shall be caught here in this minefield in daylight and picked off like sitting ducks.'

With mortar bombs from enemy weapons in Alam Nayil crashing around them, the paratroops hurriedly scraped holes in the stony soil of the dry wadi.

'Hübner, get your battalion ready to resume the advance', the brigade commander ordered when the engineers reported to him. And as soon as a lane had been cleared through the minefield Hübner's battalion moved into the lead. But the mine-free lane was under observation from Alam Nayil and an artillery and mortar barrage enveloped it as the paratroops moved up. Breaking into a run most of Hübner's men manged to get through this curtain of steel, and the minefield, to fight their way up on to Deir el Musassid ridge. They had attained their objective and there they dug in, and as soon as the brigade was under cover Ramcke ordered dummy positions to be dug 200m in front of the established line of defence.

On the morning of 2 September Generalfeldmarschall Rommel visited the brigade, and expressed his satisfaction with its location and the paratroopers' defences. Turning to Ramcke he asked 'Well Ramcke, how do you think the situation will develop now?'

'In my view, Feldmarschall', Ramcke replied 'the enemy would be stupid *not* to counter-attack in this sector. Their artillery has already started ranging on our dummy positions, and I am expecting them to attack any time now'.

'I think you're right, Ramcke', said Rommel, as he got into the car which was to take him back to his command post, 'And I am relying on you to hold on here . . . otherwise the Afrika Korps is going to be in real trouble'.

The expected attack came one hour before last light on 3 September 1942, and Ramcke immediately went up to his command post in one of the forward positions. Hauptmann Wiechmann reported his battery was ready to go into action and as soon as the enemy infantry appeared on the skyline the brigade commander told him to open fire. The enemy retaliated with a concentration of fire which crashed down behind the German positions. Minutes later a line of figures wearing flat saucerlike helmets charged up to the paratroopers' positions and a hand-to-hand struggle ensued. The enemy had attacked in battalion strength and Lieutenant Kiebitz's company — which had been held in reserve in a counter-attack role — had to go into action before the attackers could be driven back.

But this setback did not seem to deter the enemy. Indeed the battle flared up with renewed vigour, and it gradually became clear that the British were attacking on a broad front and were aiming to smash gaps in the line held by the German 164th Light

150

Above and below: More captured Allied troops.

and the Italian Trieste Divisions. Soon after this a runner arrived at Ramcke's command post to report; 'General, the commander of 164 Light Division wants your help. His tactical headquarters has been surrounded by the enemy'.

'A job for you, Hübner', Ramcke snapped: 'Get a platoon of assault troops across to 164's tactical headquarters.' Leutnant Schäfer commanded this platoon, and Generalmajor Kleemann's headquarters were duly relieved, but Schäfer himself was killed in the action.

During the morning of 4 September an attack by the 132nd British Armoured Brigade was driven back with heavy losses — Ramcke's anti-tank guns and his artillery accounting for no less than 16 British tanks. When it became possible to take stock of the situation 80 other vehicles, which had been shot to pieces or blown up on mines in front of the paratroopers' positions, were counted. 3,500 prisoners had also been taken, among them the brigade commander Major-General Clifton. Ramcke's men had made a magnificent contribution to the Afrika Korps' latest offensive and Generalfeldmarschall Rommel came to express his thanks to Ramcke and to the Italian paratroops on the right flank. (The latter had also fought well, losing two battalion commanders, Major Rossi and Captain Carugno in the course of the battle).

Rommel learning that Ramcke had dysentry suggested the paratroop commander should be flown back to Germany. Ramcke refused. He knew there were difficult days ahead and he preferred to share them with his men. So he stayed, and was looked after by his devoted batman, Seeberger.

During the ensuing week the paratroop brigade was under constant attack by an enemy which was being steadily reinforced. Generalmajor Kleeman was wounded in one of the attacks and Rommel ordered Ramcke to take over the command of the 164th Light Division in addition to his own brigade. This meant that he was now responsible for the entire northern sector of the front, and Ramcke shifted his command post to Fort Kattara. This was a phase of operations during which the paratroop engineers were in constant demand and Leutnant Tietjen, who coped with all the tasks that were thrust on him, deserves a special mention.

The phase ended when the brigade finally was redeployed with the Folgore Division south of Alamein.

The Paratroop Brigade Slips Away

The enemy's big counter-offensive opened on 23 October 1942 with a massive air attack and an intense artillery bombardment lasting several hours. All the indications suggested that the main weight of the attack would fall on the troops deployed in the Quattara Depression area. 250 heavy bombs were dropped on Ramcke's command post, and when the bombing stopped the paratroops fully expected to see the enemy advancing towards their positions. In the event the bombing and shelling in this area was a diversion, and the enemy attacked the northern section of the front.

General Bernard Montgomery who had taken over command of the British 8th Army in August, had more than 1,000 tanks at the start of the offensive, and his air force enjoyed complete air superiority. Montgomery threw everything he had into the attack, and for several days the battle swayed to and fro. At the beginning of November, however, reports that the German line was starting to crumble reached

Above: Oberleutnant Spieler in Tunisia.

Above right: Feldwebel Erich Schuster was awarded the *Ritterkreuz* for heroism on Crete. He was killed on 11 January 1943 in Tunisia.

Right: Major Wilhelm Knoche commanded III Battalion FJR 5 in Africa and it was he who conducted the initial negotiations with the French.

Ramcke's command post and Major Kroh voiced the fear that the paratroop brigade might be cut off. If it was, then there was little hope of the main body getting away, since only the field and anti-tank artillery units were motorised.

During the afternoon of 2 November a message was received ordering the brigade to break contact with the enemy, pull back and redeploy between Duweir el Tarfa and the minefield near Deir el Quatani during the night 3/4 November. This entailed a tricky disengagement and a forced march of some 30km (19 miles) — which, in desert conditions, was no mean feat. To conceal the fact that the paratroops were abandoning their positions, reconnaissance and fighting patrols were deployed up to the last minute; vehicles waited to carry them away while the enemy was still confused by the sudden burst of activity they had provoked. Meanwhile the rest of the brigade was marching back, and nobody who took part in this march is ever likely to forget it. But the paratroopers eventually reached the predetermined area and dug in. A few men collapsed on the way, but they and a few stragglers were picked up by personnel carriers operating a shuttle service along the route. The brigade had no sooner settled in than another message ordered another move. One battalion had to go north, and as the message had been delayed and the battalion was supposed to be already on its way, the whole of the brigade transport — amounting to 40 vehicles — was hurriedly assembled and Hauptmann Straehler-Pohl's men embussed. An hour later another message instructed the rest of the brigade to move and take up defensive positions west of Fuka. As Fuka was 100km (60 miles) away, as the crow flies, this order implied another forced march and four days' trekking across open desert dominated by the enemy's airforce. It looked as if the brigade was doomed, or — at least — destined for captivity. But Bernhard Ramcke was not prepared to give in.

The *Panzerarmee* got its orders to retreat on 4 November — Feldmarschall Rommel issuing the order in defiance of a personal signal from Hitler decreeing that the El Alamein position 'be held to the last man'. Thus, while the panzer divisions were hurrying away in their vehicles, Ramcke's brigade was left sitting in the desert.

Worse was to come. As the 1st and 2nd Battalions were just about to march off, the enemy attacked the positions, manned now only by a few men. Tanks were moving ahead of enemy infantry, and the rearguard waited until they were almost on them before opening fire. These tactics succeeded. A number of enemy tanks went up in smoke and then the attack fizzled out. And while the enemy were still confused the paratroopers slipped away.

At midnight the brigade was still on the march, but an hour later Generalmajor Ramcke ordered the column to halt and rest while he, Major Kroh, Major Fenski and Leutnant Wetter made a brief reconnaissance in his staff car. Topping a rise they almost ran into a regiment of British tanks, and the car made a quick turn before they were spotted. The near presence of the enemy clearly demanded a change in direction of the German retreat and the brigade marched south into the desert. But the paratroops had gained only a brief respite. Next day British planes flew over the column and within an hour tanks were seen on the horizon. Ramcke's anti-tank guns put down their trails and waited while the rest of the column moved on. And all the enemy tanks, except one, were destroyed in the action which followed. But other tanks came to take their place and throughout the day the paratroops were under constant attack. By nightfall the anti-tank gunners had exhausted their ammunition and their guns had to be destroyed; behind them they left a trail of blackened smoking wrecks which had once been British armoured fighting vehicles.

Meanwhile the rest of the brigade was still marching, and during the night of 5 November the leading scouts reported that they had almost walked into a big convoy of British vehicles; the convoy, guarded by tanks, seemed to have stopped for the night. Generalmajor Ramcke realised that this was the one — and perhaps only — chance for his brigade. 'They'll do for us', he said.

Creeping forward in small groups some of the paratroops quietly surrounded the vehicles and at a given signal sprang forward simultaneously. Seconds later the sleeping British crews woke up to find themselves looking into the muzzles of German machine-pistols. Once their weapons had been seized they were ejected from the vehicles and their places taken by the Germans. Down the road the rest of the brigade waited to board the trucks as they rolled west towards safety. From the time being the paratroops had everything they wanted, for the vehicles contained food, water and weapons.

On the morning of 7 November the convoy of vehicles was stopped on the coast road near Fuka by a German reconnaissance troop . . . the brigade was safe. Ramcke drove on quickly to where he was told Rommel had established his headquarters, and burst in on a conference at which the Feldmarschall had just announced that he believed the paratroop brigade commander had probably been captured. 'He is alive and well . . . and still with you' Ramcke reported. And the saga ended on 16 November when the small wiry man — who had joined the paratroopers at the age of 51 — was decorated with the *Ritterkreuz* with oak leaves.

Some units of the brigade were withdrawn from Africa to be returned to Germany shortly after their dramatic escape. But von der Heydte's battalion, augmented by detachments of supporting arms into a force known as the von der Heydte *Kampfgruppe* (Battle group), stayed on. And with the 90th Light Division von der Heydte's force fought gallantly with the rearguard throughout the long retreat across North Africa. Their efforts staved off defeat and allowed many men of the Afrika Korps to get away. Harassed by tanks of the British 8th Army von der Heydte's paratroops held part of the line across the salt marshes of Mersa Brega, and on 18 December near Nofilia they attacked New Zealand troops — men who in Crete had been their toughest adversaries. For this action, of which General Montgomery wrote: 'It was a savage fight . . .', von der Heydte was awarded the Italian silver medal for bravery.

So ended the story of Ramcke's brigade in Africa, although elements of it remained in Tunisia until May 1943.

Current Plans

While Ramcke's brigade was in Africa and most of the remaining paratroop formations were fighting in Russia, General Student was working on plans for more airborne operations. One was for the capture of Batum, the Black Sea port close to the Soviet oil fields. Student believed that if an airborne task force could establish a bridgehead in Batum it should be possible to extend it and hold on until the spring of 1943 when it was expected a German offensive in the Caucasus would reach the city.

If the worst came to the worst and the enemy did endanger the bridgehead before this happened, internment in neutral Turkey was open to the paratroops. The initial drop would be a brigade group from 90 converted He111s. Student wanted to have Heinkels rather than Ju52s because in terms of armament and speed they could match anything the enemy had. However this plan came to nought because it seemed too much of an aerial Utopia.

Another plan put to the German High Command, postulated the occupation of the Fisher peninsula on the Murmansk front. Because it was considered to be too ambitious it too was not approved. Nor were General Student's ideas for an airborne panzer division of 126 tanks, two paratroop regiments and an airborne panzergrenadier division to attack armaments factories in the Soviet Union received with much enthusiasm; 150 *Gigant* gliders and 300 normal gliders would have been needed for such an operation, and Student's argument that an airborne panzer formation supported by a fighter and fighter-bomber force could smash the Soviet supply system very quickly, was rejected. Yet there is little doubt that industry in some areas of Russia could have been brought to a standstill by such operations, and the enemy would have been compelled to withdraw troops from the front in order to deal with the invaders in his industrial hinterland.

The use of an airborne panzer division in the Nile Delta to cut the 8th Army supply routes was also suggested. But Hitler maintained that Africa was a secondary theatre of war and the German High Command supported his view that operations of this nature would waste resources sorely needed elsewhere. The fact was that after Crete the German High Command was not prepared to countenance the sort of airborne operations which Student wanted. The result was that the German paratroops were used as conventional infantry and frittered away in minor operations. As the saying goes — *Man kleckerte auch hier, wo man hätte klotzen müssen* (It is no use slobbering if you can afford to spit).

CHAPTER 14

From Tunis to Fortress Europe

The 5th Paratroop Regiment in Africa

While *Panzerarmee Afrika* was retreating westwards towards Tripoli, Anglo-American forces landed in Algeria. At 1400 on 8 November 1942 the commander of the Allied task force had received the signal 'Play ball'; and the Allies' Operation Torch had begun. A total of 107,000 men were deployed on the operation, whose purpose was to provide the second arm of a gigantic pincers in which Rommel's *Panzerarmee* would be squashed.

Following a series of discussions the Allies had concluded that the Russians would be unable to withstand another German offensive unless the pressure on them was relieved by the opening of a second front. This was something the Russians had been persistently demanding for some time. So an Allied expeditionary force had been assembled, and — for appearances sake — the overall command was vested in an American: General Dwight D. Eisenhower. Following a great deal of discussion and hesitation, Casablanca, Oran and Algiers were selected as the first objectives. A plan to land in the Bizerte-Tunis region was considered by the planners but rejected on the grounds that it posed too many problems. In view of the fact that there was not a single German soldier in this area, the Allied rejection of this plan may thus be seen as conceding victory in Tunisia in 1942. The *Panzerarmee's* supply line could immediately have been severed from Tunisia, after which the defeat and elimination of the Axis forces in Africa was a foregone conclusion.

The fact that France was neutral did not deter the Allies. Marshal Pétain and Premier Laval had collaborated with Germany *because* they wished to retain the French colonial territories of Morocco, Algeria and Tunisia. French troops stood ready to defend the soil, while French warships with steam up waited in the harbours ready to sail and sink an invading armada. If the Allies had hoped that the landings would be unopposed by the French sea, land and air forces in North Africa, they were sadly deluded. At Casablanca ships of the French Navy and French artillery put up a stiff resistance and it was 11 November before Admiral Davidson was able to report that French resistance had been overcome and Casablanca was in Allied hands. At Mehadia, French coast defence batteries put up a stiff resistance, and at Sebou —

where seven French destroyers sallied forth to do battle with the invasion fleet — it was the early hours of 10 November before American Rangers were able to get a foothold ashore. But once they had secured a bridgehead General Patton, commander of the Allied Forces in Morocco, poured in 37,000 soldiers and 250 tanks. There was only token resistance at Algiers, but part of the US 1st Armoured Division under Colonel (later Brigadier-General) Robinett at Oran met determined resistance, and the invaders were not able to start their advance towards Tunis until 10 November.

Turning now to the German side. The German High Command was not altogether surprised by the reports that Allied troops had landed in North Africa, although it was convinced that French North Africa was not in danger. Hitler heard about the invasion during the night of 8 November when his train stopped at a wayside station in Thuringia. He and his entourage were travelling from the Wolf's Lair to Munich where he was to deliver his traditional 9 November speech in the Bürgerbräu-Keller. When the implications of the news were discussed next day the Führer flatly rejected the idea of giving up North Africa, despite the fact that the *Panzerarmee* was in full retreat and Fuka had been lost. 'To give up Africa, *meine Herren*', his advisers were curtly told, 'means to give up the Mediterranean' — this from the man who had said Africa was a secondary theatre of war, and who, in refusing to let Rommel have another panzer division, forfeited victory in 1942. Telephoning Generalfeldmarschall Kesselring in Rome shortly after the Allies had landed in Algeria, Hitler asked 'What troops can you get across to Africa, Kesselring?'

'Two battalions of the 5th Parachute Regiment and my own headquarters defence company', came the reply, which drew the response 'Well, send what you can'!

Hitler had transferred to Kesselring the responsibility for stopping the allies marching straight through from Algiers to Tunis.

The 5th Parachute Regiment, a new formation, had moved to Italy in November 1942. Commanded by Oberstleutnant Walther Koch its nucleus was the old 1st Battalion of the Parachute Assault Regiment; and when the regiment moved to Tunisia Hauptmann Jungwirth was commanding the 1st Battalion and Captain Wilhelm Knoche the 3rd. In the event these battalions were preceded to Tunis by a force under Hauptmann Sauer, formed from paratroopers who had served in Ramcke's brigade. (Recruited in Athens they were moved first to Brindisi and flown from there to Catania in Sicily, where they were organised and equipped, before flying on to Tunisia.)

Landing in Tunis on 10 November, Sauer's force was put under the direct command of Oberst Harlinghausen, the newly appointed Air Commander Tunisia, and Hauptmann Sauer was ordered to take over and hold the two airports La Marsa and El Aouina, pending the arrival of more airborne reinforcements. Considering that a division of French troops was deployed around the two airports, Hauptmann Sauer can be said to have performed a difficult task in an exemplary fashion. Kesselring's HQ Defence Company, AA units and a rag-bag of army troops, which the Generalfeldmarschall had collected and put into planes, were among the first to arrive, and these were put under command of Sauer. And, on 14 November with more men at his disposal, the gallant Hauptmann extended his control over the region, first the southern part of the town and then, the following day, the whole of Tunis. At this time, if the Allies had suddenly decided to land at Cape Bône, Sauer's men would have been

Above left: Feldwebel Peter Arent, the hero of El Bathan.

Above right: Sanitätsfeldwebel Zimmermann of FJR 5. One of the best!

Below: A forest of posters on the outskirts of Tunis.

the only Germans they would have met. In the next few days, however, the situation changed with the fly-in of the Italian Superba Airborne Division.

Other reinforcements were now landing in Bizerta. On 11 November a section of paratroop engineers under Oberfeldwebel Peter Arent spearheaded the arrival in Tunis of the 'Field Engineer Battalion Tunis' (in reality No 16 Battalion), and when the first company of this battalion was complete it flew on to Bizerta. On arrival Leutnant Wolff, the company commander, was under the impression that he was the first German to land there but he was quickly disillusioned when the crew of a Ju52 and two of Arendt's men came across to welcome him to Tunisia. The Ju52 had flown in and landed without an objection from the French — something that could only have happened because Admiral Darlan's troops had stayed loyal to the Vichy cause.

The 5th Parachute Regiment now began to arrive, and a brief review of its background seems desirable at this point. Soon after its formation in May 1942 at Gross-Born, the regiment's 2nd Battalion, under Hauptmann Hübner, was sent to reinforce Ramcke's brigade, so it was not new to Africa. Meanwhile the two other battalions under Jungwirth and Knocke had been earmarked for the invasion of Malta. In Normandy — where companies and platoons were based at Avranches, St Lô, Genets and St Jean de Thoma — that old warrior Oberstleutnant Walter Koch had worked hard to weld them into a fighting force worthy of paratroops' traditions, and they had spent much of their time on exercises at Mourmelon. News of the Allied landings in North Africa brought a warning order to prepare for service overseas and the regiment entrained for Caserta near Naples. The 3rd Battalion (FJR 5) was the first to arrive in Caserta on 10 November, and Leutnant Baitinger's No 10 Company was the first sub-unit of the battalion to fly in to Tunis. With a motorcycle and sidecar, one *Sanitätsgefreiter* (corporal in Medical Corps) and one machine gun, this platoon went straight from the railway station to Naples airport, and if the aircraft in which they were to fly had not suffered a mechanical defect, the platoon would have been in Tunis that same night. As it was they landed at El Aouina airport on 11 November. Straightaway Baitinger was ordered to go through Tunis town and take up a position on the main road to the west. Having selected a position and settled his men into it Baitinger sent the Sanitätsgefreiter, Victor Fink, back to the airfield to report his orders had been carried out, and the Austrian-born Fink could claim the record of being the first German soldier to ride in a Tunisian tram.

Back at the airport the first Me321 *Gigants* had now landed and the first heavy weapons were being unloaded. And back in Italy where the men of the 5th Regiment now learned that the Allies had landed in North Africa, there was a flurry of activity as the advance parties of the two battalions No 3 Company under Hauptmann Langbein and No 9 Company under Hauptmann Becker prepared for their flight to Tunis that evening, In the event, the two companies under the overall command of Hauptmann Schirmer of the Regimental Headquarters, flew first to Catania and on to El Aouina next morning. On arrival Oberst Harlinghausen ordered their immediate deployment around El Marsa airfield, to ensure that the fly-in of further reinforcements should proceed smoothly.

'Schirmer Force' was formed next day (13 November) when some of the independent Army and AA units were attached to the two paratroop companies which had flown in with him. Meanwhile on 12 November the Regimental HQ staff and the

Regimental signal section, together with Leutnant Jahn's No 10 Company, one third of No 12 Company of the 3rd Battalion under Hauptmann Knoche had flown to Trapani, where they stayed the night — continuing their flight to land at El Marsa on the morning of the 13th. What now constituted a composite battalion then marched to the Marshal Foch barracks, vacated by the French.

At a conference called by Oberst Harlinghausen and attended by Hauptmanns Knoche, Sauer and Schirmer, areas of responsibility for the security of Tunis were allocated:

Schirmer Force would secure the western sector, while Sauer Force would secure the southern half of the town. Consequently on 13 November paratroops occupied all the important buildings, the harbour, the airfields and the main road arteries. At the same time patrols were sent out to reconnoitre the terrain up to the line thrown round the town, harbour and airfield by the French. An attempt to persuade the French to move back failed when the French brought up tanks.

The remainder of the 3rd Battalion (FJR 5) was flown to Tunisia on 14 and 15 November and the 1st Battalion also landed on the 15th. At another conference that day the paratroop officers decided that the French were playing for time, and because a hostile confrontation at this time would be to the Germans' disadvantage it was decided to play the same game. The paratroops were sitting on a powder keg and it needed only one spark to blow them sky high.

During the morning of 16 November Hauptmann Knoche, accompanied by his adjutant Leutnant Quednow and Leutnant Klein, the company commander of one of the infantry companies attached to the paratroops (14/IR 104 — No 14 Company of the 104th Regiment) took a motorcycle and sidecar and drove round the chain of French positions encircling the town. Taking a wrong turn during their reconnaissance they suddenly found themselves in a French camp and surrounded by French soldiers. Fortunately Leutnant Quednow spoke very good French and he was able to persuade the local commander to take the three Germans to the district commander, Colonel Le Couteux, at the latter's headquarters in Teboura, 25km (15miles north-west of Tunis). Asked what the Germans had been up to, Hauptmann Knoche told Colonel Le Couteux that they had done nothing without the approval of the French High Command. Referring to a directive recently issued by Marshal Pétain, Knoche told the Frenchman that he must withdraw his troops from the whole of Medjerda sector as far as Medjel el Bab and permit the German paratroops to establish three outposts — one at Djededa, one at Tebourba and the other at Medjez el Bab — on the far side of Medjerda, in case the Allies attacked. The French Colonel refused, saying that he took his orders from the French Command HQ at Béja. So as it was obvious that the Germans were going to get no further with him, Knoche suggested — in true paratroop fashion — that he should drive to Béja himself to discuss the problem with General Barre and negotiate a solution. (He was not authorised to negotiate, of course, but he saw his opportunity and nominated himself as arbitrator.) Le Couteux agreed, and Hauptmann Knoche was taken to the French HQ in Tunisia for discussions with the French Staff. Finally the French said they were prepared to evacuate Tebourba and Djedeida, and to pull back to Medjez el Bab. But under no circumstances were they prepared to give up Medjez el Bab, where the old main Carthagenian road to

161

Tunis crosses the Medjerda River and of which Hannibal had said 'Who has Medjez el Bab has the key to the door of Tunis, and is master of all Tunisia.'

Subsequently it turned out that French reluctance to yield Medjez and their stubbornness during Knoche's negotiations could be explained by the fact that British paratroops, near Souk el Apba, had gone on to occupy Béja. These paratroops, who belonged to the 2nd Battalion, The Parachute Regiment, had already occupied the important harbour of Bougie on 9 November. It had taken them two more days to get from there to the port of Bone, but from Bone to Bizerta it was only 190km (120 miles).

While Captain Knoche was trying to wring concessions out of the French, Ju52s, carrying the Regimental Headquarters of the 5th Parachute Regiment to Africa, were landing at El Aouina aerodrome. Oberst Walter Koch, the regiment's Senior Medical Officer Dr Weitzel and the Signals Officer Hauptmann Graubartz were in the first plane. Behind it came a constant stream of other transports which touched down to unload their cargoes of soldiers and weapons, and after a brief engine and instrument check, take off and fly back to ferry more reinforcements across the Mediterranean to Tunisia. That same day (16 November) also, Oberst Koch ordered Hauptmann Becker to march No 10 Company to Djedeida and hold the bridge across the Medjerda river. Where he was there had so far been no contact with the enemy, but their forward troops were expected to clash with the FJR 5 outposts next day.

This was to be a 'Poor Peoples' war', and it will be worthwhile taking a look at the situation from the viewpoint of the commanders of the forces involved.

The Creation of the XC Army Corps

On 9 November General Walther K. Nehring, one of Germany's leading tank specialists and Rommel's second-in-command in North Africa recovering from a wound in Wünsdorf hospital in Berlin, was told that he was wanted on the telephone. The call was from Generalmajor Gause, the *Panzerarmee's* Chief of Staff, and its purpose was to tell Nehring that Hitler had nominated him commander of the Axis forces in Tunisia. Five days later General Nehring and his staff — Major Moll, Major Hinkelbein and Leutnant Sell — were in an aircraft bound for El Marsa. The plane crashed on landing but nobody was hurt and Oberst Harlinghausen reported to the new commander. The town of Tunis, the harbour and the airfields had all been occupied by the paratroops, he said; and the French had not attempted to interfere. Furthermore General Barré — the Bey of Tunis's Minister of Defence as well as commander of the French troops in Tunisia — had pulled his division back to Béja. Satisfied that things in Tunis were under control, General Nehring flew on to Bizerta to see the commander of the German forces there and tell him to move his troops as far forward as possible. From Bizerta Nehring flew back to Sicily in a Ju52, and in Frascati he gave Feldmarschall Kesselring a resumé of his views on the situation, ending with a list of what he must have if he was to hold Tunisia. Kesselring agreed to meet his demands: XC Army Corps was conceived and the scramble for Tunisia had begun.

Paratroops in action in Tunisia

The 21st Battalion of the Parachute Engineers (*Fallschirm Korps Pioneer*

Oberfeldwebel Heinrich Schäfer of FJR 5 who defended the cactus farm and whose section knocked out 48 tanks at point blank range.

Bataillon 21) under command of Major Witzig, arriving in Tunis soon after the 5th Paratroop Regiment, was deployed in the northern sector. And when the vanguard of the British 78th Division, headed by the Royal West Kent Regiment, advanced up the valley road through Djebel Abiod they clashed with the paratroop engineers. Two Italian SP assault guns manned by Witzig's men opened fire on the British column, hitting one armoured carrier and causing the rest of the enemy transport to disperse on the road sides. Dismounting, the enemy infantry deployed quickly to seize the hills above the road and the paratroops found themselves under fire from the heights above their positions. But they had blocked the advance of the 78th Division and for the next 48 hours continued to do so, fighting as they had fought at Eben Emael. (Many of these men had lived through that battle.) Later they were reinforced by a company of German panzers and the 92nd Infantry Regiment of the Italian Superba Division. It was at this stage that the Luftwaffe was called in for the first time, and as the planes bombed and strafed the enemy locations Major Witzig's men were able to move into positions more favourable for a protracted defence. The northern tine of the enemy's three-pronged attack was broken short.

On the south the second enemy column of British paratroops from the 6th Parachute Brigade commanded by Brigadier Derek Mills-Roberts, was pushing up from Béja towards Oued Zarga. Here the enemy paratroops linked up with the third central enemy column known as Blade Force a composite self-contained force of tanks with supporting elements commanded by Colonel Hull.

Following the enemy's capture of Oued Zarga one brigade of the 78th Division turned south to join in an attack on Medjez el Bab, while the 11th Infantry brigade again turned to overrun Witzig's positions and force his men back on to the city of Tunis. When units of this enemy brigade, supported by R Company of the British 1st Parachute Battalion tried to outflank Witzig's positions by swinging up through the steep Djoumine valley they were thwarted again. At Sidi Nsir, Witzig's men with their two Italian assault guns stopped them.

Next day General Anderson sent his tanks to attack Djebel Abiod, and Witzig's men again had to pull back. This time they organised their defences around the Jefna railway tunnel a location which gave them ample scope to use their skill as engineers. As had happened before, the British were stopped again by the 21st Battalion of the Parachute Engineers.

On 18 November elements of the British 78th Division were approaching Medjez el Bab from the west while on the other side of the river Medjerda German paratroops — No 12 Company, under command of Leutnant Hoge — was also moving towards the town. As they got near to the river the paratroops came under fire, and Hoge saw that the fire was coming from positions manned by the French on the east bank. The outcome of this was an order to Hauptmann Knoche to occupy Medjez el Bab the following day. His attack was to be supported by Stukas and he was told that if he found the opposition too strong, he must occupy the dominating features east of the town to prevent the enemy getting any further towards Tunis. Back at Djedeida on 19 November, the men of Captain Becker's No 9 Company were clearing the airfield ready for the landing of German fighter bombers.

Meanwhile, a drama, which had its beginning on 17 November and which was illustrative of the behaviour of the paratroops, had been played out. That morning

164

The meeting of two worlds.

Briefing at FJR 5; second from left Oberstleutnant Koch.

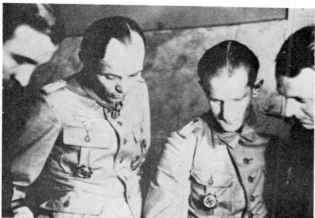

A Tiger in position near Tebourba.

Leutnant Kempa, one of the platoon commanders in the 10th Company (FJR 5) had ordered his platoon to assemble at the El Marsa airfield. This particular unit was a cyclist platoon, and while Kempa was being briefed in one of the airport buildings the men, wearing full kit, stood and waited with their cycles on ground muddied from rain which had fallen the night before. None of them knew where they were going until the platoon commander returned.

'Comrades, we're going to fly south, land on Gabes airfield on Gabes Gulf and take it over. That's all!'

'What, just us?' queried a Gefreiter from Mannheim.

'No 3 Company from the Kesselring Defence Battalion will be coming along as well', replied the Leutnant, grinning when the Gefreiter muttered, 'That makes us a proper little army!'

In due course 12 Ju52s carrying 50 paratroops and about 100 men of the Defence Battalion took off and headed for Gabes. It was a smooth and uneventful flight until the planes were about to land. Then all hell was let loose as anti-aircraft shells burst around the planes and the sky was lit by machine gun tracer. Some of the planes were hit and Leutnant Salg, the Defence Company commander, shouted to his pilot to climb and get away from the neighbourhood of the airfield. Other Ju52s also turned away and the six planes carrying Salg's men flew off north. The other six, with the paratroops aboard, circled and Hauptmann Grund, who was supposed to act as the commandant of Gabes when Kempa's men had captured it, turned to the latter: 'What do you suggest we should do now'?

Kempa did not ponder on the problem: 'We ought to drop somewhere close by, and then try to chase the French off the airfield, Herr Hauptmann', he replied.

'Good idea! Tell the pilot to find somewhere else to land'.

The radio on Kempa's plane crackled out the message to the other five Ju52s and shortly afterwards all six of them glided down on a stretch of open country 40km (25 miles) from Gabes. All but one of them were in good shape after the landing; the one which was not had a broken undercarriage. The paratroops scrambled out and Leutnant Kempa took over: 'Recce patrol to Gabes', he ordered. Within three minutes the reconnaissance section of his platoon was cycling away up the road. Outside Gabes, when they were stopped by a troop of French tanks, which promptly opened fire, the paratroopers turned back. They were saved by a caravan of camels which shielded them while they took refuge in a wadi.

Meanwhile Kempa, tired of waiting for the patrol to return, had sent another one after it. Like its predecessor, however, this patrol of seven paratroopers under the command of Gefreiter Kuntze, ran into the tanks. And they did not get away. Having been taken to Gabes they were interrogated by a French Major. When it came to Kuntze's turn to be questioned he told the major he would be well advised to surrender the airfield at once, because if he tried to defend it Stukas would come and blow everything to smithereens. The Frenchman responded by having all seven paratroopers thrown into jail.

Next morning — the date was 19 November — the paratroopers were brought back for further interrogation. The questioning had no sooner begun than there was a roar of aircraft overhead: the Ju52s which had turned away the previous day were back, and this time they had fighters with them. The sight and sound was more than enough

166

Above: Conference between armoured elements and their accompanying troops.

Left: Cemetery in Africa.

Für Freiheit
und Zukunft des Reiches
gaben sie ihr Leben

for the French commandant of the airport, and within minutes his men were scrambling into vehicles and driving off as fast as they could go, leaving their seven erstwhile prisoners free to signal-in the Ju52s. Gefreiter Kuntze even managed to find the signal pistol taken from him by his captors. With this he fired the flare which indicated the airfield was not occupied. The first American tanks put in an appearance at Gabes two days later. The paratroops shot at them with everything they had, the tanks ground to a halt and there was a respite during which two battalions of 'L' Brigade under General Imperiale arrived to reinforce the paratroops of the 5th Regiment.

In the Tunisian theatre there were many instances of this kind of surprise attack. On 18 November, for example, French troops near Medjez el Bab were standing-to opposite the outposts of the 3rd Battalion (FJR 5). These troops consisted of one regiment of French infantry, supported by armoured carriers, armoured cars and an AA battery. Hauptmann Knoche saw that four American tanks had joined the French. His own battalion, dug in about one kilometre east of the town, was under strength, but five anti-tank guns and two AA troops had been sent up to him as reinforcements. Knoche ordered his men to be prepared for an attack the following night and at 0400 on 19 November his company commanders reported that their men were ready. As arranged, Stukas arrived at 1130 to bomb the French positions and the paratroops joined in the strike by firing every weapon available to them. Hauptmann Knoche now gave the order to attack.

Under the cover of a machine gun barrage laid down by their own weapons the paratroops charged into the town to occupy the houses and blast out the enemy who had barricaded themselves in. Almost the entire urban area east of the Medjerba was overrun and only the station remained in French hands.

'Leutnant Bundt will take a fighting patrol across the river', Hauptmann Knoche now ordered. Bundt, the company commander of No 10 Company, selected the men who were to go with him on this patrol, and then they set off — steering well clear of the machine gun nests which covered the eastern Medjerda bank. Moving cautiously down the river bank they waded across, water up to their necks and a machine gun firing at them from a dug-out on the opposite bank. During the crossing two men of the patrol, Gefreiters Seidel and Heine, were wounded.

As soon as the remainder of his men had reached the far side Bundt led an assault on the offending machine gun post and when this was captured the wounded were sent back with the French prisoners he had taken. The patrol was now set to continue its advance, but as soon as Bundt's men moved they came under fire from unidentifiable sources, and Bundt was compelled to lead them along the water's edge towards the bridge. At a bend in the river the bank which had provided them with a modicum of protection flattened out and as the patrol made a dash for cover among the houses near the bridge they again came under heavy fire. Bundt, shot in the head, was killed and only four men of the patrol survived to swim back across the Medjerda and report what had happened. At 1800 the Stukas returned, and soon afterwards Italian troops and a section of anti-tank gunners arrived on the scene. Oberst Koch appeared a little later, bringing with him from Tunis a load of explosives with which he hoped the tactics used at Eben Emael might be repeated. Ten patrols were detailed, and their members issued with explosive packs, sticky bombs and blast grenades. The patrols,

Paratroop positions
in the Blue
Mountains of Bou
Arada.

Tanks on the road to
Tebourba.

Take cover!

which were to infiltrate Medjez el Bab during the night, were each given an individual objective, and at midnight they set out. One of the most daring paratroop operations ever to take place in Africa was about to begin. At 0100 — if Koch's calculations were right — all hell would be let loose in Medjez el Bab.

It was exactly 0100 when 10 explosions indicated that the patrols had completed their tasks successfully. Flames shot up from the French installations and in the light they produced the patrols blazed away with their machine-pistols at anything which moved. The morale of the French was severely shaken and they interpreted the raid as an attack by strong German forces which had crossed the Medjerda.

In consequence the air at first light resounded with the noise from the engines of heavy vehicles and tanks. As columns of trucks and tanks were seen disappearing in clouds of dust up the Oued Zarga-Béja road, it was clear that the French were abandoning the town. Most of them got away, but the paratroops did succeed in knocking out two of the tanks with sticky bombs. When the sun rose on 20 November 1942 Medjez el Bab, the 'key to the gate of Tunis' was in the paratroops' hands, and Hauptmann Knoche, who had not slept for four days was able to snatch some rest. Hauptmann Schirmer now took over, pursuing the enemy as far as Oued Zarga. He would have gone further, but a message from regimental headquarters ordered him to take his battalion back to Medjez el Bab. Schirmer's next task was to block the road running from Medjez to Beja, and with the support of the 12th (Heavy) Company this was effectively carried out, American troops being the first casualties when they advanced towards Schirmer's positions.

The following night a group of Spahis on horseback — easily distinguished by their white horses — tried to attack one of the German outposts on a farm near Smidia in the northern suburbs of the western part of the town. The attack faltered and broke when German mortar bombs started to fall among the Spahis and German machine guns joined in. Next morning while scrounging around for food, Oberinspektor Hans Hahn of FJR 5 'discovered' four Englishmen in one of the sheds of a French supply depot 2km outside Medjez el Bab. Englishmen were not quite what he had been looking for and, but for the Oberfeldwebel of No 10 Company, he was on his own. Undaunted, Hans yelled to an imaginary German squad: 'Surround the shed; 20 men round to this side... quickly!' Then he went in to the shed and told the four British soldiers that it was useless to resist. Hands above heads, and covered by Hauptfeldwebel Lippold's machine-pistol they emerged from the shed and climbed into the truck which one of them had to drive back to Tunis and captivity.

Hauptmann Knoche slept long and deeply. When he woke he went to the Tebourba-Djedeida area to take over command of the defences there. His own No 9 Company and that of Hauptmann Becker were already there; with men from Nos 10 and 12 Companies, miscellaneous sub-units of Army troops, AA gunners and an Italian company, there were about 2,000 men manning the positions. A regimental order created a 2nd and 3rd Battalion out of this composite force — the new 2nd Battalion being commanded by Hauptmann Knoche and the new 3rd by Hauptmann Schirmer. In the days to come each of these battalions was to function as an independent battle group, and elements of Hauptmann Jungwirth's 1st Battalion arriving piecemeal joined them later.

The first units of the 10th Panzer Division to arrive in Africa from the South of

El Bathan — a name that evokes powerful memories for the troops of FJR 5.

The six-engined *Gigant* transported vehicles for the paratroops.

Wounded drive back.

France were sent to relieve Knoche's battalion which had been pitched into the fighting which had developed around El Aroussa on 21 November. That same day Schirmer's battalion had been forced to evacuate Medjez el Bab. Enemy tanks were endeavouring to encircle the town and General Nehring decided to pull the whole front back to a line about 30km south-west of Tunis.

No 1 Company of FJR 5, under command of Leutnant Schuster, landed in Tunis on 21 November, and was driven round the town in order to create the impression that at least a regiment had arrived.

Next day the company moved via Ain el Asker-Bin Mcherba-Teli el Kaid-El Kasbate-Depienne, to Port du Fahs and left to fend for themselves; the company was soon to have a surprise.

In the meantime more reinforcements had arrived in the area — among them came the Luftwaffe Regiment 'Barenthin', under command of Oberst Walther Barenthin, an engineer officer who had been on Crete on the staff of Fliegerkorps XI. As Engineer commander of the XIth Parachute Corps, Major Witzig's 21st Battalion came under his control; all his other major units were paratroop battalions.

As Force Commander Mateur, Oberst Barenthin took over command of the northern sector of the front. Witzig's 21st Battalion was on the advanced right flank of the sector in the Sedjenane region; cyclist riflemen and engineers occupied the central area south of Djebel el Arkmas and the rest of the line was held by the 5th Paratroop Regiment. Thus the defensive line around Tunis was manned mainly by paratroops, and the proportion was increased when Sauer Force was brought in as well. Motorised patrols of paratroops swept the surrounding country, penetrating as far as 240km (150 miles) on occasions.

'All the precautions we took at this time', General Nehring said later, 'were like a drop of water on a hot stone.' To the commander of the Axis forces in Tunisia the important thing was to maintain contact with, and keep the road open, for Rommel's retreating *Panzerarmee*. If the enemy severed this link, the main reason for standing in Tunisia would have gone. The Germans had only gone to Tunisia to forestall the Afrika Korp's encirclement and to keep open its main supply line. According to General Nehring's records the situation in these critical days was as follows:

a   FJR 5 was deployed in a fluid defensive role in Medjez el Bab area to prevent the enemy advancing via Medjez el Bab to Tebourba, Protville or Tunis.
b   Major Witzig's engineer battalion was blocking the roads leading to Bizerta and Mateur.
c   The Italian Superba Division deployed south of the town protected Tunis.
d   Armoured (panzer) units deployed along all roads leading to Tunis were there to counter any surprise moves and for counter-attacks.

In the next few days the scramble for Tunis took a dramatic turn. The 5th Parachute Regiment was pulled back towards Massicault and the regiment's advanced positions were at Ksar Tyr and covering the road junction 15km north-east of Medjez el Bab. While inspecting trenches the men had dug, Oberstleutnant Koch saw the Oberjäger Karlinger had not shaved — in the past few days he had had no time to do so, so Karlinger said. 'What if you're killed here', asked Koch, 'do you want to meet the good

Left: An observation post on the outskirts of Tunis.

Below left: A mortar at Djebel Djaffa.

Below centre: Observers using the 'scissors' (artillery observation binoculars).

Below: Mountain paratroops with their mounts!

Left: Convoys bringing supplies to Africa accompanied by Me110 fighter protection.

173

Lord like this?' The Oberjäger hurriedly began to shave; it appears that he was convinced of Oberst Koch's reasoning.

Strong enemy forces had been gathering in the Tebourba area. According to reports by Arabs, the enemy had landed 2,000 men at Cap Serrat, with the obvious intention of destroying Witzig's engineers. But it was a message saying '1,000 paratroops have been dropped in the area north of Zaghouan' which really shook General Nehring. The enemy was threatening the weakest place in the defensive ring around Tunis, and if the situation was to be saved, something would have to be done immediately.

The paratroops who had landed were men of the 2nd British Parachute Battalion of the 6th Parachute Brigade — whose 1st and 3rd Battalions had already been in action. Major Frost had been dropped in the Pont du Fahs area with orders, it was understood, to seize the airfield north of the town; then, advancing northwards, destroy the airfield at Depienne; and finally occupy the airfield at Oudna. After that the battalion was to move north west and rendezvous with tanks of the 1st British Army at St Cyprien.

The British 2nd Parachute Battalion set out in Dakotas at 1230 on 29 November, and as there were no German soldiers at Depienne the drop was successful. Depienne was captured and in the early hours of 30 November the battalion marched towards Oudna where the airfield was deserted. En route the British paratroops had been strafed by low flying Me109s.

As soon as the Germans appreciated what was afoot part of the 1st Battalion of FJR 5 and an armoured reconnaissance troop under Feldwebel Fred Hämmerlein were sent to deal with the situation. Leutnant Jahn, the force commander, pushed the mechanised element of his column on past Depienne while Hauptmann Jungwirth moved in for a frontal attack with the 1st Battalion infantry. And as soon as he got within striking distance of the British, Jungwirth led a charge against them. Struck down by bullets from an English machine gun the Oberleutnant died within three minutes. *This* was the first real encounter between German and British paratroops. The conflict of Red Devils and Green Devils had begun.

The British fought with desperate courage until 1 December. The 1st Army which should have come to their aid failed to do so, and Major Frost's men were simply written off. A small group of them sought refuge in a farm 5km (3 miles) south of El Bathan where they were besieged by a force under Leutnant Ismer, Hauptmann Knoche's adjutant. Ismer was killed in the attack and the British who survived were all taken prisoner.

On the evening of 2 December Major Frost and the rest of the survivors came on French sentries near Medjez el Bab. The Red Devils had lost 16 officers and 250 men, and one of the officers who came back, Captain Richard Spender, marked the mood of the unit which had been senselessly sacrificed: 'Silence fell over the Medjerda Valley.'

Paratroops in the Battle for Tebourba

The struggle for Tebourba, one of the key battles in the fight for possession of Tunisia, started on 1 December 1942. General Nehring threw everything he had into the battle; only 30 soldiers were left in Tunis, and there were only a couple of 88mm AA guns to guard the south-western approaches to the city.

In Tebourba itself a company of Barenthin's paratroops a platoon of paratroop

174

Paratroops knocked
out this US Sherman
tank.

Me110s over the sea
off Libya...

...and over the
Libyan desert.

engineers had been complete surrounded by the enemy since 25 November. The enemy's advanced positions were on the Djedeida-Tebourba road and when they were forced out of these Hauptmann Nolde's Tiger tanks (of the 1st Company 501 (Heavy) Tank Battalion) were waiting to meet them. The American-built enemy tanks were shot to pieces and the wrecks of nine of them remained on the battlefield. The fight continued throughout 2 December with more tank duels in which the German 10th Panzer Division inflicted further heavy losses on the enemy — virtually annihilating the British 11th Armoured Brigade which lost a total of 34 tanks and 6 armoured cars.

On 30 November a patrol from the 5th Parachute Regiment, which had been ordered to man the reserve positions, captured a dozen prisoners, and when these men were interrogated it was learned that the enemy in Oberstleutnant Koch's sector near El Bathan were part of the British 78th Infantry Division. That night Koch sent out another patrol under Peter Arent with orders to sneak through the enemy front line and occupy a bridge 4km (2½ miles) west of El Bathan. Next morning (11 December) in a concerted attack the rest of the regiment tried to batter its way forward to El Bathan but concentrated enemy fire stopped them getting very far towards their objective. The attack is notable because it was the first occasion in which the Jungwirth, Knoche and Schirmer battalions had combined in a single operation and in which the men of the three battalions had advanced shoulder to shoulder.

Leutnant Kautz's platoon were the only men to get into El Bathan, and Kautz did this by making a wide detour round the village to approach it from the rear. Dodging around the houses the paratroopers spotted the American headquarters and made for it. Before they could get to it however, a column of Sherman tanks, their guns spitting flame, rumbled towards them. 'Attack', yelled Leutnant Kautz, making a dash towards the American HQ, and the rest of his platoon ran after him. A burst of fire from one of the tanks killed Kautz and two other paratroopers, Bohley and Vogel, but the rest ran on hurling grenades into the houses.

During this time another battle was raging on the outskirts of the village. German tanks which had penetrated the enemy line, were systematically destroying an enemy artillery battery which was still in action when they arrived. Shortly after this the British and American units broke and fled towards the Medjez hills. Leutnant Wöhler's No 12 Company headed the column which pursued the scattered enemy and the paratroops got as far as Djebel Lanserine before they were stopped by fire from enemy positions there and on a neighbouring feature — Djebel Bou Aokaz. Meantime the Engineer platoon had reached the river crossing at El Bathan and the Feldwebel had positioned his two machine guns left and right of the bridge while mines were put down on the road across it.

It was not long before a column of British vehicles coming from Medjez el Bab were seen approaching the bridge; the machine guns opened up and first one vehicle, then a second struck a mine. The second vehicle, which apparently contained ammunition for the enemy at Tebourba, blew up with a spectacular roar. The bridge was effectively blocked and as the enemy abandoned their other vehicles the machine guns took a heavy toll. But the 11th British Armoured Brigade needed the replenishment supplies carried by the column that was stuck on the wrong side of the bridge, and after dark the enemy made a second attempt to break through. This, too, was repulsed —

repulsed by the mere handful of paratroops holding a strategically important point. Arent and his engineers had been isolated behind the enemy lines for over 24 hours when the attempt to recover the bridge was made. A party of enemy crossing the Medjerda upstream tried to sneak up to the paratroopers' position. But Arent was on his guard and the enemy assault group was greeted with a shower of hand grenades. (In this action Oberjäger Kraczewski showed that he was a bomb thrower par excellence, hurling his grenades at least 30m.) The enemy was driven back and Arent's engineers held the bridge until the tanks of the 10th Panzer Division had rolled over it. Both the engineers at the bridge and the crews of the first tanks cheered as the panzers crossed the river.

When the enemy abandoned Tebourba on 4 December, the German forces concentrated in the Medjez Hills, and the paratroopers of the 5th Regiment, Witzig's engineers and men of the Barenthin Regiment were among them. Peter Arent did not make it however, on its way back to the regiment, his platoon was shot up by the enemy on Pt 154 — Khoumet Ed Diab, and Arent fell with a shot through the head; he was buried in the military cemetery at La Mornaghia, and the *Ritterkreuz* he had been awarded for his action at El Bathan earlier in the day was placed on his coffin by Oberst Koch, who had been with him at Eben Emael.

The paratroops, and the crews of Baron Nolde's Tiger tanks of the 10th Panzer Division who had fought alongside them, fought magnificently at Tebourba. And the enemy suffered heavy losses there: the wrecks of 134 tanks littered the battlefield and 1,100 Allied soldiers were taken prisoner. Blade Force and Combat Command B no longer existed, the British 11th Armoured Brigade and the 18th Regiment of the US 1st Armoured Division had been shattered; and 40 guns and the ammunition which were captured were put back into service on the German side. In three days the enemy had also lost 47 aircraft over Tunisia. As the Official Allied History of the war in North Africa says: 'The Germans won the race for Tunis.' In winning the race the role of the paratroops was outstanding.

Although the Allies had undoubtedly lost the race for Tunis they still held the Medjez Hills and over the next six months — until the campaign ended on 12 May 1943 — the paratroops were deployed time and again wherever danger threatened. Barenthin's Regiment and Witzig's battalion in the northern sector, and the FJR 5 at places like Fourna or on Pt 107 on the main Tunis-Medjez el Bab road behind Ksar Tyre. Most of these places will be best remembered by the paratroops by the names given to the locations where they installed themselves — 'Christmas Farm', 'Tin-can Farm', 'Koch Farm'. In the Blue Mountains around Bou Arada they took part in a dramatic operation in which Leutnant Erich Schuster died, and was replaced by Leutnant Kleinfeld.

Meantime the *Panzerarmee* had pulled back to Gabes, and it was from here that Rommel undertook his last big raid via Gafsa through the Faïd Pass to Tebessa. The object of the raid was a daring one, since Rommel intended to cut off the enemy in Tunis from his supplies and so turn the page in the Tunisian saga. After several abortive attempts, tanks of the Stotten Battalion, the 8th Panzer Regiment, swept through the Kasserine Pass; beyond it the road appeared to be open, and the way clear to Tebessa — the enemy supply centre. Only the Djebel el Hamra Pass remained to be negotiated, and it looked as if the scramble for Tunisia might well have been not just to secure the *Panzerarmee's* exit route but a step towards final victory in Africa.

The day of decision came on 22 February 1943. The enemy threw everything he had into the gap which the Germans had created and 'Combat Command B', under Brigadier General Robinett, ultimately forced a conclusion. Another factor which played its part was the drama being enacted south of Gabes where what remained of Rommel's *Panzerarmee* was preparing for an attack by the British 8th Army. Feldmarschall Kesselring, after flying over from Frascate to discuss the situation with Rommel saw that the *Panzerarmee* had no alternative but to draw in behind the Mareth defences. On 23 February Kesselring sanctioned a reorganisation of the command structure in North Africa, and the *Heeresgruppe Afrika* [Army Command Africa] came into being, with Rommel its first commander. Rommel's successor was General von Arnim, commander of the 5th Panzerarmee — formed in Tunisia from the XC Army Corps.

When the final battle for Tunis began the paratroops were again in action on all fronts. (Witzig's battalion, for example, was attached to Manteuffel's Division.) In Operation Ochsenkopf [Bull's Head] where the force attacking in the south consisted of the FJR 5 and the 10th Panzer Division, German and British paratroops clashed for the second time. The troops involved were from Captain Jungwirth's 1st Battalion (FJR 5) and the British 1st Parachute Battalion (1 Para Commando 6 under Brigadier Mills-Roberts) which was then part of the 11th Brigade of the 78th Infantry Division. Following a hard-fought battle the British paratroops withdrew to regroup and when tanks of General Evelagh's 78th Division were sent up to support them the Germans had to give up their attack.

When Hauptmann Schirmer's 3rd Battalion (FJR 5) overran a British supply dump near Kir el Briouigue the enemy was completely taken by surprise. Continuing the advance, with Leutnant Gasteyer's No 12 Company leading, the battalion came under fire at the top of the Bir el Krima Pass. Twelve tanks of the 10th Panzer Division under Hauptmann Hofbauer which were moving up behind the paratroops now came up and exchanged fire with the enemy. Gasteyer was all in favour of pushing on to El Aroussa as quickly as possible. But it took four hours for the tanks and paratroops to assemble and regroup near the summit of the Pass — by which time the 3rd Battalion had been reinforced by sub-units of the 1st. So it was afternoon before the advance could be resumed, and by that time the enemy had been assembling his forces. Just before El Aroussa the vanguard of the German force ran into an ambush and nine of the twelve tanks were knocked out by British anti-tank guns. There was no option but to fall back on the Pass. There the paratroopers installed themselves in a position suited to all-round defence, and when enemy patrols probed towards it they were sent reeling back. Hours later the British launched a set-piece attack with infantry supported by tanks. Schirmer, however, had asked for air support and the Stukas which flew to the scene broke up the attack and destroyed some of the tanks. The Pass was defended until 28 February. The following day, 1 March, the enemy attacked with tanks and when this armour broke through the German positions Schirmer's paratroops pulled out and withdrew in good order to Goubellat which they reached on 3 March. Operation Ochsenkopf had failed.

On 5 March the FJR 5 became part of the Hermann Göring Jäger Division and was renamed 'Jäger-Regiment 5 Hermann Göring'. Meanwhile the paratroops continued to fight in North Africa as they had fought before Hermann Göring decided to change their regiment's title. Between Sidi Salah and Goubellat they were opposed by an enemy ten times their strength, and they defended Djebel Jaffa at the cost of many of their lives.

Before the final battle, Witzig's paratroop engineers had scratched their way into the ground on the Djebel Achkel near the coast north of Tunis. And when the enemy attacked the engineers stopped him. Further south a lone platoon of paratroopers, 48 men under command of Oberfeldwebel Heinrich Schäfer held up a whole division at a place codenamed Cactus Farm. Cactus Farm was surrounded by a minefield and 37 enemy tanks were destroyed. Schäfer and his men held on until 1 May, and then withdrew to a position south of Massicault where their war ended. (On 8 August 1944 in a prisoner of war camp at Harne in Texas an American colonel handed Oberfeldwebel Schäfer the *Ritterkreuz*. It had been sent on to him via the Red Cross.)

Oberst Koch had been ordered to return to Germany, and on 30 April the acting regimental commander Hauptmann Schirmer was evacuated following a severe attack of malaria. Hauptmann Zimmermann, who had only been in Africa since April now took over command of the Regiment and Hauptmann Hoefeld commanded the 3rd Battalion from then on.

On 12 May 1943 General Cramer, General der Panzertruppe and last commander of the Afrika Korps despatched the following radio message to the German High Command in Berlin:

'To OKW: The last round of ammunition has been fired. Weapons and supplies destroyed. In accordance with your orders the Afrika Korps has fought to the bitter end.'

So ended the campaign in Africa. 130,000 German soldiers were destined to spend the next few years in captivity. Among them were many paratroopers who had been in the thick of the fighting throughout the months of this 'Poor Peoples' War'. 322 others who were laid to rest in the war cemeteries at La Mornaghi, remained in Africa.

CHAPTER 15

The Battle for Sicily

The Months Between

During the winter of 1942/43, while the 5th Regiment was fighting in Africa, the 7th Air Division was re-named the 1st Parachute Division (*1 Fallschirmjäger Division* (FJD)). This title, which was effective from the end of November 1942, remained unchanged throughout the rest of the war. Towards the end of January 1943 a second parachute division — 2 FJD — was raised from a nucleus of paratroop training centres, reinforcement details and various minor units — including some of FJR 5 which had not been sent to Africa. Generalleutnant Ramcke was appointed to the command of this division, which was formed in the Wehrmacht training area at Coetquidan. (From here at the end of April what was left of the Pietzonka Battalion — transferred from Russia to Mourmelon in October 1942 — was flown to Africa.) Once the organisation of the 2nd Parachute Division had been completed the commander of Fliegerkorps XI had, for the first time, two paratroop divisions at his disposal, and at the end of June the Corps became the OKW's (German High Command's) operational reserve — with Corps HQ at Nîmes in the south of France.

In the two years which had elapsed since the invasion of Crete, the problem of the paratrooper jumping with 'the weapon on the man' had been resolved. By this time the paratroops were even jumping with heavy mortars. Thus Fliegerkorps XI, with 30,000 well trained and well equipped soldiers, was the OKW's strongest mobile reserve. In September 1942 General Eugen Meindl had been ordered back to Germany to take command of Fliegerkorps XIII. His old formation — now known as 'Division Meindl' — continued to fight on in the central sector of the eastern front where, it will be recalled, the Parachute Assault Regiment had proved its worth time and again. But Meindl's staff went with him to Grossborn and it was here, and in the Bergen area, that the first 10 Luftwaffe 'Field' Divisions (*Felddivisions*) were formed. Twenty-two such field divisions were eventually raised, but not by Meindl. He wanted to get back to the paratroops and his wish was shortly to be fulfilled.

The Enemy Lands on Sicily

On 12 May 1943 — the day the war ended in Africa — the headquarters of the British

8th Army moved back to Cairo. The Egyptian capital was the location of the planning headquarters of 'Battle Group East' — the Allied force which was to prise open the gates of Fortress Europe in July 1943 by an invasion of Sicily.

Five phases were envisaged during the campaign in Sicily — codenamed Husky:

1 Naval and air forces would neutralise enemy (German & Italian) air and sea bases, and prevent the establishment of new ones.
2 Airborne and seaborne landings to secure airfields and the ports of Syracuse and Licata would then take place.
3 These operations would be exploited to establish a firm base from which the ports of Augusta and Catania, and the airfield complex of Gerbini could be attacked.
4 The capture and occupation of the objectives set out in phase 3.
5 Finally the occupation of the whole island.

The invasion was to be carried out by two forces: The 7th US Army under General Patton would land along the Gulf of Gela between Licata and Scoglitti. (See Appendix: The Sicily Invasion Forces). The British 8th Army, under General Montgomery would go ashore on Pachina peninsula and on the eastern coast along the Gulf of Noto. The aim was to divide the island into two — the western half to be taken by the 7th US Army and the eastern by the British 8th Army.

On the other side of the hill, the Italian Sixth Army Headquarters with coastal and defence responsibilities was in Sicily and the Army commander was General Guzzoni. The Italian forces under him consisted of two army corps organised into five coast defence divisions, two coast defence brigades and one independent coast defence regiment. 30,000 German troops on the island were also under his command. Originally these were uncoordinated miscellaneous units of AA, Luftwaffe ground personnel, and reinforcements intended for the Africa theatre. On 6 May, however, Oberst Ernst-Günther Baade had been ordered to bring together all German Army, Navy and Air Force installations, and form a support group. From this 'Kommando Sicily', a panzer grenadier division, was to be raised. And when the division came into being Generalmajor Rodt took over command of what was then called the 15th Panzer Grenadier Division. During this preparation period also the Hermann Göring Panzer Division moved down to Sicily.

These then were the Axis forces on the island on 9 July 1943.

The invasion of Sicily started on the night of 10 July 1943, and the staff of Fliegerkorps XI was alerted as soon as the news came through. General Student promptly suggested an airborne response, for which he had 3,000 picked paratroops already standing by. These, he reckoned, could be dropped into the areas where the enemy was landing and smash his forces when they were most vulnerable. Because it was considered too much of a dare-devil idea, Student's suggestion was rejected.

Meantime the units of Fliegerkorps XI were standing to, waiting impatiently but knowing that their services would be required before long. At midday on 11 July the first call on them came through when General Student was ordered to move the 1st Parachute Division to Italy. General Heidrich, the divisional commander, and his tactical headquarters staff flew immediately to Rome and reported to the Italian Southern Command HQ at Frascati. The 3rd Parachute Regiment under Oberst

Heilmann, emplaning at Avignon and Tarascon, followed close behind, and after them came the 10th Parachute Machine Gun Battalion, the 1st Engineer Battalion, and finally Oberst Leutnant Walther's 4th Parachute Regiment with field artillery and anti-tank artillery batteries.

General Heidrich was at the airport when the He111s carrying Heilmann's regiment landed at Rome, and Heilmann was told that his men would be taking-off again next morning and be dropped on the Catania plain.

'Three more paratroop groups will follow you', the divisional commander said to Heilmann. A machine gun battalion and the divisional signals section will be in the next drop; the engineers, anti-tank artillery and the 4th (Parachute) Regiment will be in the second; and the 1st Regiment and the field artillery will be dropped last.' In the conversation before and after this Oberst Heilmann gained the impression that Heidrich was convinced that driving the enemy back into the sea was quite feasible.

Meanwhile Hauptmann Stangenberg, a staff officer from the 1 FJD's HQ, together with the operations officer from Feldmarschall Kesselring's HQ, and Hauptmann Specht — who as the 1 FJD administrative officer was responsible for making the requisite administrative arrangements prior to the arrival of the division — had flown to Sicily. The He111 carrying them touched down on Fiumicino airfield in the middle of an air raid. Stangenberg's job was to select a dropping zone for FJR 3 and his reconnaissance south of Catania was interrupted by another air raid which forced him to take cover in a ravine. Back at Catania, after the raid Stangenberg telephoned General Heidrich to say that he had found a dropping zone and to pass its map reference coordinates to Oberst Heilmann who was ready to take off. While Stangenberg had been looking for a dropping zone Hauptmann Specht had been rounding up vehicles and arranging for them to be driven to Catania where Heilmann's paratroops could pick them up. The stage would then be set for their advance to contact the enemy.

All the arrangements ran smoothly and General Heidrich radioed a message to General Student: 'Dropping zone Statione Di Passe — Martino. The aim is to reinforce Group Schmalz'. (Group Schmalz was a reinforced regiment of the Hermann Göring Division deployed at Syracuse to prevent an Allied breakthrough into the Catania Plain.)

Four and a half hours after Captain Stangenberg had taken off, the paratroopers emplaned and flew to Pompigliano airfield south of Naples where the aircraft refuelled. Because the airfield had been devastated by an enemy air raid the refuelling operation took longer than expected, and this set the drop back several hours. The paratroopers' aircraft were also pounced on by 20 P-38 Lightnings over the Messina Straits. But as the enemy fighters were at the limit of their endurance and had to break off in order to get back to their African bases, it seems that on this occasion the gods of war were smiling on Heilmann and his men.

The Boschhorns, signalling it was time to jump, sounded at exactly 1815 on 12 July. Heilmann, in the leading plane, was first out; his 1,400 paratroopers followed. Had it not been for a high wind which led to several of the paratroopers being injured when they landed, the drop went off better than an exercise. There was no shooting during the descent, and within 45 minutes of leaving his aircraft Heilmann had collected his regiment and was marching them south. Reaching the rendezvous, where the vehicles collected by Hauptmann Specht were waiting, the regiment embussed and drove to the Lentini region. There, when they arrived at 2000, they met some of the Schmalz Group which had been falling back under great pressure from the enemy. During the night Heilmann ordered his men to take up a position between Carlentini and the sea; but under the orders of Oberst Schmalz, the 2nd Battalion (FJR 3) marched to Francfonte to help fill the gap between the Schmalz Group at Lentini and the Hermann Göring Panzer Division at Vizzini.

The Allies send Paratroops

On the evening of 11 July 2,000 paratroops of the US 82nd Airborne Division took off from Tunisian airfields in 144 C-47 aircraft. They were to jump over the Farella airfield which the US 1st Infantry Division had occupied. As Allied aircraft had come under fire from ships of the Allied naval forces during the first night, the Second US Corps had warned all ships by radio of the impending operation. Anti-aircraft gunners in the vicinity of the dropping zone had also been specifically told to show restraint and they were to open fire only on clearly recognisable Luftwaffe and Italian Air Force targets. As the C-47s headed towards Sicily some Allied shops north of Malta fired a few rounds of light AA at them but without inflicting damage. Shortly before midnight however, they were flying at an altitude of 600m (2,000ft) over the invasion fleet at anchor in the Gulf of Gela. There was no cloud and no wind, and everything would have gone without a hitch if German bombers had not suddenly appeared over Gela and launched a massive attack on the fleet.

From his HQ — previously a Caribinieri station in Scoglitti — General Bradley watched as the AA guns of the Allied ships shot down two of the German bombers. When the rest of the bombers turned and flew away the AA guns ceased firing. And as the guns went silent the leading flights of American air transports flew in over the Gulf of Gela, heading towards the dropping zone. Everything appeared to be going well, with the invasion fleet and the rest after the raid. Then suddenly, one of the AA guns opened fire and within minutes every Allied gun in the beachhead and offshore was blasting the slow moving columns of aircraft. General Bradley was still watching as some of the planes were knocked out of the sky, and here is what he said about this incident:

'While I was watching, helplessly from the beach, the whole sky appeared to explode in a roar of AA fire. Shrapnel smacked down on the tiles of our roof. The planes scattered like flights of quail, and raced away as the pilots tried to get out of the area. When the first planes were hit the paratroops tried to get out of the doors to jump. Some who managed to get out were taken for German marauders and shot up after landing. Many were killed in their parachutes as they descended. Of the 184 planes that departed Tunisia 23 never returned. Half the others that did manage to struggle back to Tunisia were unserviceable. But the full extent of the whole gruesome expisode was only apparent on the morning of 12 July when the wrecks of some of the planes which had been shot down were seen drifting off shore. During the night more than twenty per cent of the paratroops were lost. And *without* the enemy doing anything. I attribute this whole tragic affair to the Navy's lax fire discipline'.

183

More German Paratroop Landings

Flying to Sicily on 12 July Feldmarschall Kesselring visited the Italian Sixth Army Headquarters to discuss the current situation with General Guzzoni and his deputy, Generalleutnant Fridolin von Senger und Etterlin. Among other things Kesselring wanted to make sure that command and control of the battle was being properly coordinated. After a frank and cordial discussion both Kesselring and von Senger flew up to the front and Kesselring summed up his impressions of the whole trip in the following words: 'After my visit to Sicily I was pessimistic about the prospects there. Apart from deficiencies in organisation and equipment and a weak chain of command, the Italians appeared to have completely ignored the plan we had agreed for the defence of the island. In consequence the German troops — whose tasks were almost impossible anyway — were almost worn out.'

In the afternoon of 13 July an aircraft carrying Major Schmidt, CO of the 1st Parachute Machine Gun Battalion, landed on Catania airfield in the middle of an air raid. Schmidt went straight to Oberst Schmalz's command post to report the arrival of his battalion and the battalion advance party, which had also landed, was marched by Hauptmann Laun towards Primasole and told to dig in on the edge of an orange grove near the village. In the orange grove the presence of the paratroopers could not easily be spotted from the air, and as things turned out, Laun's decision to dig in there was a wise one.

Shortly before noon (on 13 July) there was a second air raid on Catania airfield, Flying Fortresses laying a carpet of bombs across the landing strip while the planes carrying the rest of the Machine Gun Battalion had just touched down. Two transports had been lost in the first raid, and two more — both Me321 *Gigants* crammed full of anti-tank gunners this time — were destroyed in this second attack. The net result was that the anti-tank battalion of 1 FJD was now considerably under strength.

Landing in Catania shortly after this incident, Leutnant Fassel the officer in charge of divisional signals company was about to carry on with his task of establishing radio communications when he was called across to the divisional commander. Hauptmann Stangenberg had just reported from Catania harbour that the Italian garrison had deserted and General Heidrich wanted Fassel to take his men there and defend the waterfront.

Meanwhile the 15th Panzer Grenadier Division, the Hermann Göring Panzer Division, and the Schmalz Group with its three attached paratroop battalions had been involved in heavy fighting. And this fighting had intensified on 13 July. But it was considered that the line running from the southern edge of Lentini to Ninella and Casteluzzo had to be held until at least 14 July, as this rested on the last natural obstacles before Catania.

When Major Schmidt reported to Oberst Heilmann after a visit to Oberst Schmalz, Heilmann told Schmidt: 'Something is bound to happen tonight. The enemy will try to break through to the Catania plain, and to do so he'll send in more troops — either by sea or by air. If he manages to land then in our rear and to dig in, then we're cut off here. So your battalion will remain south of Catania. Hold the bridge over the Simeto and put one company between there and the sea.'

That night Oberst Heilmann waited in vain for the 14th Anti-tank Company which was urgently needed to ensure that his position was secure. However, the pace of the

Paratroop engineers of No 1 and No 3 Companies recover wounded British soldiers on the morning of 18 July 1943 at the tank scrapes in front of Catania.

Gravely wounded British receive immediate treatment.

Sicily is in sight for returning elements of FJR 5 from Africa.

185

advance and the hot sun had tired the British troops and the 8th Army's thrust in the east had slowed during the day (13 July). Nevertheless General Leese's 30th Corps had gained ground towards Vizzini, and Montgomery was intent on forcing a break-through at Zentini and getting to the Catania plain with the 13th Corps. With that end in view he now threw in a paratroop brigade and a commando unit. These fresh troops were to seize the two bridges which constituted a prerequisite to his break-through operation. The first bridge was the Ponte dei Malati north of the Lentini Hills, the second spanned the Simeto near Primasole.

The British 1st Parachute Brigade under Brigadier Lathbury was told to seize the Primasole Bridge and establish a bridgehead on the north bank of the river, while the Commando unit, after landing from assault-craft on the coast west of Agnone, was to occupy the Ponte dei Malati.

The plan for this airborne operation ran as follows:

'At 1100 hours the Primasole Bridge will be seized by a combat force from the 1st Battalion and the 1st Field Squadron Royal Engineers:
Two platoons of the 3rd Battalion will be dropped at H-hour plus 5 minutes to eliminate the AA battery on the north-west corner of the bridge defence complex.

'The remainder of the 1st Battalion will then take up defensive positions at and on the bridge; while the 3rd Battalion (less two platoons) will establish the bridge head north of Primasole.

'Meanwhile the 2nd Battalion will occupy a feature south of the bridge and provide covering fire for the other group on and in front of the bridge.'

Towards sunset on 13 July the Dakotas carrying the paratroops took off from six airfields between Kairouan and Sousse; 30 Horsa gliders, towed by 19 Halifax and Stirling bombers and 11 Albemarles, flew with them. The latter were being used mainly to carry heavy weapons and jeeps to the operational area — to give the paratroops more firepower and greater mobility. Shortly after take-off the first untoward incident occurred when three of the planes carrying paratroops and three of the ones towing gliders had to turn back with engine failure. The second setback came when the aerial convoy flew over the Allied invasion fleet. Having been under constant attack by the Luftwaffe the ships were taking no chances. Minutes before the British planes arrived Ju88s had bombed the port of Augusta and the ships opened fire again. Several of the leading aircraft were shot down in flames, and the planes which continued on course ran into a solid wall of anti-aircraft shells from German and Italian batteries once they crossed the coastline. Horsas, full of ammunition exploded in midair; the pilots of some aircraft — each with a full load of paratroops — turned back; while the pilots of others simply dropped their troops where they were and banked away to safety.

Even the planes which did get through to Primasole were unlucky. Hauptmann Laun had concealed the Machine Gun Battalion in an orange grove and when the planes were within range the German paratroopers opened fire. One platoon, whose guns covered the direct line of the aircraft flight path shot down three gliders each of which was carrying an anti-tank gun and a Jeep. The machine guns of a second platoon accounted for three of the Dakotas and the vest of the aircraft had to turn away.

By this time, before the ground operation had even started, some 20 British planes had been destroyed, many more had been damaged, and a large number of the paratroops they carried had been dropped into the sea where the majority drowned. In and around Primasole the Machine Gun Battalion captured 82 men by midnight and — including these prisoners — the losses sustained by the 1st British Parachute Brigade were about 300 men. Despite all the losses and mishaps however, about twenty-two per cent of the paratroopers dropped near Primasole and throughout the night the Germans could hear groups of these men shouting passwords and pass-phrases to each other. To 'Desert Rats' came the response 'Kill the Italians.'

When the British paratroopers did manage to assemble, Brigadier Lathbury had about one fifth of his original force. These men succeeded in getting to the bridge without meeting opposition — one group reaching the southern end almost at the same time as another party which had forded the Simeto attacked and overran the Germans who were guarding the north end of the bridge. British sappers promptly went to work disconnecting and removing the explosive charges which had been put under the bridge in case it had to be blown. (Some of this explosive was thrown into the river, the rest was used to supplement the mines which Lathbury's men laid in a semi-circle around the bridgehead on the northern bank.) The first Germans to learn that the British were now in possession of the bridge were the drivers and escorts of four trucks taking supplies up to the Schmalz group and which were shot to pieces as they neared the southern end. But the news did not reach the German paratroopers until after another incident next morning. About 1030 a German motorcycle despatch rider carrying a message from Hauptmann Stangenberg to Oberst Heilmann at HQ FJR 3 approached the bridge. Halted by a hail of bullets he turned round and rode back to Catania and reported to Stangenberg that the British and seized the bridge and were blocking the route between FJR 3 and Group Schmalz.

Stangenberg reacted immediately. Taking 20 paratroops with him he drove back down the road taken by the messenger and when his vehicles were stopped by a burst of fire about 200m from the bridge his men took up positions covering it. A couple of guns from a heavy AA battery in Catania and a miscellaneous collection of staff officers, clerks, orderlies and others were rushed up to deal with the situation. But Stangenberg wanted more men, so he drove back to Catania and put a call through to Rome to tell General Heidrich that the enemy had occupied the bridge over the Simeto. He had only 80 men and he needed the divisional signal company. Heidrich said yes, and by 1500 Leutnant Fassel's technicians had joined the German force massing at the south end of the bridge.

While the drama was being played out at the bridge, Lieutenant-Colonel Slater's 3rd Commando had been making for the Ponte dei Malati bridge. The 2nd Battalion FJR 3 had spotted the commando's assault boats as they approached the beach and had opened fire. But this had not stopped the commandos getting ashore at Agnone. The first Germans they ran into were from the tactical headquarters of the 3rd Regiment and Hauptmann Vetch's paratroopers there were a match for the commandos. However, while part of Slater's force was skirmishing with Vetch's men Major Young and the rest had pushed up the Lentini valley. Reaching the bridge about 0300 his men removed the explosive charges under it and threw them into the river. By this time Slater and the other commandos had joined Young's party and a defensive position was taken up on the northern bank of the river. Attempts to secure the other end of the bridge were thwarted by a Tiger tank of Group Schmalz which effectively prevented the commandos crossing the bridge.

During the morning the solitary Tiger was joined by a strong contingent of German troops who drove the lightly armed British raiders off the bridge. From the British point of view however the commando operation was completely successful because the Germans did not have time to replace the explosives and blow up the bridge before the arrival of the British 50th Infantry Division.

But for the fact that they had been delayed at Carlentini the advancing British troops would have reached the Primasole bridge before the morning of 15 July. In the event when they did arrive the bridge had been abandoned a few hours earlier. The men of the 1st Parachute Brigade had run out of ammunition and so had no choice but to retreat.

The Odyssey of the 3rd Parachute Regiment

The 1st Engineer Battalion (FP Battalion) and the Light Field Artillery (Light FAAbt) under Hauptmann von Bültzingslöwen were dropped near Catania during the course of the battles which have just been described. Both units were told by Oberst Schmalz to get into contact with the 1st Machine Gun Battalion but to stay where they were, occupying prepared positions at the northern edge of the plain.

Meanwhile the drop of FJR 4 under command of Oberstleutnant Walther had been made immediately after that of the Machine Gun Battalion — Walther's men landing near the coast north of Acireale. (This, by the way, was a second good reason for holding the Primasole bridge). The regiment now took up positions along the northern bank of the river inland from the coast with Walther's 1st Battalion deployed on both sides of the bridge. During the night of 14 July this battalion was joined by the machine gun battalion which had pulled back westwards from Primasole — s.Giorgio back on to the Simeto. The location into which they now settled flanked the FJR 4 on the left (west), while Group Schmalz which had also pulled back was on its right. The withdrawal went according to plan and Oberst Schmalz's men had settled in to their new positions by the morning of 15 July. But part of the group was missing. What had happened to the FJR 3?

It will be recalled that Colonel Slater's commandos on their way to their objective the Ponte dei Malati had run into Oberst Heilmann's FJR 3 HQ and there had been a brief engagement with the regimental commander and his staff. (During this action the commando captain leading the 60 men who attacked the headquarters was taken prisoner). Subsequently, when the 5th and 50th British Divisions reached Carlentini Heilmann was ordered to withdraw. However, as he had not heard from his 2nd Battalion near Francofonte he was reluctant to pull out there and then. It was afternoon before the regiment was ready to move and there was still no news of the 2nd Battalion. But Heilmann decided he could wait no longer, and enemy tanks were actually rolling up the road behind him when the last of his vehicles drove off towards Catania. A British naval force was shelling the coast road but Heilmann was hoping his column would be able to slip through the marshy region between the beach and the road. When this was seen to be impossible Heilmann decided to march westwards through the night.

Moving up the Lentini valley the regiment emerged on the Lentini-Catania road near Principe, south west of the Ponte dei Malati, on the morning of 15 July. Reconnaissance patrols which were sent forward returned to report that the road ahead was blocked with British vehicles, including tanks. So Heilmann decided to wait until nightfall before trying to effect an escape, During the day an enemy patrol actually passed through the orange grove in which the Germans were sheltering, but nobody noticed them. Nor did the personnel of a British HQ which picked Heilmann's orange grove as a suitable site for its activities. They did not see Heilmann, but Heilmann's binoculars were trained on them.

With columns of enemy tanks and trucks rumbling past, the regimental commander summoned his battalion and company commanders to a conference. 'We are not going to move anywhere near the road tonight', he told them. 'We will cross the Lentini and slip along the far bank under the bridge. You, Kratzert, and your 3rd Battalion will lead the way. The mortars and Regimental HQ will follow; the 1st Battalion will bring up the rear.'

Leaving the 70 prisoners they had taken earlier in the charge of some slightly wounded paratroopers, Heilmann's men crossed the Lentini and stole along the river bank towards the nearby bridge. The men of the 3rd Battalion slipped quietly under its girders; so too did the regimental staff. Then a fusillade of shots rang out, and the 1st Battalion — throwing caution to the winds — stampeded across the road. On the other side the column started to run, scurrying down into a mushy ravine and bending low among the reeds as enemy bullets cracked around. But the paratroopers were out of danger now. Soon after this they came to a railway line and after marching along it for a while they reached a deserted railway station where they regrouped. Still following the railway they entered a tunnel which caused some concern when it turned out to be 2km (1¼ miles) long. They emerged on to a short stretch of open country beyond which another belt of scrub offered more cover. Beyond that they came to a deserted airstrip where the weary paratroopers were happy to crawl into the tents the ground crews had abandoned some time before.

Throughout the day columns of enemy armour drove past the airfield, and the regiment stayed under cover until nightfall, before resuming the march through the coastal plain. At 0400 they had to go to ground once more when more tanks passed close by. And as it was too dangerous to move by day they remained where they were until nightfall. But that night brought the end of their adventure. A few hours' more marching brought them finally to where Group Schmalz had re-established the German line. A few more hours and the 800 paratroopers whom the rotund little Oberst Heilmann had led to safety were being congratulated by their divisional commander Generalleutnant Heidrich and Feldmarschall Kesselring himself.

When the 1st Canadian Infantry Division captured Piazza Arminia on the night of 17 July, the enemy also tried to seize the Primasole bridge, which was vital to a breakthrough into the Catania plain and hence to Messina. Here at Primasole bridge the Red Devils again fought the Green Devils.

Oberstleutnant Walther, the regimental commander of FJR 4, had repeatedly tried to have the bridge demolished. And Major Paul Adolph, the CO of the Engineer Battalion, who had tried to drive a truck load of explosives on to the bridge, was killed in one such attempt. In the end the British 23rd Tank Brigade arrived and took possession of the north end of the bridge, where they were joined by a force of British paratroops which had crossed the river 500m west of the bridge and shot its way up to the tanks. As this combined force pressed forward Walther's men were compelled to fall back until they reached ground near a small stream where they were able to re-establish a proper defensive position.

Meanwhile the British XIII Army Corps was sending more and more tanks up to the bridge and the British bridgehead was extended over 2.6km (1.5 miles) opposite there were just five *Fallschirmjäger* battalions. General Dempsey ordered his troops to break through on the evening of 17 July, and after a bombardment lasting two and three quarter hours the 50th Infantry Division and the 23rd Armoured Brigade advanced to the attack. By throwing in what remained of his reserves Oberstleutnant Walther managed to stem the attack and to drive the enemy back to his starting point. The British in this sector of the front had failed to make any headway, and despite their numerical superiority they did not take any more ground here until 3 August.

General Montgomery now concentrated his major effort on a thrust by the 5th Division which was to cross the river and push up towards Misterbianco.

Meanwhile on 27 July, however, Generals Patton and Bradley received from General Alexander the directive which was to initiate an operation to end the battle for Sicily.

This directive ran as follows:

'To bring about the quick collapse of the remaining German troops on Sicily, you must exert a strong pressure on their northern flank and continue to sustain the pressure relentlessly.

'To ensure the operations of the Seventh and Eighth Armies are properly coordinated the pressure is to be applied as soon as possible; by 1 August at the latest.'

The British thrust was directed northward against Centuripe, a village at an altitude of 733m (2,400ft), in front of which, near Catenanuova, a Fortress battalion had been deployed. The flank next to Catenanuova was secured by the 1st Battalion FJR 3 and the two battalions had been put under the command of Oberstleutnant Carnap, the operations officer of 1 FJD. Carnap had been told that his task was to stop any advance up the Dittaino Valley. The 2nd Battalion of FJR 3 under Hauptmann Liebscher was in Centuripe itself and the 3rd Battalion was back at Regalbuto.

The British attacked on the night of 30/31 July, and within an hour troops of the British 78th Infantry Division and the Canadian 3rd Infantry Brigade had smashed their way into the Dittaino Valley and were behind the 1st Battalion FJR 3 — Oberstleutnant Carnap being killed in the massive artillery bombardment which preceded the attack. But the British hesitated in front of Centuripe giving time for the whole of the 3rd Parachute Regiment to concentrate there. As a result when the British did assault the village on the evening of 31 July they were sent reeling back. General Leese demanded air support and towards noon on 1 August heavy bombers answered his call. However, between the time the ground attack was called off and the air strike Hauptmann Liebscher had pulled out his battalion, redeployed it south of the town and ordered it to dig in. Consequently although the air raid reduced the village to a smoking ruin, Liebscher's men were unharmed.

190

As expected the air strike was the prelude to another attack and men of the 36th Brigade (of the 78th Division) advanced towards Centuripe, and when they reached Pt 698 below the slope east of the village the British artillery opened fire. Storming forward under cover of this bombardment the British troops came up to Centuripe cemetery where the paratroops were waiting for them, and the battle which now developed lasted all night. Not until the morning of 2 August did the British manage to penetrate the village itself and no sooner were they in among the ruins than Allied bombers flew over to drop more bombs. This time the bombs landed on the British who suffered heavy casualties before they withdrew, leaving the paratroops to return and reoccupy their old positions as soon as the air raid was over. The 36th Brigade had taken a heavy knock and was no longer fit to fight.

So the 38th Brigade was brought up to assault Centuripe at 2000 on 2 August. And in a matter of hours the village was in British hands. There was little resistance as Oberst Heilmann had ordered his 2nd Battalion to withdraw from Centuripe and pull back to Regalbuto to support what was left of the 1st Battalion FJR 3 — 120 soldiers in all. Between Centuripe and Regalbuto these 120 paratroopers were trying to ward off attacks of the 3rd Canadian Brigade, and as soon as they got to Regalbuto the 2nd Battalion found itself under attack by the famous 231st (Malta) Brigade. Inside Regalbuto the 3rd Battalion under Hauptmann Kratzert was also having a rough time but holding its own in spite of air raids and almost constant artillery bombardment. But the situation could not continue like this for ever and when the 1st and 2nd Canadian Brigades were thrown into the battle the remnants of the three paratroop battalions were pulled back to the Etna line.

The British 50th Division returned to the attack on Walther's force at the Simeto Bridge on the night of 4 August. The paratroops fought desperately but by the afternoon of 5 August the British had advanced on a 7km (4 mile) front. South of Catania other paratroops who were also putting up a gallant resistance had to withdraw and abandon Catania during the night of 6 August. Next morning the British entered Paterno and reached Misterbianco.

Meanwhile the 78th Division on the left flank of the British 8th Army had thrust towards Salso during the afternoon of 3 August. Advance elements of the 3rd Regiment fought a delaying action but were ultimately forced back across the river. The British advance now threatened the main German position on the Etna.

The British 30 Corps now advanced towards Adrano, and there were numerous air strikes in support of the move. The greater part of the Army Corps crossed the Salso river on both sides of the Centuripe-Adrano road during the night of 5 August, and the German forces slowly fell back. On 6 August the first enemy formations reached the outskirts of Adrano and circumvented the town to reach the road to Bronte. The next night FJR 3 was ordered to pull back again, and when the battalions left their positions, the 78th Division was on the paratroopers' heels. Next day (8 August) they had to abandon the positions they had taken up to block the upper Simeto valley.

The loss of Adrano meant that the main German defence line across northern Sicily had been breached and the Axis forces continued to retire towards Messina. To keep this route open Generalmajor Rodt's 15th Panzer Grenadier Division, defending Troina had to fight off the British advancing up the Ragalbuto-Adrano road. On 4 August this division also had to face an attack by American troops with powerful artillery and air support. In the course of this action the 15th Panzer Grenadier Division lost 1,600 men — 40 per cent of its fighting strength.

During this period Generalmajor Fries's Panzer Grenadier Division had been deployed on the coast in the San Stefano area, and Fries' troops held their positions until the Troina position had to give up. Two American assault landings behind this division were repulsed, but the situation had deteriorated to such an extent, that General Hube, the former commander of the XIV Afrika Korps, now in overall command of the island, ordered his staff to work out a plan for the ultimate evacuation of the German troops from the island to the Italian mainland. As there were about 50,000 German soldiers on Sicily and the enemy air forces would be able to bomb the evacuation points at will, this was not an easy undertaking.

As Allied pressure forced the Axis troops back towards Messina the defence lines shortened and the plan that was drawn up visualised a methodical withdrawal over four nights. When the troops moved back from the 5th to the 4th line of resistance 8,000 soldiers would be released to be ferried across to the mainland. This process would continue from line to line, with the final evacuation taking place when the last defence line was abandoned. When Oberst von Bonin, the XIVth Corps Chief of Staff, submitted the plan to the German High Command in Italy, Feldmarschall Kesselring approved it and told Bonin that the Corps HQ would have a free hand in its execution. Two days later the OKW confirmed Kesselring's approval and Day X in the plan became 10 August. This meant that the evacuation was to start on 11 August; until then, however, the three German divisions and the paratroops had to hold on.

Following the fall of Bronte FJR 3 withdrew to Maletto, and this so far as Oberst Heilmann was concerned was where the pathetic remnants of his regiment would make their last stand. The 1st Battalion was down to 120 men but these men fought like tigers to hold the village until 12 August. Walther's force and Group Schmalz stayed where they were when Catania fell, and on the evening of 8 August both were still fighting 8km (5 miles) north of Catania.

Maletto was abandoned, and the Americans reached Randazzo on 13 August. But try as they might the Allies could not get to Messina before the Germans, and so they were unable to pull tight the string of the bag in which the German forces were now caught. Only on 14 August, when Walther's force and Group Schmalz withdrew further north, was the way open for the 50th Division to take Taormina, the 51st Division to occupy Linguaglossa, and the 78th Division to clear the roads running from Randazzo to the coast. In an attempt to cut off Walther force an enemy sea-borne group landed behind Walther during the night of 16 August. The attempt failed because Walther had pulled out five hours earlier and was now holding a position north of where the cut off party had landed.

The evacuation went so well that it was decided that it should be operated by day was well as by night. The AA batteries deployed on the two sides of the Messina Straits made it impossible for Allied aircraft to approach the embarkation and debarkation points. An immense concentration of flak created a curtain of steel which the enemy could not pierce, and under its protection the ferries crossed to and from the Italian mainland without loss.

Over the last two days it was the paratroopers and men of the HG Panzer Grenadier Division who bore the brunt of the pressure coming from the west and south. Oberst

Schmalz and his staff were ferried across to the mainland in one of the last assault boats to make the crossing on the morning of 17 August and in the *very* last one — that indomitable solider who had made his name in Russia, and who had vowed that he would return only when the last of his troops was safely away — was Panzergeneral Hube.

On both sides the losses on Sicily were high:

The Allies lost 19,739 dead, wounded and missing.
The Italians lost 160,000 dead, wounded and missing (most of whom it transpired later had been captured.)
The Germans lost 32,000 dead, wounded, missing and captured.

Here on Sicily, as elsewhere, the paratroops had shown that they knew how to fight and how to stand up to an enemy many times numerically superior. And the fact that the German Command managed to save so many troops and salvage so much material was largely due to the paratroops. In the final analysis however, the Allies accomplished what they had set out to do — conquer Sicily and push open the gate to Fortress Europe. Now, before they took their first step through that gate there had to be a sober assessment of the lessons of the campaign.

CHAPTER 16

The Battle for Italy

A Strange Task for General Student

While the greater part of the 1st Parachute Division was fighting in Sicily — with one regiment, FJR 1, in reserve in the Naples area — the 2nd Parachute Division, under Generalleutnant Ramcke, was stationed in the south of France where the German High Command was expecting more Allied landings.

In the late afternoon on 25 July General Student was called to the telephone, and an hour later he was on a fast plane bound for Rastenburg airfield and the Führer's Headquarters. The flight took five hours and when he reported to the Führer about midnight he was taken straight to the war-room where, a year later, the abortive attempt would be made on Hitler's life. General Student recorded that Hitler announced:

'"I have selected you and your paratroops for a very important task. Today the King of Italy has dismissed the Duce and he has been put under arrest. That means that Italy will probably try to get out of the war and may join the enemy camp. Get as many of your paratroops to Rome. I am making you responsible for seeing that Rome will be held. It *must* be held, otherwise our men in southern Italy and Sicily will be cut off. In Italy you and your men will come under command of the C-in-C South, Feldmarschall Kesselring, who has already been told of your impending arrival..."

'A detailed briefing followed, towards the end of which Hitler blurted out the instruction I had been expecting: "One of your special missions will be to locate and liberate my friend Mussolini...Of course, he is supposed to be extradited by the Italians (to the Americans)..." Hitler said somewhat pathetically but in a raised voice.

'I left for Rome early in the morning accompanied by the hitherto unknown SS Obersturmführer Skorzeny. During the night he and his 40 strong commando had been allotted to me for special police tasks.

'In Frascati I reported to Feldmarschall Kesselring who gave me more detailed information on the situation in Italy, and offered to put me up in his quarters. I accepted his invitation and enjoyed his hospitality until mid-September when the battle for Rome ended.'

The paratroops were flown to Italy almost immediately, and within two days 20,000 of them who landed at Pratica di Mare Airport south of Rome were bivouacking in the Pontine Marshes.

In Rome itself General Student immediately set about finding out where Mussolini was. When Feldmarschall Kesselring had asked King Victor Emmanuel about him the King had merely said that the former Duce was under his royal protection and that he was well. Beyond that there was absolutely no news at all; it was almost as if Mussolini had disappeared from the face of the earth. Then suddenly the searchers got a lead. Oberst Rübke, the Chief Signals Officer, told General Student that one of his NCOs had reported seeing Mussolini. Apparently, when this Unteroffizier — who was stationed on one of the Pontine islands — had landed at Gaeta the air raid alarm had sounded. Most people had promptly gone to the air raid shelters but there had been no signs of enemy air craft. And in the interval between the sounds of the alarm and the eventual 'all-clear' several cars and an ambulance had driven up to the harbour. According to the NCO Mussolini had got out of the ambulance and had been marched on to a cruiser tied up at one of the jetties. All this had happened in the space of a few minutes and it was doubtful if many people had noticed because they were all in the shelters.

When the news was passed back to Hitler, the Führer ordered the Unteroffizier to report to him at Rastenburg. His story was believed, and other corroborative evidence reaching General Student suggested that Mussolini had been taken to the island of Ponza. Things now began to move quickly. When SS Sturmbannführer Kappler, the Police Attaché in Rome, confirmed that Mussolini was indeed being held on Ponza, Student asked the Führer to give him a free hand in mounting a rescue operation. Hitler agreed.

For the proposed operation three patrol boats and a submarine commanded by Kapitän zur See Kamptz were put at Student's disposal, and the 3rd Battalion of FJR 1 in Eboli was taken off all duties. Oberst Karl-Lothar Schulz wanted to take command of the rescue party in person, but questions of who should do what in the raid let alone who should command it had not been settled when this rescue attempt had to be called off. Mussolini had been moved to Maddalena.

As soon as he heard the news Hitler summoned Student to Rastenburg once more. In the course of his discussion with the Führer Student asked permission to use Skorzeny in another rescue operation. Again Hitler agreed, and preparations were in full swing for a raid on Maddalena when Skorzeny told Student that he had learnt that Mussolini had vanished for a second time. The search was resumed and eventually Kappler's secret police reported they had heard a whisper that Mussolini was being held in a hotel, the Campo Imperatore, in the mountain resport of Gran Sasso. This time Student did not bother to seek Hitler's consent. On 8 September 1943 he sent a medical man, Stabsarzt Dr Krutoff, to have a look round at Gran Sasso, and Krutoff returned with the news that the Campo Imperatore Hotel had recently been closed.

When the news reached Student however, the latter's mind was more occupied with what was happening in Rome than with the rescue of the erstwhile Duce. On 8 September the Italians capitulated, and Kesselring's headquarters in Frascati and those of von Richthofen in Grotta Ferrata were bombed. Over a thousand civilans were killed in these two raids, which completely destroyed the two principal German headquarters in Italy. Only the HQ of the XIth Fallschirmkorps continued to function as the battle for Rome began.

The Battle for Rome

Men of the 2 FJD heard about the treachery of their Italian comrades during the evening of 8 September, and the news spread like wildfire. Major Mors, who had picked up an American news broadcast from Palermo, was probably among the first to know about the capitulation, and when he told General Student the whole division was ordered to stand to. Student himself hurried off to confer with Feldmarschall Kesselring. When he returned to his headquarters Student had Kesselring's permission to act as he thought fit; and within a matter of minutes a paratroop task force was driving north towards Rome. No less than seven Italian infantry divisions were encamped around the 2 FJD but nobody made any attempt to stop the paratroops. Nor did anybody try to put any obstacles in the way of General Gräser's 3rd Panzer Grenadier Division — also on its way down to Rome from the north. The paratroop task force, six battalions strong, was under Major von der Heydte; back at the Pontine camp Oberstleutnant Meder-Eggebrecht was in command of the remainder of the division as General Ramcke had fallen ill. (Soon after von der Heydte's force moved out, Meder-Eggebrecht's men systematically disarmed the Italians in the area.)

Von der Heydte's instructions on reaching Rome were clear and simple: 'Approach Rome from the sea side. Any resistance offered by the Corpo D'Armata di Roma (Rome Garrison) is to be broken'. That there would be some resistance became apparent when the leading German units entered the suburbs on the south-west of the town. Fired on by men of the Sardinia-Grenadier Division the paratroops halted while their gunners (2 Parachute Artillery Regiment) were called forward. The 3rd Battalion of FJR 6 under Major Pelz had been stopped in front in a castle-like building, and while Pelz was discussing what artillery support he needed with Hauptmann Milch one of the paratroop commanders, Major von der Heydte drove up. 'What's happening, Pelz?' he asked.

'My battalion is pinned down in front of that castle', Pelz replied. 'It blocks the road to Rome'.

'What we ought to do', suggested Hauptmann Milch, 'is to get round the blind side and blast the place to pieces.'

'Good!', said von der Heydte, 'Then what are you waiting for? Don't stand around here.'

Firing over open sights at a range of 200m two 10.5cm (4 inch) gun-howitzers shot the building to pieces, and the paratroop column rolled on; von der Heydte sitting on the roof of his patrol car was well to the front. And whenever there was any hold-up he was there urging his men on. At the Rome Radio Station, for example, Milch wanted to stop and seize control. 'Don't stop here, get on into Rome, Milch', von der Heydte ordered.

'Wouldn't it be better to wait here and let the infantry catch up, Her Major? If we get involved in street fighting we might find ourselves in a difficult situation'.

'That's a risk that has to be taken, Milch', von der Heydte replied. 'I'll drive on ahead and you can follow on with your guns'. So the column drove on — von der

196

Above: During the withdrawal up the Adria, Oberfeldwebel Schmitz destroyed a Sherman tank with a *Panzerfaust* (near Tomba, height 203, before Cattolica).

Below left: Oberfeldwebel Schmidt, the man who recovered Calvary Hill.

Below right: Karl-Lothar Schulz as an Oberst and commander of 1 FJD in Italy.

Heydte's car leading with another car behind, and Hauptmann Milch in a motorcycle tractor (a Kettenkrad) behind that. The story is taken up by Hauptmann Milch:

'We drove on peacefully into Rome, and at one point Major von der Heydte stopped at a market to buy grapes which we ate straightaway. When we drove on again, however, we saw a posse of motorcyclists in Italian uniform in front of us. They rode on as we approached, keeping a respectful distance ahead and making no attempt to hinder our progress. However we decided discretion was the better part of valour and I took the lead in my *Kettenkrad* and the task force commander dropped back to become number 3 in the convoy. Anyway, just before the famous obelisque in the Via Ostiense — quite close to the Coliseum — I saw some tanks in a side street and the barrels of their guns were following our movements. We had driven into a trap.

'To warn the two vehicles behind me I fired a shot from my rifle at the nearest tank — and got a salvo of shells in reply. Then the tanks started to chase von der Haydte's patrol car, which turned round and drove back towards my guns. These, in accordance with my orders, had followed slowly and warned by my shot, they were ready for the tanks. The result was a battle between my guns and the tanks which lasted all afternoon.'

Major von der Heydte remained in command of the task force until 11 September, when all the Italian troops in Rome lay down their arms. Shortly after that a Fieseler Storch taking him on a reconnaissance flight, crashed near Rome and von der Heydte was seriously injured.

But we must again turn back the clock and see what had happened to the rest of the paratroops.

Dropping into the Italian HQ at Monte Rotondo

Among the 20,000 paratroops flown into the Rome region was the 2nd Battalion of FJR 6 under the command of Major Walther Gericke. Gericke's battalion had been deployed to protect the airfields near Foggia, but during the afternoon of 5 September — three days before Italy's defection — General Student sent for Gericke.

'Gericke', the conversation started, 'I have a special mission for you and your battalion. It is a secret Reichs affair. We have to reckon on the possibility that Italy will get out of the war sooner or later and change sides. In case this should happen we have to consider what steps need to be taken to safeguard the German Army in Italy. So here are your orders:

'If Italy capitulates your job will be to knock out the Italian HQ in Monte Rotondo. By parachuting in to the place your battalion will be able to paralyse the whole Italian Army's chain of command. You will be entirely on your own, I'm afraid. For security reasons there can be no question of support either before or during the operation.'

Walter Gericke was not too happy about his mission. But he drove back to Foggia, ordered his battalion to prepare for an operation, while he studied a large-scale map of the location of Monte Rotondo north-west of Rome. According to this the Italian HQ was on a hill 160m (500ft) high, and completely surrounded by a thick and formidable belt of defence works — obstacles and anti-tank traps on the roads covered by strong points inter-connected by an elaborate trench system. AA guns and field artillery were included in these defences.

Gericke wanted to know more, so without asking permission he took a plane to Frascati and persuaded the pilot of a Fieseler Storch to fly him into the Italian prohibited zone near Monte Rotondo. Approaching the area two AA shells exploded near his plane; clearly this was a warning. 'Wobble your wings to show we understand', Gericke said to the pilot. So the latter wobbled the wings of the little plane, and flew round the area in a wide circle so that Gericke could get a look at what he was up against. But that was not enough for Gericke. He wanted to get inside the HQ to see what things looked like on the ground. So he considered the feasibility of going as Feldmarschall Kesselring's driver, when the latter went to discuss something with the Italian Chief-of-Staff. Concluding that an inquisitive German driver wandering around inside Monte Rotondo would certainly attract attention he dismissed this idea in favour of one which actually worked. Drawing on his imagination Gericke conjured up a mythical regiment, marching to Rome via Monte Rotondo. To avoid trouble it had halted nearby while he, Gericke, went ahead to consult the Germans' 'brothers-in-arms' about a route which would take them round the prohibited area. Carrying a map marked with the route of the imaginary regiment, Gericke simply drove up to the entrance of Monte Rotondo. As he passed obstacles and crossed anti-tank ditches he made a mental note. Eventually, arriving at the main line of defences he was held up — just as he had expected. Then, after a few minor formalities he was allowed to drive on, escorted by one Italian officer and four men. And on the way back he was allowed to drive alone. So he left Monte Rotondo with most of the information he had set out to acquire.

Gericke got the order to put his operation into effect on 8 September, and at 0630 the following morning the battalion took off for Monte Rotondo in 52 Ju52s. As the aircraft approached the prohibited area the Italian AA guns opened fire causing the first casualties of the day. In fact these were of less consequence than the fact that groups of the battalion were dropped outside the target area — some as much as 4km away from Monte Rotondo. But those who landed where they were supposed to land went into action and fought their way forward into the very heart of the Italian HQ. Gericke himself, with his own specially selected section of paratroopers, made straight for the tower which he suspected housed the Italian command staff, while a second group tackled the signal centre.

Those inside the tower put up a fierce resistance and there was a tough fight before it was overcome. Inside, when it was captured, were 15 senior Italian officers and 200 soldiers. But General Rotta, the Italian Army's Chief-of-Staff, was not among the captured officers. He had slipped away in time and was actually at Pescara, waiting to fly to the Allies, when Gericke reported completion of his mission. By the end of the day a total of 2,500 Italians — of whom 100 were officers — had surrendered to Gericke's paratroopers, and as the HQ was no longer functioning it must be concluded that Gericke's mission had been successful.

But the operation was not over, and that afternoon it took an ugly turn. An Italian armoured division, deployed near Rome, had been ordered down to Monte Rotondo to restore the situation there. As its move weakened the force opposing the paratroops in and around Rome the latter may be considered to have benefited from an easing in the pressure on them. It was a different matter for Gericke however. His battalion was in no position to stand up to an armoured division and it was clear that he would have to negotiate a withdrawal. In the event he did not have to do so because General Student had already opened negotiations with the Italians at a higher level. The results of these negotiations were set out in a radio message to Gericke:

'Following the fighting in and around Monte Rotondo the Italian Army Command and the German High Command South (Feldmarschall Kesselring) have agreed to a truce on the following terms: after an exchange of prisoners, the recovery of wounded and dead, all arms will be laid down. The Gericke task force will then be allowed to move north through the Italian lines. All Italian authorities and military units will permit Gericke Kampfgruppe to pass without hindrance and they will be responsible for the protection and security of the German column'.

Before these arrangements could be put into effect however, the Italians in Monte Rotondo turned awkward. Only a few paratroops were guarding a vast number of prisoners; when some escaped others followed and there was some shooting. Gericke ordered his machine guns to go into action and the situation appeared to be deteriorating rapidly when one of the prisoners, an Italian captain, ran across to his compatriots waving a white sheet. The Germans had agreed to an armistice, he told them. After that the situation quietened down and Gericke's battalion left Monte Rotondo during the afternoon, linking up with German units around Rome that evening. Meanwhile the Italian troops inside the capital had thrown in the sponge. Gericke's operation had helped to undermine their morale, and persuaded them to give up far sooner than had been expected.

Mussolini is Freed

General Student was now able to turn his attention to his plans for the Duce's liberation from Gran Sasso. And on 12 September, one day after the signing of the armistice, the operation to free Mussolini was set in motion. The Paratroop Training Battalion (Fallschirm Lehr Battalion) under Major Mors was to conduct the operation; Skorzeny, as deputy of police, was to fly in with the battalion.

In his first orders for a surprise attack on the Pratica di Mare airfield General Student impressed on the men of Leutnant Freiherr von Berlepsch's company that...'Not a single shot must be fired until your gliders have landed on the obective. The gliders will go in quietly; there will be no steep dives and no use of the braking parachutes. The whole approach will be one of "imperturbable calm".'

The towing planes took off towing 10 gliders behind them and the operation went almost exactly as planned. Nine of the gliders landed directly on top of the rocky hill and their arrival completely surprised the enemy. (The tenth glider crashed on the steep slope of the hill opposite the objective but there were only a few casualties.) The Italian guards offered no resistance and Hauptmann Gerlach was able to set down a Fieseler in front of the hotel. Mussolini and Skorzeny — who had gone in with one of the gliders — then climbed into the Fieseler and flew to Rome. Finally a Heinkel took

Albert Kesselring who is remembered for campaigns in North Africa, Sicily and Italy.

Oberst K.-L. Schulz reports to Feldmarschall Kesselring in Italy.

Oberst K.-L. Schulz takes off for Vibo Valencia on the Italian south coast. The enemy was certain to attack here!

Mussolini and Skorzeny to the Führer's HQ at Rastenburg where Skorzeny was acclaimed as Mussolini's liberator.

The Air Landings and Paratroop Action on Elba

During the night of 17/18 September the 2nd Battalion of the 7th Parachute Regiment was ordered to occupy the port of Portoferraio on Elba and to clear the enemy from the north-west of the island. When that had been accomplished a Wehrmacht-battalion would be shipped in to Portoferraio. Both battalions would then co-operate in an operation designed to bring about the capitulation of the Italian garrison.

This operation was mounted because the OKW (German High Command) were expecting the Allies to land on Corsica and Sardinia as well as on the Italian mainland.

The 2nd Battalion, under command of Major Friedrich Hübner, started out from the Ciampino airfield near Rome in the early morning, and was dropped — according to plan — at the south west of Portoferraoi Bay. Stukas had bombed the island just before the drop took place, and the garrison was quaking. As a result the commander offered to surrender after only a short battle and the Wehrmacht battalion which was ferried across did not have to do any fighting. By the time it arrived the paratroops had taken possession of Portoferraio and 10,000 Italian soldiers on Elba became prisoners of war.

Italy's unconditional surrender presented the enemy with new opportunities for prosecuting the war — not only in Italy. Bases in the Balkans and on the Greek and Italian islands were now possible, and the fact that the enemy missed out on Corsica was due entirely to the action taken by Oberstleutnant Pietzonka, commander of FJR 7. Nevertheless the enemy did seize the opportunity to grab the islands of Kos, Leros and Samos in the Aegean.

The Germans counter-attacked — first against Kos which was wrested from the Allies by German troops on 3 October 1943. The second counter-attack against Leros was lauched on 12 November, when a seaborne force landed from German TA boats and transport vessels. Later, when the enemy resistance stiffened the 1st Battalion of FJR 2 was dropped on the island. Led by Major Kuhne the paratroops jumped into the middle of the enemy's defences. A fierce battle developed at the end of which Leros was in German hands. Finally, when the enemy abandoned Samos the Aegean islands were free again. By this time the battle for Rome had been decided. But what of the regiments of 1 FJD in the South of Italy?

The 1st Fallschirmjäger Division in Southern Italy

Montgomery's 8th Army landed at the southernmost point of Italy's toe in 3 September 1943. Two days later men of the 1st Air Landing Division disembarked from boats in Taranto harbour and American divisions landed the same day in the Gulf of Salerno.

Two days after these invasions — on the morning of 7 September — the 1st Parachute Regiment under Oberstleutnant Schulz set out to march from the Naples region to Francaville on the Brindisi-Taranto road. Schulz was at the head of the column when towards noon it arrived at a road block manned by Italians. The column halted and waited — until the following day. Then the paratroops learned the bitter truth; that Italy had capitulated, and that Marshal Badoglio had secretly sold the Italian Navy to Britain. Thus, because the paratroops stayed behind the Italian road block and did not continue on to Taranto, the British were able to occupy the town without opposition when they landed there in force during the morning of 9 September.

Once it was known that the Italians were out of the war, Schulz marched on and when his battalion clashed with the enemy the latter's progress was slowed from a run to a crawl. Until 20 September the British gained very little terrain, and when they did break through the German line on that day Schulz was quickly on the spot to reform it and organise a counter-attack. An enemy 'Jabo' (fighter-bomber) riddled his command car with cannon and machine gun fire, killing the driver and wounding the adjutant. But Schulz himself was unhurt, the counter-attack went in as he had planned, and within two hours the paratroopers had recovered the ground they had lost. They had also taken a number of prisoners and among those brought before the regimental commander was a captain who introduced himself as Lord B———. Addressing Schulz in a typically English manner he said 'Would you be so kind as to tell my unit that I am here? Otherwise my family will get worried!' Smiling at the request, Schulz agreed to do so. And a few days later his kindness was returned when a radio message emanating from the British Air Landing Division said that one of Schulz's reconnaissance patrols which had been captured by Italian partisans had been freed by the British.

Inevitably the regiment had to give ground and fall back. The battles around Foggia lasted until 27 September and there was some nasty street fighting in Garignola.

On 18 September Generalleutnant Richard Heidrich had the whole of his division under his own command for the first time since 1 FJD left France on 11 and 12 July. His orders were: 'The First Parachute Division will defend the Apulia area'.

It was here that Heidrich showed that he knew how to command a division. His men fought for three weeks in the Ofanto sector and south of Foggia and the withdrawal battles that were fought in Apulia were models of their kind. Writing of this period Feldmarschall Kesselring said: 'One has to admire the qualities of leadership and endurance displayed by the 1st Parachute Division in Apulia.'

In fact the division still had to face its most critical challenge. 1 FJD was on its own in Apulia and the enemy, trying to reach Pescara on the east coast of Italy threw the British 22nd Army Corps against it — attacking on a 50km (30 miles) front. The paratroops fought like tigers, spurred on by Richard Heidrich who seemed to be everywhere. Extraordinary feats were performed but when FJR 4 was defeated near Motta the division withdrew behind the Biferno.

A Further Withdrawal Towards the North

In December 1943 Montgomery's forces crossed the Moro. Their objective was Ortona, and on 14 December they succeeded in breaking through the German defences covering the town. General Herr, commanding the 76th Panzerkorps called for reinforcements and the 3rd Parachute Regiment under Oberst Heilmann was the first formation to arrive.

On 15 December, Oberst Heilmann, on a reconnaissance mission around Ortona, found that Canadian troops were already in the town. The 2nd Battalion of his regiment under Hauptmann Liebscher was ordered up to restore the situation and a report to divisional headquarters resulted in Generalleutnant Heidrich deciding to concentrate the burden of his resources in the Ortona sector. (As the New Zealanders had entered Orsogna on 3 December a counter-attack had to be staged in this area also. This was successful and the enemy was evicted from Orsogna.)

Christmas 1943 will be remembered by paratroopers who served in Italy and survived the war for the intense bombardment which rained down on them. At Ortona where the Canadians launched a massive attack some of the fiercest fighting of the campaign lasted for seven days and seven nights. 1 FJD fought for every metre of the town until Heidrich ordered them to withdraw to prepared positions 2km from the built-up area.

The British 8th Army had suffered a severe defeat and their plans had been disrupted. Montgomery handed over the 8th Army to Sir Oliver Leese, while he himself flew to England to take over command of the 21st Army Group which was preparing for the invasion of NW Europe. Sir Oliver did not wish to renew the battle for Pescara, or for his men to fight Heidrich's paratroops. What he planned now was a breakthrough at Monte Cassino.

On 5 February 1944 Richard Heidrich was awarded the *Eichenlaub zum Ritterkreuz* (Oak leaves to the *Ritterkreuz*) for his part in the battles around Ortona.

Meanwhile the 2nd Parachute Division had set off on a journey from which many would not return. The division had been transferred to Russia.

CHAPTER 17

The Second Parachute
Division in Russia

When Italy surrendered to the Allies the men of the 2nd Parachute Division were more concerned than ever about their future. Where would they be employed next? In Southern Italy? Or — as some of those who claimed to be in the know would have it — in Russia?

A new Soviet offensive in November 1943 brought the answer. On the Ukranian front the 30 Soviet infantry divisions, 24 armoured brigades and 10 motorised brigades which were suddenly hurled against the weak German 3rd Army, effected a breakthrough. Kiev fell on 5 November, Zhitomir and Korosten less than a week later, and by 11 November the Red Army had reached Radomysl, 85km (50 miles) west of Kiev. 2 FJD, which had been standing by to move since the fall of Kiev, was now told that its destination was Zhitomir.

In the event the first regiment of Generalleutnant Ramcke's division to arrive in the Ukraine on 26 November was put straight into the front line to relieve a Waffen SS Regiment where a battle was raging west of Marjanovka. (This was FJR 2 under command of Major Pietzonka; Oberstleutnant Hans Kroh had been sent back to Germany because he was ill.) This particular battle raged for 12 days with the enemy being continuously repulsed. Then on 12 December — by which time the rest of the division had reached the Ukraine — FJR 2 was pulled out and driven to Zhitomir which had been recaptured by General von Manteuffel's 7th Panzer Division on 19 December.

From Zhitomir the regiment was flown to Kirovograd to cope with a sudden crisis which could only be resolved by a 'fire-brigade' of paratroopers. On 13 December the regiment was told that it was to attack Pervomaisk and for the next four days reconnaissance patrols probed the enemy positions. The attack was launched on 18 December and the enemy was dislodged from the dominating features on which he had installed himself. Three days later another attack at Novgorodka drove the enemy from Pt N167 overlooking the town, but this could not be held. Oberstleutnant Kroh rejoined the regiment and resumed command of the regiment about this time.

On the 22nd day of what the paratroops were now calling Bloody December, Pt N167 was captured for the second time in less than a week. Success came after some bitter fighting and in the Kirovograd sector it was the medical officers who earned everybody's respect and praise. One of them, Stabsarzt Dr Schmieden, deputy commander of the 1st Sanitary Company and his medical orderlies literally dragged every casualty out of the line themselves and tended to their wounds immediately.

Pt 159.9 near Kirovograd can be likened to a rock in the middle of a strip of ground against which waves of Russian attackers broke and surged away. The Russians tried hard to capture this height, and the fighting for it reached a climax shortly after Christmas when Leutnant Erich Lepkowski's 5th Battalion (FJR 2) took over from the 6th Battalion (FJR 2) who had been holding it until then, and during the next few days the 5th Battalion went through hell while the enemy bombarded its positions. The Russians were preparing for a massive assault on Pervomaisk on the Bug river, which, it was planned, would include the encirclement of all the German units in the triangle Kanyev on the Dnieper, Kirovograd on the Ingul and Pervomaisk on the Bug.

The Soviet 2nd Ukrainian Front under Marshal Koniev and the 1st Ukrainian Front under General Vatutin launched the offensive on 5 January 1944, and an attack on the German outpost at Pt 159.9 opened with a massive bombardment by heavy artillery, mortars and rocket launchers. Red Army infantry then assaulted simultaneously from three sides; the 2nd Battalion (FJR 2) deployed on the slopes right and left of the 5th Battalion in the centre was pushed back. But the men of the 5th were steadfast and from the firm base thus provided Obertsleutnant Kroh was able to recover the lost ground. So at the end of the day, 6 January, the hill was still in the paratroopers' hands.

That night (6/7 January) the Russians attempted a surprise attack and the paratroopers lost some positions — only to regain them soon afterwards. But the situation was deteriorating rapidly. On 8 January three German divisions of the 47th Army Corps had been surrounded in the Kirovograd area and it looked as if the 2nd Parachute Division would soon be sharing their fate. So when the enemy broke through on both sides of Pt 159.9 in divisional strength, Major Ewald, the CO of the 2nd Battalion was ordered to withdraw. The 5th Battalion on the height was already completely surrounded so there was no question of it getting away at that time. Next night, however, Leutnant Lepkowski sent Oberjäger Müschenborn out to find a way through the Russians, and when Müschenborn returned and reported that he had found a gap in their lines, Lepkowski decided to try to lead what was left of his battalion back to the German lines. The group of paratroopers slipped quietly down the hill and made for the bridge across the Ingul. The roads were chock-a-block with Soviet vehicles and when they reached the bridge the paratroops found that it had been blown up (by their own regimental engineers). But some of the girders were still standing and the men were able to swing themselves across to the other side. Soon after this Lepkowski was able to report to Oberstleutnant Kroh, who told him that his stand on Pt 159.9 had saved the 2nd Parachute Regiment from destruction. Stabsarzt Dr Marquard who had been on the hill was told to write a report which Oberstleutnant Kroh forwarded to the divisional commander. After reading it General Ramcke recommended Lepkowski for a *Ritterkreuz*; months later this was presented to him in Brest.

The division retreated west fighting hard and retrieving the situation on many critical occasions. At the beginning of March when General Ramcke fell ill the command passed to Kroh, who had been promoted to Oberst.

Towards the end of March 1944 2 FJD reached the Dnieper bend and here they halted to stem another Soviet offensive. Having repelled one massive attack the paratroopers themselves returned to the offensive and for the last time in Russia they counter-attacked. When this attack ended more than 10,000 prisoners had fallen into their hands, the Russian offensive had been put out of phase, and the German divisions on the flanks of 2 FJD were no longer in danger of being encircled. For his part in the re-establishment of the German front line Hans Kroh was awarded the *Eichenlaub* to the *Ritterkreuz*.

This action in the Dnieper bend marked the end of the fighting on the Eastern Front for 2 FJD. In April what was left of the division was sent to the West to be brought up to strength and to re-equip. Under Major Friedrich Wilhelm von der Heydte a new regiment, FJR 6 raised in January 1944, was already training at Wahn, and when General Ramcke — fully recovered now from his illness — visited this regiment on 6 May, 1944 the 3,000 paratroops gave him an enthusiastic welcome.

Hauptmann Gerhard Schirmer, subsequently promoted Oberst and Regimental Commander FJR 16, on the Eastern Front.

CHAPTER 18

The Second Parachute Corps

At the end of 1943 the old Fliegerkorps XIII, which had raised 22 Luftwaffe Field Division, became II Parachute Corps (II Fallschirmkorps), and Generalleutnant Meindel the corps commander was back with his beloved paratroops. His chief of staff was Oberstleutnant Blausteiner.

For technical and training purposes the new Parachute Corps was responsible to General Student's Fallschirmarmee-Oberkommando 1 (1st Parachute Army HQ) whose headquarters at this time were split between Berlin and Nancy. Operationally the Corps came under the C-in-C West, and then two new divisions 3 FJD and 5 FJD were added to the Corps on 12 May 1944, General Meindl was directly responsible to the GOC 7th Army with headquarters 120km (75miles) east of Brest.

General Meindl was now ordered to bring the two new divisions to fighting pitch and to raise all the independent corps troops needed to make the corps a first-line formation. To do this Meindl needed:

Corps Reconnaissance Abteilung 12
Corps Intelligence Abteilung 12
Assault gun Brigade 12
Corps Reinforcement Unit 12
Field Surgical Unit
Paratroop Training Depot 12

At this time 3 FJD commanded by Generalleutnant Schimpf was at full strength. 5 FJD, under Lt General Wilcke was 80 per cent up to strength. 2 FJD, reformed in Brittany duing May 1944, was also destined for this Corps.

The Corps AA Regiment 12 and the Corps Artillery Regiment 12, whose organisation was the responsibility of II Parachute Corps were raised in Germany. But these units never saw service with the Corps. Under General Meindl's direction the rest of the Corps trained hard, and exercises included action against simulated airborne attacks.

On 6 June 1944 — D-Day of the Allied invasion of Normandy — II Parachute

General Meindl who commanded the FJStR (*Fallschirmjäger Sturmregiment*) on Crete and who later was GOC II Fallschirmkorps.

Corps was ordered to move to the St Lô area. To begin with only 3 FJD and the corps troops moved immediately; units of 5 FJD remained at the garrison stations where they were currently deployed. But the transfer of 2 FJD to its operational area now began.

The Transfer of the 2nd Fallschirmjäger Division

On 11 June 1944, the sixth day of the Normandy invasion, General Ramcke was in Wahn, when he was called to the telephone. The call came from Nancy; General Student, C-in-C of the 1st Parachute Army, wanted Ramcke to report to him in person the following morning. Moreover he was to travel to Nancy by car and *not* by plane.

So Ramcke drove to Nancy and reported to General Student who had sent for him to give him details of what was expected of his division.

'Now then, Ramcke, the 2nd Fallschirmjäger Division will move immediately to Brittany. You can carry on with your training programme, but your operational role is to deny Brest to the enemy. He may well try to land there — either by sea or air — and you must stop him. You will be under command of 25th Corps in Pontivy and the Corps Commander will give you detailed instructions. I have already ordered your operations officer, Major Schmidt, to get things moving, and Schmidt had been told to meet you in Vannes. The first convoys will leave Wahn tomorrow morning. And I want you to get down to Brittany as fast as you can — tomorrow morning at the latest. My administrative officer is attending to the question of your accommodation.'

In his usual way Student, anticipating what had to be done, had everything worked out.

Thus on 16 June General Ramcke reported to the commander of the 25th Army Corps, Generalleutnant von Choltitz, and the two men discussed how the greater Brest area would be defended. Ramcke spent the next three nights at Landivisiau, a small town on the Elorne, and then moved to Lampaul and his headquarters were set up there.

Leaving the trail of 2 FJD and II Parachute Corps we must now return to the old 1st Parachute Division and the newly raised 4th Division of the 1st Parachute Corps. Both divisions had been in the thick of the battle, and we must see what had happened.

210

CHAPTER 19

The Battle for Monte Cassino

The First Battle of Cassino

The battle for Salerno convinced Feldmarschall Kesselring that it was futile to think in terms of driving the enemy back into the sea. What he had to do was to contain the enemy in the south, so preventing him establishing air bases within range of the German frontier. Thus it was decided to prevent any further advance by standing on what was to become known as the Gustav line, across the narrow neck of the Appenine Peninsula. Here the Garigliano river provided a good natural obstacle in front, with the river Sangro and the mountainous Abruzzi in the rear and on the left flank. Another advantage of the Gustav position was that the Liri valley, up which the enemy was expected to advance with overwhelmingly superior armoured columns, was dominated by the two rock cones of Monte Maio in the south and Monte Cassino in the north.

To protect the Benedictine Abbey at Monte Cassino, Kesselring insisted on the German defence works being sited at the foot of the mountain on which the ancient abbey stood, and the area round it was declared a prohibited area. Furthermore, before the fighting erupted on 14 October 1943 the artistic treasures of the abbey were taken into safe custody by Oberstleutnant Schegal, the CO of the Divisional Repair Detachment (*Instandsetzungs Abteilung*) of the Hermann Göring Panzer Grenadier Division. Don Gregoria Diamare, the Father Abbott, and the Convent both agreed to the treasures being removed, and on 8 December Schegal handed the entire collection — 120 lorry loads of works of art — to a representative of the Holy See in Rome. Painting from the picture galleries in Naples, including some European masterpieces, which had been transferred to the abbey were among the treasures handed over to the Vatican. It was a precautionary measure which was destined to save the treasures from destruction.

The enemy now tried to envelop Monte Cassino by attacking on a broad front. Following the Allied landings in the Anzio-Nettuno area, the attack was intended to trap the German forces between two fires and close the pincers on the entire German 10th Army in Southern Italy.

The British 10th Corps started to attack Cassino on 17 January 1944, and on the

211

first day the 5th and 56th Divisions penetrated the defences of the 96th German Infantry Division and crossed the Garigliano. This forced the Germans back into the Acrunic Mountains, and the Monte Maio positions were threatened. Feldmarschall Kesselring promptly called his reserves and counter-attacked with the 29th and 90th Panzer Grenadier Divisions (PGDs). These two divisions stopped the British advance but they were not able to eliminate the enemy bridgeheads on the north bank of the Garigliano. Then on 20 January 1944 the 5th US Army under General Clark attacked the German positions held by the 15th PGD covering the lower stretch of the Rapido river. The attack was not successful, however, and the American 36th Division 'Texas Boys' were thoroughly 'serviced', losing 1,700 men in the process.

It was now the turn of General Juin's 3rd Algerian Division which attacked north of Cassino town on 24 January. Juin's objective was Monte Cassino from where he hoped to push down into the Liri valley and ultimately to block the Via Casilina — the German 10th Army's supply route. The 44th Division — the *Hoch-und Deutschmeister* — bore the brunt of this attack. Tunisian units and the Algerian Division managed to seize the Belvedere but the 44th stopped them getting any further.

On 28 January Generalleutnant Ernst Günther Baade's 90th PGD relieved the 44th Division and two days later the Americans returned to the attack. On 30 January men of the US 34th Division acquired the village of Cairo north of Cassino and by 2 February they were in the northern outskirts of Cassino itself. As they were now poised above the Via Casilina, the *Feuerwehr* (Fire-Brigade) was brought up. The *Feuerwehr* was in fact the Schultz Battle Group — the 1st Parachute Regiment (FJR 1) and attached troops, which included the 1st Parachute Machine Gun Battalion under Major Schmidt, and Hauptmann Kratzert's 3rd Battalion of the FJR 3. This was the first time the paratroops had intervened in the battle for Monte Cassino.

Oberst Schulz deployed the machine gun battalion on the slopes of Monte Cassino, while Kratzert's battalion dug in on the Calvary Hill (Hangman's Hill). And in the desperate fighting which developed shortly after the paratroops got into position the men under the command of the hero of Rotterdam and Heraklion did not give up an inch of ground. Karl-Lothar Schulz's Battle Group defended the 'Monte' to the limit of their capacity. When the enemy dropped leaflets saying that the German paratroopers were trespassing on the Abbey's sacred soil and accusing them of using the monastery as an observation post and strongpoint, Schulz broadcast a radio message denying the accusations. At the same time he informed General Heidrich who reasserted that none of his soldiers was to set foot in the Abbey grounds. The 211th Regiment of the 71st Infantry Division was defending Cassino town, when on 11 February the Americans attacked for the last time in this sector. The US 34th and 36th Division had been ordered to clear the town and go on to seize Calvary Hill. Once again the enemy was sent reeling back with a bloody nose, and when the attack was called off the 2nd US Corps had lost a vast number of its soldiers.

The first battle of Cassino was now drawing to a close. As a grandiose and cruel finale, however, 142 B-17 Flying Fortresses took off from the airfields round Foggia on the morning of 15 February and flying over the Abbey about 1000 dropped 353 tons of bombs. They were followed by 47 B-25s and 40 B-26s which dropped a further 100 tons of bombs. At the end of the raid the Monte Cassino Abbey was in ruins. Karl-Lothar Schulz and his paratroops survived this vicious bombardment, and

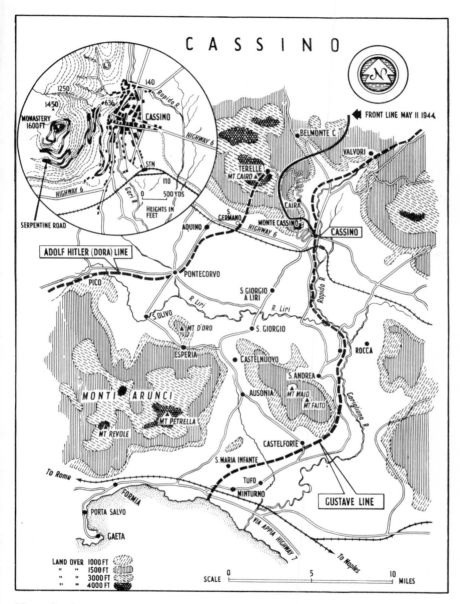

Monte Cassino.

the paratroops had no losses; indeed the only casualties were among the civilian population. From a military point of view the bombing was senseless. Oberst Schulz had the Father Abbott and the monks escorted to a safe place on 17 February and then — and only then — did the paratroops install themselves in the Abbey ruins. Next day, 18 February, each of the battalions of the 7th Indian Brigade took turns to attack the 'Monte' and all of them were bloodily repulsed. Their defeat marked the end of the first battle of Cassino. Schulz's Battle Group was now withdrawn for rest and recuperation; it had stopped the enemy penetrating the Gustav line, and Karl-Lothar Schulz himself received the *Eichenlaub zum Ritterkreuz*.

The Allied Landings at Anzio-Nettuno

The 4th Parachute Division commanded by Oberst Trettner was raised in the Perugia area during January 1944 when the Parachute Corps was expanded. Survivors of the former Parachute Assault Regiment and the 2nd and 6th Regiments were the nucleus of this new division; the rest of the troops came from disbanded Luftwaffe field divisions and superfluous Luftwaffe ground personnel. Trettner the commander, who had originally been on Student's staff, quickly welded these men into a first line formation.

On 18 January 1944 Trettner was ordered to nominate a 'special duties' battalion from each of his 10th, 11th and 12th Regiments. These battalions were required for a plan, codenamed Richard, which had been drawn up to cope with an enemy landing behind the Cassino (Gustav) line. Oberst Trettner went straight to the 11th Regiment on 19 January and appointed Major Gericke, the regimental commander, to take command of these three groups from 4 FJD.

Plan Richard was put into effect when the US 6th Corps landed in the Anzio-Nettuno area and the three special service battalions, known now as *Kampfgruppe Gericke* (Gericke Group) moved quickly up to the Allied bridgehead. So began the 4 FJD's war with the Allies in Italy; within a few weeks of being raised this division was submitted to the supreme test of battle.

Gericke Group, which with other German formations would contain the enemy bridgehead and stop the Allies marching on Rome by way of the Via Casilina and the Alban Hills, moved to Aprilia. Meanwhile there was nothing to stop General Lucas, the commander of the US 6th Corps from marching straight from Anzio to Rome, and by not doing so he lost his chance of victory. Instead of marching he preferred to wait until his troops had assembled and all their vehicles and supplies had been brought ashore. Inside 14 days he had 18,000 vehicles, 380 tanks and 70,000 men within the narrow confines of the bridgehead. Churchill, well known for his sarcasm, commented: 'We must be superior in numbers of drivers. But I am shocked to hear that the enemy has more infantry than we have'.

Major Gericke reported to General Schlemm's Corps HQ at Grottaferrata three days before the landings and was told that his formation would '... remain in the Isola Farnese area and continue its training programme. Its full complement of ammunition and patrol stocks could not be made up until 22 January; until then all available supplies were needed by the 10th Army.'

Gericke returned to Isola Farnese where at 0530 on 22 January he was handed a signal: *'Achtung!* The enemy has landed on both sides of the Nettuno. One battalion will move immediately to Albano; the Group Commander will accompany.'

Hauptmann Hauber's battalion was turned out and at 0900 it set off for Albano; Major Gericke had already set off for Corps HQ where, when he arrived at 0730 he was informed that: 'The enemy landed on both sides of the Nettuno in the early hours of the morning. The 2nd Battalion of the 71st Regiment (GR 71) guarding the coast was unable to stop the landing and was driven back. Nothing more is known about the extent of the invasion.'

During the day (21 January) all troops in and around Rome were stood to and to ensure co-ordinated action the various units were put under Gericke's command. Meanwhile the first enemy troops who had come ashore on the coastal strip between Caesare S Lorenza and Torre Astura had penetrated as far as the railway station at Campo do Carne and occupied the village of Gorgemontello.

Gericke did not wait for his group but deployed every unit as it arrived and reported to him — blocking the main roads to stop a motorised enemy advance. The Nettuno-Aprilia and Las Fossa-Ardea were obviously the most likely axes of such an advance and they were given priority. By noon nearly all of Gericke's units had reported to him and had been deployed — the last to arrive, at 1730, being Major Kleye's battalion from the 11th Regiment.

Directly after this General Gläser, the divisional commander of the 3rd Panzer Grenadier Division, arrived at the house in Albano where Gericke had set up his command post. And at 1905 an order was received from Corps HQ: 'Weak enemy force advancing on Ardea driven back by 2nd Battalion 71st Regiment. Ardea town still in our hands. One battalion of Gericke Group will occupy and hold Ardea and La Fossa.'

By 26 January the rest of the 4th Parachute Division had concentrated in the coastal strip, and the enemy had still made no attempt to break out of the bridgehead. Contained now by 4 FJD and the 3rd PGD the dangerously explosive situation created by the existence of the bridgehead had largely been defused.

General von Mackensen, C-in-C of Army Group C, now ordered a counter-attack, and on the night of 8 February Gericke Group and two regiments of the 65th Division assaulted the enemy positions at Carroceto. The paratroops succeeded in penetrating as far east as Pt 80 and Carroceto station, but General Schlemm, GOC 1st Parachute Corps (1FschKorps) was not satisfied and on 9 February he ordered Gericke to capture Pt 80.

The attack began on 20 February with Kleye's battalion making a wide outflanking move to assault from the north. Kleye was killed in the fighting but the attack was completely successful and Pt 80 was captured.

To link up with the 3rd PGD which was simultaneously attacking Carroceto, Leutnant Weiss, the company commander of Kleye's No 2 Company, led 60 men in an assault on a group of houses north-west of the station. The enemy occupying the houses were overwhelmed, 180 Scotsmen were captured, and the impetus of the assault carried the paratroops into the railway station. But the enemy hit back with tanks and Leutnant Weiss's group disintegrated. Weiss himself, with 12 other men, successfully defended the station and at the end of the day the station, Carroceto and Pt 80 were still in the hands of the paratroops. But Kleye's battalion had lost four officers and 287 other ranks.

Over the next few days Gericke Group remained in the forefront of the battle. The operation to wipe out the bridgehead which had begun on 16 February had to be called off on 18 February and a second operation — ordered by Hitler himself — collapsed during the afternoon of 1 March.

Meanwhile the enemy, now commanded by General Truscott, was preparing to break out of the bridgehead, and when it was learned that an all-out attack was to be launched on Aprilia — and would thus be directed against the 4th Panzer Grenadier Division — Oberzt Trettner issued an Order of the Day. Dated 27 March this order said among other things:

'. . . . The main battle line (HKL) is to be held, and if the enemy does break through, the line must be restored by counter-attack. Early recognition of enemy concentrations, through observation, reconnaissance and fighting patrols, is essential, so that they can be destroyed by artillery and mortar fire. Reserves are to be kept well forward. Support weapons must be sited for all round defence, and every man in the division must be psychologically prepared for the coming attack and ready to hand out the same sort of treatment as the 1st Parachute Division has handed out to the enemy at Cassino . . .'

Five German divisions round the bridgehead now faced nine Allied divisions inside it, but it was some time before the expected attack developed. In effect General Truscott had ordered that it should begin on 23 May, and his aim was to cut the main withdrawal route of the German 10th Army at Valmonte die Via Casilina.

When the Allied offensive opened on 23 May, FJR 12, under Major Timm, was defending a sector of the German line at Velletri. Timm managed to stave off attacks by the US 34th Division but the battle swayed to and fro and during the night of 31 May the Allies broke through the 76th Panzer Corps over the Monte Artemisio. In consequence the German 14th Army front collapsed, the Allies gained access to the Alban Hills, and their advance on Rome developed rapidly. The 4th Parachute Division now became the 14th Army's rearguard and as the paratroops retreated they held up the enemy time and again. And when the advance guard of the US 88th Division drove into Rome's Piazza Venezia at 1915 on 4 June FJD 4 had successfully completed its mission by making possible the withdrawal of the 14th Army.

Of these men who had stood at the Anzio-Nettuno bridgehead, and who had been the last German soldiers to leave the Eternal City, Eric Linklater wrote: 'The thoroughness and military know-how displayed by the Germans at the Anzio bridgehead was even more convincing than at Monte Cassino.'

And what had been happening at Monte Cassino?

The Second Battle of Cassino

In the lull between the ending of the first battle for Cassino and the time the second began, Generalleutnant Heidrich regained control of his entire division, and Feldmarschall Kesselring ordered him to take over the defence of the Cassino sector.

Generalleutnant Heidrich at his tactical HQ on Cassino. Oberst Heilmann, whose FJR 3 was the linchpin of the defence, is in the middle.

On 15 March the paratroop engineers were in action in the town of Cassino. This was Schmitz's base. The wounded are being evacuated.

The last German assault gun standing in front of a dug-out.

On the Allied side the New Zealand Corps had also taken over from the US 2nd Corps which went into reserve.

This time it was to be Oberst Heilamm's 3rd Parachute Regiment which was to be in the forefront of the fighting, for it was this regiment which now deployed in defence of Cassino town and the Abbey mountain. The 2nd Battalion and No 10 Company of the 3rd Battalion FJR 3 were in the town and the 1st Battalion was deployed on the Abbey mountain; in the hills behind the Abbey General Heidrich had positioned the 1st and 4th Regiments.

The battle started on 15 March 1944 with a heavy air attack. Six hundred aircraft flew over to drop their bombs on Cassino while the Allied generals watched the spectacle from a viewpoint on Monte Trocchino. When the aircraft flew off 750 guns and mortars took over to soften up the defences even further before the infantry attacked. Most of this fire was directed on Cassino town where Major Foltin's 2nd Battalion suffered heavy casualties — 220 paratroops alone being buried under the ruins. Only one company (No 6) sheltering in rock caves 5km behind Cassino escaped unscathed.

The assault was led by 400 tanks as the New Zealand infantry advanced on Cassino from the north. They got as far as the town centre but there they were held up. The tanks could not get over or through the ruins and the infantry were mowed down by small-arms fire from the paratroopers who had survived the air strike and the artillery bombardment.

Next night the 4th Indian Division attacked, overrunning the Rocca Janule and storming up the Abbey mountain. In the early morning of the 16th Gurkhas were on Pt 435 — a feature 400m behind the defenders of Monte Cassino. However a counter-attack by the 1st Battalion of FJR 4 routed three battalions of the 5th Indian Brigade and restored the situation. The New Zealanders had captured two thirds of the Abbey ruins but pockets of paratroopers in the remaining ruins continued to hold out. And on 22 March General Alexander ordered his men to call off the attack.

The Third Battle of Cassino

At the end of March Feldmarschall Kesselring took the battle-weary 1st Parachute Division out of the front line to give it a week's rest. But then it had to go back to Monte Cassino. This time however it was Oberst Walther's FJR 4 with the 1st Machine Gun Battalion which took over the defence of Cassino town and the Abbey mountain. FJR 3 took over the mountain sector which included Calvary Hill, the Colle S. Angelo and Monte Caira; and the Ruffin Group — a composite force of mountain troops from GJR 100 and the 4th Battalion Hochgebirgs (high mountain troops — were attached to the regiment specifically for the defence of Monte Caira. The 1st Regiment was in divisional reserve in the rear.

Because each of them had been required to give up their 3rd Battalion to form the nucleus of the new 5th Parachute Division, all three regiments were under strength when the third battle of Cassino started. The Allies on the other hand, who intended to attack with four army corps this time, had no less than 16 fully-equipped divisions available.

As the BBC London time signal pipped 11pm on 11 May 2,000 enemy guns opened fire and a thunderous barrage descended on the four weak German divisions in the

Still in action.

Assault gun in front
of the ruins.

This is what Cassino
looked like after the
Allied bombing.

Cassino area. From the upper valley of the Rapido down to the coast there was a flickering wall of flame, and the ground was ploughed up by exploding shells and mortar bombs for the third time.

When the Allied soldiers moved in to assault the German defences Oberst Heilmann's 3rd Regiment found itself fighting the 2nd Polish Corps. The Poles were repulsed at most places, but the focal point of their attacks was Calvary Hill occupied by Major Böhmler's 1st Battalion. Böhmler's men had an impossible task. No 3 Company, manning the centre of the Calvary Hill positions, had to withstand repeated attacks by the 2nd Polish Armoured Brigade; No 1 Company, holding the summit of the Hill was eventually overrun by Polish mountain troops (*Karpathenjäger* — the Carpathian Mountain Div) — although the No 7 Company was brought up to help. The reserves, 1st and 2nd Battalions of FJR 3 made four counter-attacks to try to recover the Hill, but they failed to do so. However, on the evening of 12 May a fighting patrol from No 14 Company, under command of Oberfeldwebel Karl Schmidt, succeeded in re-establishing a foothold on Calvary Hill and eventually in driving the enemy off it. Schmidt was the hero of the day and for his bravery he was awarded the German Cross in Gold. When the fighting died down at nightfall the enemy had only one officer and seven men still on the Hill; General Anders had had to withdraw his Polish troops, and that night they were back behind the start lines they had left that morning. For his part in the gallant defence of Calvary Hill Major Rudolf Böhmler was awarded the *Ritterkreuz*.

The battle continued until 17 May. In the six days which it had lasted General Heidrich showed that he really practised what he preached. Dashing into the middle of the battle to recover wounded he personified the paratroop maxim he had coined: *Kameradschaft — Können — Korpsgeist* Comradeship — Knowledge — Esprit de Corps). The general, who had received the *Schwerter zum Ritterkreuz* (Swords to the *Ritterkreuz*) on 25 March knew that his men were not defeated. But in the early morning of 18 May 1944 his division was ordered to withdraw from Monte Cassino. A French force had crossed the Aurunci Mountains the day before and broken through to the Itri-Pico road. As they were now 40km (25 miles) north of the Cassino line, the 1st Parachute Division was in danger of being cut off. General Juin's advance sealed the fate of Monte Cassino and compelled the 10th Army to retreat.

It was against this background that General Heidrich assumed command of I Parachute Corps, and Oberst Karl-Lothar Schulz — soon to become a Generalmajor — took over the 1st Parachute Division. Schulz commanded the division during the retreat which, by the end of August, had taken it almost back to Bologna on the Adriatic. Here at Bologna on 10 September the US 5th Army launched a massive attack, and it seemed as if the town was doomed when Generalmajor Schulz's paratroops entered the lists. The enemy was halted and on 27 September the American 5th Army called off the attack and withdrew. Schulz, dashing from one threatened sector to another in a little red Fiat, made a significant contribution to this success and he was awarded the *Eichenlaub zum Ritterkreuz*.

While the two divisions of I Parachute Corps, 1 FJD and 4 FJD were engaged in Italy, the 3rd and 5th Parachute Divisions and the 6th Parachute Regiment were also fighting in the bitter battles of Normandy.

CHAPTER 20

The Battles on the
Western Invasion Front

Von der Heydte's Regiment at Carentan

Major von der Heydte was appointed to the command of the 6th Parachute Regiment when it was raised in Wahn. At the beginning of June 1944 the regiment moved to Normandy and became the Corps reserve of the 84th Army Corps; regimental headquarters were in Carentan.

When General Student visited the regiment on the evening of 5 June, Major von der Heydte had just gone off to see one of his units. However the orderly officer quickly organised a celebration dinner for their 'old man', Kurt Student — commander-in-chief of the Parachute Army now — and after the meal General Student delivered a brief talk to the officers who had dined with him. He concluded this talk with a prophetic phrase *'Seid Wachsam'* (Be on your guard).

That night American planes flew over to drop paratroops on Normandy. Oberfeldwebel Peltz captured one major, two captains and 73 men in his area alone, and in the early hours of 6 June Major von der Heydte drove to Carentan to question these prisoners. It turned out that they belonged to the 501st Regiment of the American 101st Airborne Division. 'This is the invasion, Viebig,' von der Heydte said to his adjutant, before picking up the telephone to report to the operations officer (General Marcks) at the HQ of the 84th Corps.

Standing on a hill near St Côme-du-Mont at 0900 and scanning the coast through his binoculars, von der Heydte saw the great Allied invasion fleet off the 'Utah' beach. Calling forward his headquarters to St Côme-du-Mont, he ordered his regiment into action. In the first instance he tried to get to the coast at Medeleine by way of St Marie-du-Mont and Turqueville. The 1st Battalion reached St Marie-du-Mont without trouble, and if the 2nd Battalion could have got to Turqueville and turned in towards the beach across the flooded fields in that area, the routes from the American landing beach would have been blocked. But it was already too late. A message from Hauptmann Mager's 2nd Battalion reported that the enemy was already in St Mère Eglise and the 2nd Battalion paratroops were under heavy fire from there.

From St Marie-du-Mont, where he had ridden on a motorcycle, Major von der Heydte issued fresh orders. Mager was not to turn in, but to attack St Mère Eglise, capture it, and so eliminate the threat to his flank. In the event the attack failed and on the morning of 7 June von der Heydte told his battalions to dig in and prepare for a protracted defence.

The position taken up by the 6th Parachute Regiment now constituted a security belt, 20km (12 miles) long and 15km (9 miles) deep, across the entrance to the Cotentin Peninsula. But the enemy was pouring reinforcements into the beachhead and if the regiment stayed where it was, sooner or later it would be encircled. This danger really became apparent in the middle of a *Lagebesprechung* (briefing) at Regimental HQ when enemy tanks rolled up and started shooting at the house while the regimental commander was giving his views on the situation. Grabbing their weapons the Headquarters staff — cyclists, radio-operators, runners and clerks — sallied forth to deal with the tanks.

Time and again the Americans thought they had trapped the paratroops, and time and again the latter slipped away to reappear in the enemy's rear. With his right arm in a sling and a stiff shoulder — both after-effects of his plane crash — Major von der Heydte led his men through swamps and across rivers, and then stood to fight with them. And some of his confidence undoubtedly pervaded his men as the following story will testify: one of his paratroops captured by the Americans escaped and walked all across France armed only with a knife just to be with his *Haufen* (crowd) again.

On the evening of 8 June the regiment pulled back to the suburbs on the east and northern outskirts of Carentan. Here in new positions on the Route Nationale 13 the paratroops stood between the two American bridgeheads, and Carentan became the scene of some of the bloodiest fighting of the invasion. The paratroops fought to the limit of their endurance. Inevitably however, there came a time when both men and ammunition were almost exhausted. When this time did come, 10 June, the 1st Battalion broke contact but the US 101st Airborne Division had been defeated but at high cost to the paratroops. The 700 strong battalion was almost wiped out. It was on this day, 10 June, about noon, that an emissary from General Taylor asked von der Heydte to surrender. Just as the emissary returned to the American lines, Ju52s dropped food and ammunition, and the paratroopers fought on. On 11 June a Wehrmacht communiqué announced: 'FJR 6 under command of Major von der Heydte distinguished itself in the heavy fighting round the enemy beachhead.'

That day the regiment had been put under command of the 17th SS Panzer Grenadier Division *Götz von Berlichingen* and von der Heydte had asked the divisional commander, Brigadeführer Ostendorff, to reinforce his paratroops round Carentan. When Ostendorff declined to do so, von der Heydte decided he could no longer hold Carentan and at 1700 on 11 June he ordered his men to pull out of their positions and fall back. With them went the vital block between the 'Utah' and 'Omaha' beachheads. Fighting continued in and around Carentan, at the Hotel du Commerce and the railway station during the withdrawal, but on 12 June it was all over.

After the withdrawal what was left of the regiment was deployed along the Carentan-Periers road, where they performed a Hussar's trick. A cyclist company — 20 men on cycles accompanied by a borrowed tank — successfully ambushed a US infantry battalion capturing 13 officers and 600 men.

Following the American breakthrough at St Lô the regiment, as part of the 2nd SS Panzer Grenadier Division *Das Reich* withdrew from Coutances and marched south to join the 353rd Infantry Division near Garray; von der Heydte, who had been promoted to Oberstleutnant, had brought his paratroops to safety.

On 12 August FJR 6 was finally pulled out of the fighting, after an action north-west of Vire in which 3,000 of the paratroops were killed, wounded or taken prisoner. Posted to Gustrow (in Germany) they were brought up to strength and put under command of Army Group B for 'fire-brigade' duties in the north of Belgium and south of Holland.

The 2nd Parachute Corps in the West

Following the Allied invasion on 6 June 1944 II Parachute Corps was put under the command of the 84th Army Corps (LXXXIV AK) and an 'Army Abteilung' was created by this formation on 12 June.

At St Lô an American attempt to encircle the 3rd Parachute Division (FJD 3) was foiled. Meanwhile the 15th Parachute Regiment under Oberst Gröschke, moved straight from Germany directly into the fighting in the 84th Army Corps area. Although raw and unblooded the regiment performed exceptionally well in the battles against the Texans of the US 90th Infantry Division. Major von der Schulenburg, commanding the 13th Regiment was killed in this fighting on 14 July. A massive attack towards St Lô by the Americans (1st US Army) east of Vire was stopped by II Parachute Corps, and the 5th Parachute Division which had suffered from heavy air attacks took up positions on the Corps front. It now functioned as a division; up to this time it had been deployed piecemeal. In the violent air strike directed on the Panzer Lehr Division on 26 July, the Heintz Group — composed of men of the 13th and 14th Parachute Regiments — suffered heavy casualties.

For three days and three nights the corps was involved in heavy fighting. Although General Meindl threw in his last reserves, the 15th Regiment, the enemy broke out of his narrow beach-head, and the paratroops of Major Noster's 14th Regiment had to claw their way into the ground in the Marigny area.

At the Lemesnil-Herman crossroads the Parachute AA Battery 12 under Hauptmann Göttsche successfully foiled an American attempt to capture the divisional staff of the 352nd Infantry Division by knocking out 12 Sherman tanks. General Meindl's paratroops were able to hold the right flank of the front but the left wing of the 84th Army Corps was cut off and there was nothing to stop American tanks rolling towards the south between the two formations.

As the situation deteriorated the location of Corps HQ changed almost daily. The only light to shine in this darkness was on 1 August when the 3rd Parachute Division compelled the enemy to give up Torigny-sur-Vire. The withdrawal continued until 19 August, each bit of ground that was given up by the paratroops being due largely to a crisis in adjoining areas. Eugen Meindl, who had been promoted to General der Fallschirmtruppe at the beginning of August, spent the worst battles in the front line with his soldiers. Up to 20 August the later destroyed 606 enemy tanks at close range, and shot down 75 enemy aircraft with small-arms fire.

It was 28 August before General Meindl was able to get his corps out of the front line — and then only because there was no artillery support for him. Both of his divisions had been in action continuously since 12 June. However, the 3 FJD had to act as rearguard for the 5th and 7th Armies. and in the withdrawal most of the division was taken prisoner, when on 4 September 1944 near Mons the Grenadier and Panzer divisions fell back too quickly and left the paratroops to fend for themselves.

In the Fortress of Brest

Before the invasion the 2nd Parachute Division was deployed in Brittany with its headquarters at Lampaul. The possibility of an Allied airborne operation to capture Brest was considered and a reconnaissance of the country around Brest led to the conclusion that to contain an operation it was essential to occupy areas and features east and south of the port. To the east the Monts d'Arrée dominated the coastal strip; south of Brest, control of the Crozon peninsula was essential to the control of the Brest anchorage, and the Menez Hom feature was the key to the Crozon peninsula. South of Chateaulin the flat terrain provided an ideal dropping zone, and it was therefore necessary to turn this region into a killing ground.

General Ramcke issued the orders for the redeployment of the division personally:

'The 2nd Regiment will move to the Chateaulin area and occupy the Menez Hom Heights and the region south of Chateaulin.

'The 7th Regiment will move to the Sizun region and occupy the Monts D'Arrée, centring on Pt 384 at Commana.

'The Engineer Battalion will be responsible for Douarnenez Bay, and a battle group from the 2nd Battalion of the 7th Regiment and an anti-tank battery will take up a position north-west of Brest.

'The troops will organise the defences in their respective areas and continue training.'

One aggravating feature of the current situation arose from the fact that the bridge over the Loire near Nantes had been destroyed. This meant that supplies for the 2nd Division had to travel via Dijon to the south of France and be reloaded on to smaller vehicles for the last part of the journey.

Towards the end of July the division had to detach a battalion for the Normandy front. No sooner had this battalion gone than orders were received for the whole division to move to Normandy. Then, on the second day of the move, the order was countermanded and the division was told to stay where it was.

Next day units of Oberst Kroh's 2nd Regiment and Oberst Pietzonka's 7th Regiment were attacked by American tanks advancing from Avranches towards Brest. A fierce battle developed and from the heights near Commana General Ramcke directed and controlled the German efforts. Anticipating the enemy moves Ramcke switched anti-tank guns from one sector to another and the paratroops wrought tremendous damage with *Panzerfausts* and *Panzerschrecks*. In the middle of the battle the divisional commander pinned an Iron Cross to the tunic of a Gefreiter who had destroyed two Sherman tanks, one after the other in the space of a few minutes. For three days the enemy tried to overrun the Monts d'Arrée but lost 32 tanks and was driven back. And Oberst Pietzonka, to whom much of the credit for this successful action was due, was awarded the *Ritterkreuz*.

224

On 7 August 1944 General Ramcke was ordered to occupy Brest itself. The order reached him as American troops were advancing south west towards the port from Lesneven 22km (14 miles) away. The American advance guard occupied Guipavas airfield — only 8km (5 miles) from Brest — next day, and promptly sent emissaries into the port to demand its surrender. Oberst von Mosel, the garrison commander, refused and the 2nd Division arrived to occupy the fort next day. Three days later, on 12 August, by order of the OKW, Hermann Ramcke was declared Fortress Commander, Brest.

Between 29 July and 12 August 50 paratroopers were murdered by guerrillas and more than 200 were wounded; another 100 who were reported missing simply vanished and have not been heard of since.

Allied aircraft had bombed Brest on a number of occasions since 5 August and on 12 August there was a particularly heavy raid. General Ramcke, worried about the civilian population, decided the time had come to do something and a radio message was sent to General Middleton, the commander of the US 8th Army Corps which was attacking Brest. As a result of this a cease-fire was arranged and on the four days when this became effective between 0700 and 1100 hours trucks of the division moved the civilian population out of the town. The evacuation was carried out without any display of friction on either side. A few Frenchmen refused to go and went into hiding, and the sick who were unfit to travel were moved into improvised hospital wards in tunnels where they were looked after by their own doctors.

The garrison of Brest was completely surrounded by this time, and Ramcke himself and his staff moved across to the Crozon peninsula with the units remaining north of the anchorage. Responsibility for the southern part of the Fortress was transferred to Generalleutnant Rauch and Kapitän zur See Richter, the commander of the Naval AA units was designated artillery commander of the Fortress. The naval commander Brest, Admiral Kähler, put the guns and the crews on board the ships in harbour at Richter's disposal.

General Ramcke now sent an emissary to General Middleton under a flag of truce, with a request that all the hospitals marked on a map handed to the American general would be spared. He also asked for the village of Le Fret near Cape Espagnol, where American prisoners of war would be housed, to be respected as a neutral zone. General Ramcke had done everything humanly possible in the situation and General Middleton agreed to the requests.

On 26 August the American artillery opened the attack on the fortress with a bombardment of the defences manned by the 1st Battalion of FJR 7. To Oberstleutnant Moeller, the division's operations officer and Hauptmann Dr Hoven the intelligence officer, this suggested that the enemy intended to try to break in at Gouesnou.

As soon as General Ramcke was told of their conclusion he shouted for his driver Dietinger and his aide, Hauptmann Kamitschek, and drove to Major Hamer's command post. The CO of the 1st Battalion FJR 7 had been expecting him and as the car slowed down he leaped on to the running board and Dietinger drove on into the area where the shells were dropping. From one of the observation posts tanks could be seen manoeuvring on the plain in enemy territory. Moreover they were advancing.

'What are the forward positions looking like, Hamer?' Ramcke asked the battalion commander.

'They are manned by only a few of the old paratroopers', Hamer replied. 'They'll let the tanks go over the top of them and then hit at them with explosives and *Panzerfausts*, Herr General.

'What then?' queried Ramcke.

'As soon as the second enemy wave has crossed our front line, we shall counter-attack from the flank. The counter-attack force is under cover at the foot of this hill. Apart from that I also have a company with mortars in reserve. And as soon as the time is ripe I will use it to attack from the other side.'

'Good', said Ramcke. These were his paratroops who knew how to act independently and in a manner of which he wholeheartedly approved.

The battering of the forward positions continued and not a single German gun had so far responded: the enemy tanks were not yet in range.

'Herr Major, the second enemy wave has crossed', reported the man at the binoculars. Hamer glanced across to Ramcke who nodded. The major then raised his signal pistol and fired. Almost immediately the German guns all opened fire, and flames flickered from the muzzles of 88mm AA guns, 75mm anti-tank guns, 37mm Quadruplets field-guns and light artillery. The leading tanks were hit and stopped with flames spraying out of their hatches and engine compartments.

Then from positions on the flanks which the American infantry following the tanks had already passed, there was a crackle of MG 42s (machine guns). As the enemy dived for cover Major Hamer gave the order to counter-attack. His reserve company hurled itself at the enemy's left flank and a brief battle developed among the tanks, as the tank-destroyer parties tackled them with *Panzerfaust* and explosive charges. (These parties consisted of four men, two of whom sprayed the infantry accompanying the tanks with their machine-pistols, while the other two dealt with the tanks).

When volunteers manning a couple of Shermans which had been captured undamage drove them into the enemy flank the Americans decided they had had enough, and at the end of the day 500 of them had been taken prisoner.

Shortly before the battle ended however, Oberst Kroh sanctioned a surprise operation which many ex-paratroopers remember to this day. One man of the 2nd Battalion of FJR 2 who had been captured earlier by the Americans had managed to escape and get back to the Fortress. More than 100 of his comrades, he reported, were being held in a school in the village of Braspart by an organisation of franc-tireurs and partisans. Moreover these imprisoned paratroopers were being tortured. Clearly their liberation was imperative and an operation was mounted with that end in view. The man nominated to command the group which was formed to penetrate the American lines (8th US Corps) and drive through several occupied villages to get to Braspart was none other than Leutnant Lepkowski, the man who had defended Pt 159.9 at Kirovograd. In the event the operation was a 100 per cent success — 113 comrades were released from captivity, and 40 French prisoners were taken. With 45 paratroopers Lepkowski shot his way back to Brest and he was recommended for the *Eichenlaub* to the *Ritterkreuz* and received his decoration on 22 August from General Ramcke.

When an enemy attack was launched against the western half of Brest, the

Above: 1 FJD HQ staff in January 1945.

Below left: On the Western Front the paratroops fought under Feldmarschall Model.

Below right: When they were surrounded in Breslau they were commanded by General Niehoff.

227

paratroops were expecting it, having been warned by the radio-intercept section in the port. The enemy succeeded in capturing Pt 103, but at Guipavas, Hauptmann Becker's men — joined on 4 and 6 September by men from Hauptmann Kamitschek's group — repulsed the attack. However on 7 and 8 September the Americans smashed through Becker's defences to roll up the flank of the adjoining engineer battalion. Both Hauptmann Becker and Hauptmann Kamischeck were taken prisoner in this action.

The division held on until 10 September, but the odds of four to one in numerical superiority were too much and the paratroops pulled back into the Fortress to occupy the HKL (main battle line) in Brest. In effect it was a hopeless struggle, and the submarines which could still operate and a few other boats left Brest heading for Lorient. Major Ewald led a counter-attack by the 2nd Battalion of FJR 2 when the enemy penetrated the defences in the north west and the line was restored. But the end was in sight.

On 13 September an emissary from General Middleton handed a message to General Ramcke which read:

'Inevitably there comes a time in war when the military situation does not justify a commander shedding more blood.

'I have discussed the situation of the German garrison of Brest with officers who have fought bravely with you and who are now prisoners of war. I am convinced that the military situation is hopeless and that nothing can be achieved by prolonging this fight. Therefore we agree that the German garrison of Brest no longer has any justifiable reason for holding on.

'Your soldiers have fought well, your troops are trapped in a narrow area. So you have fulfilled your duty for you people and your country. I now ask you, as one professional soldier to another, to give up this unequal battle.

'We hope, that you, as an old, responsible officer, who has served honourably and fulfilled his duty, will give your favourable consideration to this proposal.

signed Troy H. Middleton'

General Ramcke's response was:

'Herr General! — I decline your proposal.'

The Americans renewed their attack on 14 September and by the evening of the 15th they had penetrated the Quilbignon and Recouvrandre suburbs of the town. The St Pierre area north of the submarine base, held by Oberst Kroh, continued to hold out, as did the Porzig strongpoint. But on 16 September when it was clear that St Pierre could not hold out much longer Ramcke decided to pull his troops out and ferry them across to the Crozon peninsula where the fight would continue.

On 18 September the guns in St Pierre fired their last shells and were then blown up. General Mosel surrendered Brest town later in the day, but the fighting continued on Crozon. The last of the desperate fighting that marked the final stages of the battle was on the Espagnol Peninsula. Ramcke formed a battle group of 170 men under the command of Major Mehler, the CO of the Paratroop Signal Unit, and this battle group occupied the Quellenriegel. Over the next three days the enemy concentrated their artillery fire on the Quellenriegel and then attacked. Leutnant Jacobs drove off two infantry attacks — and was subsequently awarded the *Ritterkreuz* for his valour — but his men were unable to stop the Americans penetrating the German perimeter when they brought up tanks.

Relays of fighter-bombers bombed and strafed the positions on the morning of 20 September and the enemy was able to advance. When the remaining paratroops had been driven back to within 100m of General Ramcke's command post Oberstleutnant Moeller and Hauptmann Dr Hoven burned the secret files. By the time they had finished enemy troops surrounded the HQ bunker on three sides; on the fourth side there was a steep cliff.

Suddenly the shooting died down and an American brigadier-general approached the bunker. Ramcke went out to him and saluted. The American returned the salute and Ramcke spoke:

'I am General Ramcke.'

'I am pleased to meet you General', the brigadier-general replied. 'Your bunker was the last pocket of resistance in the whole Fortress. Consider yourself my prisoner . . . You are a great adversary, General!'

That was the end of Brest and the time was 1900 on 20 September 1944. For seven weeks the 2nd Parachute Division had held the fortress against an Army Corps; the paratroops had withstood attacks by bomber and fighter-bomber aircraft and they had not been overcome by overwhelming artillery. Generalleutnant Ramcke was promoted *General der Fallschirmtruppe* and awarded the *Schwerter und Brillanten* (swords and diamonds) to the *Ritterkreuz* with oak leaves.

For 2 FJD, the war was over.

CHAPTER 21

To the Bitter End

In the West

When Kurt Student was promoted Generaloberst on 11 August 1944, detachments of his 1st Parachute Army were fighting in the West, on the Eastern Front and in the South. Working from an office in Berlin-Wannsee the general himself was busy with plans for the raising of new paratroop units.

On 4 September 1944 news that British tanks had entered Antwerp triggered consternation in the *Wolfschanze* (Hitler's HQ) and the Führer sent for Student. He had thought of the paratroops and Student was told to set up a new defensive line on the Albert Canal. But where was he going to get the men from to do so?

The 1st and 4th Parachute Divisions were fighting in Italy; the 3rd and 5th had been battered to pieces around St Lô and Falaise; the new parachute regiment had only just been constituted as the 7th Parachute Division and Generalleutnant Erdmann had only just assumed its command.

In the course of his discussion at the Führer's HQ Student had managed to have a collection of 20 heavy, medium and light AA batteries allotted to him. These were artillery training units serving with the Reich Air Fleet (*Luftflotte*) and Student proposed to employ them as anti-aircraft battle groups.

On 5 September Student flew from Berlin to see Feldmarschall Model. Model was the C-in-C of Heeresgruppe B (Army Group B) to whom the 1st Parachute Army was responsible. The Field Marshal expressed himself disappointed that the whole paratroop army amounted to only 20,000 men so far. But he allotted Student an area running from the North Sea to Maastricht — which meant a front of 120km (75 miles) Appreciating that this was more than Student's 20,000 men could cope with Model also put General Reinhardt's 88th Army Corps under Student's command. This corps consisted of two infantry divisions the 719th and 176th — the latter, a *Kranken Division* (Sick Division) had not yet arrived in the area but it was on its way from Germany.

From Model's HQ General Student went on to see General Reinhardt at Moergestel and Generalleutnant Chill, the commander of the 85th Infantry Division. When he arrived at the latter's command post he was told that British tanks had crossed the

Albert Canal near Beeringen over a bridge which had not been demolished. Student ordered Chill to counter-attack and restore the situation. For this purpose Oberstleutnant von der Heydte's 6th Parachute Regiment was put at Chill's disposal.

The FJR 6 and men of the 85th Infantry Division fought against the British Guards Armoured Division and while the battle was raging there the 7th Parachute Division was brought up. In a series of bloody counter-attacks the division captured the villages of Hechtel, Helchteren and Zonhofen but the enemy's numerical superiority prevented them going further, or stopping the British 50th Division from crossing the Albert Canal near Gheel. However, just before General Student pulled his paratroops back behind the Maas-Schelde Canal, the 2nd Battalion of FJR 6 under Hauptmann Mager did manage to contain the 50th Division bridgehead. Meanwhile men of General von Zangen's 15th Army who had been cut off round Calais had fought their way through the British lines to the paratroops' positions and had been integrated into their units.

On 15 September Student moved his command post to a house near 'S Hertogenbosch south of Vught. Two days later — a Sunday, and a warm summer's day — he listened to a sound which began as a whisper and grew to a roar which drowned every other sound. In General Student's own words:

'I stepped out on the balcony, and wherever I looked I could see aircraft — troop transports and aircraft towing gliders — flying quite low over our house. They came in groups and as one disappeared into the distance another followed — flight after flight. It was a spectacle which impressed me deeply. At that particular moment I had no thought of the dangers it foreshadowed; I was only thinking of my own airborne enterprises in earlier days. If I had ever had such resources at my disposal ...!

'With Colonel Reinhard, my Chief-of-Staff, I went up on to the flat roof of the house to see where the aircraft were going. There was still an immense stream of them passing overhead and some flew so low that we ducked out heads.

'There was quite a lot of shooting going on by this time. Our clerks, drivers, batmen and the signal section had grabbed their rifles and were shooting at the low flying aircraft.

'So far as I could tell two of the three airborne divisions which were deployed in this operation flew over us.'

One of the WACO gliders in the first wave of this airborne assault was shot down near Vught and a complete set of the enemy's operational plans was found in it. A few hours' later these plans were on Student's desk with an analysis by his Intelligence staff. The enemy's ultimate objectives were the important bridges over the Lower Rhine and the British 2nd Army was to push up and break through to the corridor seized by the airborne troops. The enemy's order of battle and dropping zones were as follows:

101st US Airborne Division, General Taylor: Eindhoven-Veghel.
82nd US Airborne Division, Major-General Gavin: Grave-Nijmegen.
1st British Airborne Division, Major-General Urquhart: near Arnhem.

The operation was under the overall command of Lieutenant-General Lewis H.

Brereton, commander of the First Allied Airborne Army, second in command was the commander of the British Airborne Corps, Lieutenant-General Browning.

General Student directed the German side of the battle in his area throughout the night. The 6th Parachute Regiment, deployed on the Hechtel-Eindhoven-Valkensward triangle was ordered to move north into the Schijndel area, and here on the morning of 18 September the regiment clashed with the US 82nd Airborne Division. The German paratroops attacked immediately and although this attack did not make much headway the Americans — who said the fighting was 'very heavy' — called the action the 'Battle of the Dunes'. This battle continued until 24 September when one of von der Heydte's battle groups near St Oedenrode succeeded in cutting the American's supply route south of Veghel.

Meanwhile Student had been coping with the landings in the Arnhem area. There was some fierce fighting but the enemy did not gain his objective here. Nevertheless, although the British 1st Army was unable to break through to the airborne forces, the 1st FJ Army had been split into two parts by the landings. An important new factor began to make itself felt after 17 September 1944, however. On that day Feldmarschall Model ordered the 3rd and 5th Parachute Divisions and most of II Parachute Corps troops re-equipping in the Cologne area to move up to the battle zone and the following day these welcome reinforcements were on the march to Kleve. All German troops north of the Reichswald, the thickly forested country on the Netherlands-German border, were put under General Meindl's command. Although these troops did not amount to more than 3,400 men they were able to accomplish a great deal. When Major Becker occupied the high ground near Berg en Dal and the Fürstenberg Group pushed forward on his flank the Allies lost the strip of territory which they had earmarked for the landing of 450 gliders carrying supplies to the airborne forces.

On 20 September the Germans launched an attack to try to break up the 82nd US Airborne Division and reach the Maas-Waal Canal. Three battle groups had been formed for this purpose:

a *Kampfgruppe* Major Becker
b *Kampfgruppe* Major Greschick
c *Kampfgruppe* Oberstleutnant Herrmann

The three groups all achieved their intermediate objectives but could get no further after that. And this time it was no longer possible to recover Nijmegen. Tanks of the Guards Armoured Division of the British 30th Corps crossed the road bridge north of the town that evening (20 September). On the explicit orders of Feldmarschall Model, the bridge had not been demolished, because — he explained later — his intention was to recover it with a counter-attack by II Parachute Corps.

On 24 September Hitler ordered that the enemy in the Arnhem, Nijmegen, Mook and Groesbeek areas must be destroyed, and that the gap in the front line north of Eindhoven should be closed. Responsibility for seeing that this order was carried out fell on General Meindl, and the 108th Panzer Brigade and an extra anti-tank battery were allotted to him for this purpose. Meindl mounted an attack, which went in on 28 September and which was finally called off on 2 October when Student had to report that: 'The attack by II Parachute Corps has failed. By day the enemy's air

Above left: Major Erich Walter who died in Soviet captivity during 1947.

Above: Leutnant Gerhard Schacht.

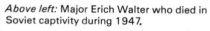

Left: Generalmajor Hans Kroh, one of the first and last paratroops, who ultimately commanded 2 FJD.

233

superiority was overwhelming, and the troops were not sufficiently well trained in night fighting.'

On 3 October Meindl's men dug in and prepared to hold the line they had reached; and the 6th Parachute Regiment which had been pulled out of the Schindel area at the end of September was ordered to stop the Canadians crossing the Schelde and keep open the access to the island of Walcheren. Near Woendsdrecht there was some desperate fighting, where four enemy attacks were repulsed before 16 October when the paratroopers were compelled to evacuate the town. In the 13 days they had been in the area they had destroyed 250 tanks — nearly all of them with infantry weapons at short range.

On 28 October Friedrich-August von der Heydte had to give up the command of his regiment to build up the Paratroop Army's Battle School (*Kampfschule der Fallschirmarmee*) in Aalten. Barely six weeks later came another call for his services in the field, for on 9 December von der Heydte was summoned to General Student's HQ. There he was told that a massive offensive was to be launched in the west and that he would command a paratroop task force which would be dropped at a nodal point behind the enemy's lines.

Van der Heydte's *Kampfgruppe* assembled in Aalten, leaving there for Sennelager on 11 December; and Oberstleutnant von der Heydte reported at the HQ of Model's Army Group in Euskirchen four days later. His task was defined as: 'Keeping open gaps in the enemy's line for the 6th SS Panzer Army'.

The Ardennes offensive began in the early morning of 16 December 1944, and the 3rd and 5th Parachute Divisions were among the formations who took part. The 5th Division, under command of Oberst Heilmann since the late autumn, crossed the river Clerf and advanced towards Wiltz. Within 24 hours the division was deep inside enemy territory; on 22 December — despite constant attacks from the south — it reached Vaux les Rosieres, 15km (9 miles) south-west of Bastogne. Here the division was hurled piece-meal into the witches' cauldron which surrounded the town. Subsequently Heilmann managed to lead his division out of the area where he was in danger of being encircled. But the division sustained heavy casualties; so too did the 3rd FJD which was under command of 6th SS Panzer Army for this operation.

The last large-scale drop of German parachute troops took place in December 1944. The enemy was reinforcing the Elsenborn area and the purpose of the drop was to block the enemy's route south through the Schnee-Eiffel — so disrupting his reinforcement programme. Von der Heydte's *Kampfgruppe* was given the task and arrangements were made for the drop to be made during the night 16/17 December.

The move to the airfields at Paderborn and Lippspringe went as planned, the Ju52s took off, and a quarter of an hour later than had been planned the first planes were over the dropping zone. The *Boschhorn* sounded and Oberstleutnant von der Heydte was the first to jump. In his own words:

'Below me the dropping zone looked eerie but beautiful; above me the planes' positional lights seemed to be glow-worms. The tracers of the American AA barrage formed a sort of pearl curtain, behind which I could see a black ribbon I knew were trees. Behind that were the white fingers of searchlight beams.

'When I touched down I was utterly alone, but I met some other men as I made my way towards the orchard near a cross-roads which was our assembly point. By dawn I had collected 125 soldiers — a little more than a tenth of the *Kampfgruppe*.

'We pulled back from the road into the forest and formed a hedgehog (position of all round defence). The radio was not working, and although a motorcyclist despatch rider we captured was found to be carrying orders for the US 18th Corps I could not pass them back. I sent a few runners — men who volunteered to try to get through the enemy lines — back with copies of these orders; but none of them got through.'

As von der Heydte's men pulled back further into the forest during the afternoon of the second day, they met another party of 150 men of the *Kampfgruppe*. A war correspondent, Leutnant von Kaiser had taken charge of these men, who had already been involved in skirmishes with American patrols. Realising that the two combined groups could not possibly complete his mission, von der Heydte decided to dissolve the unit and he ordered it to break into small parties and try to get back to the German lines. On 24 December, when von der Heydte himself was captured by the Americans, the von der Heydte *Kampfgruppe* officially ceased to exist.

In the closing months of the war on German soil the reconstituted 2nd Division under Generalleutnant Lackner, the 6th Division under Generalleutnant Erdmann, and Generalmajor Wadehn's 8th Division were all in the battles which took place between the Maas and the Lower Rhine. They were in the fighting in the Reichswald near Geldern and Weeze, Emmerich and Wegze. General Schlemm, who had taken over the command of the 1st Parachute Army, withdrew his division step by step and showed himself to be a real master of improvisation. At Gooch and Weeze, on the 'hill of the dead' at Keppeln, at Vadem and finally at the Weser bridgehead where what was left of them stood firm for 31 days, the paratroops fought bravely and stubbornly.

In the retreat through Germany to the Hunte-Ems Canal and to the Edewechter Dam between Edewecht and Friesoyte other paratroops were in action time and again. And the performance of the Paratroop Assault Gun Battery 12 which only formed in the autumn of 1944 deserves a special commendation. In this fighting Leutnant Heinz Deutsch, the commander of one assault gun section of this unit, destroyed 44 enemy tanks; for this he was deservedly awarded the *Ritterkreuz*. Another 147 tanks were destroyed by the 7th Division near Edewecht.

When the end came II Parachute Corps was in Gross-Breckendorf 15km (9 miles) south-east of Schleswig. In April, General Student, who had recovered from his illness and resumed command of the 1st Parachute Army was nominated Commander-in-Chief of the Weichsel Army Group. But he was never able to take up this appointment . . . The war in the West was over.

The Paratroops in Italy
The autumn battles which raged in Romagna presented Generalleutnant Richard Heidrich's I Parachute Corps with some difficult tasks. During the retreat there was some hard fighting at the Reno river and Panaro, but Heidrich (whose headquarters were at Bondeno) was able to cope, and the 1st Parachute Division under command of Generalmajor Karl-Lothar Schulz did not let him down. Schulz's division was deployed near Bologna, where it was joined by Generalmajor Trettner's 4th Division when the latter pulled out of the battles near Florence and Rimini. Shoulder to shoulder the paratroopers of both divisions then retreated to the River Po. At the river they

found that the bridges were down and no arrangements had been made to get the troops across. Thus it was that on the morning of 23 April General Heidrich called a conference of his senior commanders — Generalmajor Schulz, Generalmajor Trettner and the victor at Schlüsselburg, Generalleutnant Harry Hoppe. Following a review of the situation he issued the following directive:

1 I Parachute Corps will cross the Po near Felonica during the night of 24/25 April, and will deny the crossing to the enemy.

2 The 278th Infantry Division will establish a bridgehead on the south bank at the old Felonica railway bridge to protect the crossing. This division will also take over protection of the right flank of the Corps.

3 Unserviceable vehicles are to be burned, but battle-worthy equipment and vehicles are to be ferried across. Ambulances with wounded have priority. Tyres to be stripped from the vehicles left behind and given to non-swimmers.

During the crossing many soldiers drowned in the waters of the Po. And those who got through faced another long retreat during which they were continuously ambushed by partisans.

The end came on 2 May 1945, and in his last Order of the Day Generalleutnant Heidrich said:

'We have done our duty to the end, and we do not feel we have been defeated. Keep your *Fallschirmjäger* Spirit! Even if we have to undergo a temporary separation, we remain a single entity. Each of you must know that the darkest hour of our people demands manly dignity.

'Remember our dead comrades — those who died for us all.'

The End in the East

Towards the end of January 1944 Obertsleutnant Gerhard Schirmer was ordered to form a new regiment, FJR 16; the survivors of his battalion, which had been virtually annihilated near Kiev was the nucleus of this regiment. By May the regiment was up to strength with four battalions and during June it was given parachute training in night drops. And in July the regiment entrained for a move to the encircled stronghold of Wilna.

In the bitter fighting around Wilna Schirmer's paratroops demonstrated their superb fighting capabilities time and again. Enemy attacks were repulsed, tank hunting parties knocked out Soviet armour of every type, and at the end of July Schirmer's Regiment supported by the 6th Panzer Division broke through to the West. Crossing the Wilna bridge — which was blown sky-high when the last man was across — the paratroops carved a passage across to the defence line in East Prussia. There they defended a section of this line between Schlossberg and Wilkovischken until October (1944), and during this time they were visited by General Matzky, the Commander-in-Chief who came to decorate paratroops with the Iron Crosses they had won in the earlier battles. Schirmer himself received the *Eichenlaub* to the *Ritterkreuz*.

At the end of the month FJR 16 (Ost) was pulled out of the line and taken back to

Kukernese to establish a bridgehead across the Memel near Tilsit. This they held until the end of the war and subsequent captivity.

On the lower Oder in March 1945, a hurriedly raised 9th Parachute Division under command of the renowned General Bruno Bräuer — one of the very first paratroopers — was deployed to stem the Soviet advance. Driven back to Berlin, Bräuer's Division resisted until the very last.

In March 1945 also, Oberst von Hoffmann's 10th Parachute Division — equally hurriedly raised in Italy — was deployed in the St Pölten region in the Steiermark. Like so many of their comrades the paratroopers of this division fought stubbornly until they were annihilated in Czechoslovakia at the beginning of May.

The Parachute Battalion Skav, from the Schacht Special Duties Regiment, flew from Jüterbog to Breslau on 28 February 1945 and was dropped there through a Russian AA barrage. The paratroops were integrated into the units defending the town where the fighting continued until 6 May. They too then marched into captivity. This was the last recorded airborne action of World War II.

When the war ended on 8 May 1945 the German paratroops joined their comrades in prisoner-of-war camps and endured the rigours of captivity. Fate was especially cruel to some: General Bruno Bräuer, extradited to Greece, was condemned to death for no valid reason by a tribunal of hate, and was executed in 1947; Generalleutnant Erdmann died in a British prison camp, and Generalmajor Walther did not live long in Russian captivity.

The war was over. During it men had witnessed the introduction and employment of a new weapon which was to be developed and used more extensively even after hostilities ceased in 1945. And if it is 'the task of an army to march at the head of progress' as Scharnhorst used to say, then the future will see airborne armies and air-landing armoured divisions. General James M. Gavin predicted the need for them when he said 'The only way of getting to grips with a numerically superior enemy depends on one's own superior mobility.'

The airborne concept had permeated the whole world, and so long as there are attackers and defenders it will continue to exist. All the wars and conflicts which have followed World War II have proved its worth.

Index

238

240